THE AFFLUENT SOCIETY REVISITED

The Affluent Society Revisited

MIKE BERRY

OXFORD

UNIVERSITY PRESS

OXFORD
UNIVERSITY PRESS

Great Clarendon Street, Oxford, OX2 6DP,
United Kingdom

Oxford University Press is a department of the University of Oxford.
It furthers the University's objective of excellence in research, scholarship,
and education by publishing worldwide. Oxford is a registered trade mark of
Oxford University Press in the UK and in certain other countries

Published in the United States of America by Oxford University Press
198 Madison Avenue, New York, NY 10016, United States of America

British Library Cataloguing in Publication Data
Data available

Library of Congress Control Number: 2013941291

ISBN 978–0–19–968650–6

Printed and bound in Great Britain by
CPI Group (UK) Ltd, Croydon, CR0 4YY

Preface

The Affluent Society was John Kenneth Galbraith's most famous book. It was written in the middle of the long boom following the Second World War. The author was then and for a time after America's best known economist in the broader public sphere, a position he never fully lost until his death almost fifty years later. The book has never been out of print and has been widely read by people who grew up during the long boom and just after. Most were not economists but intelligent readers who wished to be informed about the serious matters that economists and governments grappled with. Though the period during which it was written has long past and economics as a discipline has moved far from the terrain laid out by Galbraith, *The Affluent Society* still resonates, still raises important questions of how economics is to be practiced and how economic policy is to be conducted. It is the aim of this book to say how and why this is so. Its very title has entered into the common language, along with phrases like "the conventional wisdom," so commonplace that many people are unaware as to their origin.

As an Australian who grew up during the 1960s, I am reminded of another book written by a fellow countryman, the writer and critic Donald Horne. *The Lucky Country*, published not long after Galbraith's book, sought to establish that Australia, as a small nation sitting on a huge land mass of natural resources with a well-educated though insular community, had huge potential to grow and prosper. The main difference was that Horne's title was meant to be ironic—Australia, he argued, was wasting its future, complacently resting on its colonial past, overly reliant on its imperial masters, Britain and the United States, living a derivative existence, and expressing what came to be called "a cultural cringe." Australians, Horne claimed, simply didn't have the balls to grab the future and run. He was infuriated that his message was taken over and reversed by business, cultural, and political elites who proclaimed that, yes we are the lucky country, so can keep on doing exactly what we have always done. Nothing needs to change.

The Affluent Society (ironically) has suffered a reverse fate. When written it was intended to identify real and emerging economic and social trends in America and other advanced economies. Instead, as we will see, "affluence" now has a deeply ironic flavor. Especially since the global financial crisis of 2008 and its lingering aftermath, the most developed economies in the world are struggling to maintain, still less improve, the material conditions of its hard-pressed citizens. As I write, more than half of Spaniards under 30 are unemployed, financial institutions in a raft of countries are barely afloat, the weaker ones already having gone under or been taken on board by their

governments, many of whom face the unpalatable choice between imposing harsh austerities on their already burdened publics or defaulting on their
burgeoning debts, putting at risk their citizens' future livelihoods. A further
irony—the "advanced" economies are increasingly dependent for their prosperity on the continuing rapid growth of the "emerging economies," Brazil,
Russia, India, and China.

I argue in the opening chapter that *The Affluent Society* is well worth a revisit,
that the themes raised and some of the insights there offered can cast light on
our current volatile present and uncertain future. Just as importantly, the gaps,
silences, and (with hindsight) errors there, provoke contemporary efforts to
grasp what is happening and why.* The approach, in keeping with the original, is challenging but non-technical and aimed at the general reader who may
appreciate a guide to decoding the often opaque and simplistic accounts of the
current predicament served up by economic commentators and policy makers.

* * *

A number of people helped during the writing of this book, some of whom
are unaware of the fact. I wish to acknowledge the stimulating discussions
over an extended period with my colleagues and students at RMIT University;
in particular, Esther Charlesworth, Val Colic-Peisker, Tony Dalton, Benno
Engels, John Fien, Robin Goodwin, Guy Johnson, Julie Lawson, Martin
Mowbray, Anitra Nelson, Manfred Steger, Rob Watts, and Gavin Wood. I have
also gained immensely from discussions over the years with Perle Besseman,
Lois Bryson, Terry Burke, Gordon Clark, Deni Greene, Michael Harloe, Kath
Hulse, Vivienne Milligan, Chris Ryan, Susan Smith, Christine Whitehead,
Peter Williams, Ian Winter, and Judith Yates. Thanks also to two anonymous
referees.

Some of the original work on the book was carried out during a stimulating period as visiting fellow at The Rockefeller Foundation Centre, Bellagio.
I thank both the Foundation for its support and the amazing collection of
creative people I mingled with while there.

Finally, thanks to my family for their loving support during difficult times.
This book is dedicated to my wife, Deirdre.

---

* Galbraith was well aware of the dangers of social prophecy and readily accepted that time
would tell on the arguments he advanced. At the end of the preface to the 1962 Pelican edition of
The Affluent Society he commented: "...there may be instances where time in its unkind way has
exposed error, and certainly if this edition remains in print for long there will be more. I haven't
attempted to either correct or to anticipate such exposure. Nor do I think one should. The author
should give his best in the first round. Then, if time shows he has been wrong, he should count
on the reader to see the mistake and make the necessary correction. I imagine that most readers
rather welcome the opportunity. They know that authors are fallible, but, within limits, to redis-
cover this elementary truth is pleasant and reassuring."

Contents

However selfish soever man may be supposed, there are evidently some principles in his nature, which interest him in the fortune of others, and render their happiness necessary to him, though he derives nothing from it except the pleasure of seeing it

(opening lines of Adam Smith (2009/1759),
The Theory of Moral Sentiments).

1

Why Revisit *The Affluent Society?*

Looking backward, the 1950s seems to be another country. Yet most western readers over fifty will have at least a hazy memory of a time when life's austerities were fading, along with memories of war and depression, mass privation, and pervasive economic insecurity. The birth rate in countries like the United States was booming, a veritable production line of today's baby boomer generation. A wave of war-induced migration was redistributing refugees and others in search of a better life to the shores of the Anglo-democracies—America, Canada, Australia, and New Zealand. Reconstruction was commenced with a vengeance, the backlog of almost two decades of stagnation to be made good. New housing, new cities, new highways, hospitals and airports, massive power generation, and a burst of school building, unseen since the late nineteenth century, emerged as the US converted the largest ever war machine to peaceful purposes at home and—via interventions like the Marshall Plan and military occupation—to Europe and Japan.

It's true that some sources of insecurity were ratcheting up. The Cold War and occasional hot wars in Korea, Malaya, and, most ominously (in hindsight), Indo-China, disturbed the single-minded pursuit of prosperity and the sense of personal well-being in the civilian economy. On the other hand, what near the end of the decade President Eisenhower would call "the military-industrial complex," consolidated its economic position and political power in the post-war world. Achieving economic growth and high levels of employment were explicitly legislated as the responsibility of national governments and increasingly became a key measure of relative success in the battle between capitalism and communism. Decolonization saw the decline and eventual fall of the British and French empires but an active policy of "neo-colonialism" embraced by both the United States and USSR carved out new spheres of influence and new fault lines across the globe. International agencies—the United Nations, World Bank, International Monetary Fund—hammered out by the victorious allies brought some order to postwar political and economic relations between countries and all policy makers believed that they had learnt the harsh lessons of the "beggar-thy-neighbor" behavior widely believed to have led to the horrors of the Second World War.

In short, at the time—and in hindsight—the 1950s seems to have been a period of quiet optimism and increasing prosperity for the vast majority of people living in the most economically advanced countries, most particularly the United States of America. The tensions at home and abroad that did exist seemed to be capable of resolution through continuing economic growth. As John Maynard Keynes's *General Theory* (Keynes, 1973/1936) was beginning to guide macroeconomic policy makers in these countries, his earlier speculations about "Economic possibilities for our grandchildren" (Keynes, 1973/1930) appeared to be within reasonable reach. Growth was to be the thing! To the obvious positive spur was added the negative worry that—in General Secretary Khrushchev's words—in a few years the economically surging Soviet Union would overtake—indeed, "bury"—America. The appearance of the Soviet Sputnik in October 1957 gave an edge to such threats.

In 1956, one of the seminal contributions to the discipline of economics appeared. The (1956) article, for which the young economist Robert Solow would receive the Nobel Prize twenty years later, provided an elegant model describing how a fully competitive market economy grows over time, and what the key variables and assumptions are. This model was seen—by the established economics profession—as superior to previous attempts to get at the dynamics of a growing economy because it was fully consistent with the dominant paradigm, neoclassical economics, and the "neoclassical synthesis" forged by Solow's MIT colleague, fellow future Nobel Laureate Paul Samuelson, interpreting Keynes within the larger foundational theory of general equilibrium.

In fact, in one of those not infrequent cases of multiple discoveries, essentially the same theory of economic growth was published independently in the same year by the Australian economist, Trevor Swan. Although Australians and other non-American economists tended to refer to the Solow–Swan model, the Australian eventually dropped off the credit sheet, not living long enough to receive a share of the Nobel Prize—a not infrequent occurrence in the history of "the prize."

Two other influential works appeared soon after the resurrection of growth theory, in some ways a return to the roots of the discipline that arose as an attempt to understand the nature and causes of the wealth of nations. The first book concentrated on the forces that constrained or blocked growth in some countries—i.e. kept them poor. Written by Swedish economist Gunnar Myrdal (also a subsequent Nobel Laureate, but not for this work), *Economic Theory and Under-Developed Regions* (Myrdal, 1957), provided a compelling analysis of *cumulative and circular causation*, demonstrating why some regions or whole economies grow while others stagnate; more importantly Myrdal suggested that these trajectories would, if unchecked, increasingly diverge. That is, richer economies would increasingly outstrip poorer ones; divergence, not convergence was, in this view, the fate of an increasingly integrated free market world.

This message, first delivered as a lecture series in Egypt where a young radical nationalist leader, Gamal Abdel Nassar, had begun to flex his political muscle, carried an ominous message to western political leaders as well as challenging an important implication of the Solow–Swan model. The latter suggested that over time the key variable—the rate of savings and, hence, investment—would fall, thanks to the pervasive effect of diminishing returns, slowing economic growth in the most advanced countries. Laggard economies, through thrift and progressively adding to their capital stock, would improve productivity and thus grow more quickly eventually converging with the most advanced economies. This benign future beckoned, as long as free markets and free trade ruled. However, if Myrdal was right and underdevelopment proceeded alongside development, then all bets were off. In this more Darwinian world poor countries would remain poor, or at least poorer than they might be under a different economic program and political regime. To the emerging economies of what came to be called the "third world" an alternative socialist path to growth and prosperity seemed possible, fuelling the Cold War competition for influence—a case of Dr. Strangelove instead of Dr. Pangloss.

The *third* contribution to the growth question published around this time was, of course, *The Affluent Society* (hereafter *AS*). First published in 1958, it shot into the US best seller list and stayed there for more than six months. At the time, its author, John Kenneth Galbraith, was an established tenured professor in the Economics Department at Harvard University. At fifty years of age, he had already produced an influential book on American capitalism, regulated prices in the US economy during the war, been a successful columnist, advised Democratic Presidential candidate Adlai Stevenson, and infuriated the US Air Force by authoring an analysis of the ineffectiveness of mass bombing over Europe during the Second World War. That his analysis of the bombing proved accurate only served to increase official displeasure and almost stopped Harvard from granting him academic tenure in 1948. In the years following the publication of *AS*, he went on to advise President John F. Kennedy, to serve as US Ambassador to India, and fall out badly with President Lyndon Johnson over the Vietnam War.

II

By his own account, Galbraith started out to write a different book—*Why People are Poor*. However, he claims in his *Memoirs* (Galbraith, 1981) that he "encountered difficulty"; he had no convincing explanation for why poverty persisted in societies that were in general becoming more affluent, why all boats were not rising with the tide. Nowhere did this seem more paradoxical than in his own country, indisputably the leading economic as well as military power in the world. The focus for his intended book thus shifted from the poor minority in America (whom he acknowledged existed, albeit fleetingly and by his later judgment, inadequately) to the phenomenon of increasing affluence among the majority. The fact that mainstream economics continued to privilege the problem of scarcity, to focus on the issues of economic efficiency and maximum material growth was, he argued, perverse in a situation characterized by affluence and expanded potential choice about the ends to which the resulting abundance could be put.

The traditional "dismal" concern of economists with lifting people out of grinding poverty was all very well for those countries where mass privation existed—most countries in the world at that time and all countries in previous times—but the United States faced the new challenges posed by affluence. He had, therefore, nothing novel to say about the dominant concern of mainstream economics, which faithfully followed the injunction of Alfred Marshall to solve the poverty problem while also paradoxically claiming to be a "value-free" science. He would leave the large and intractable problem of mass poverty, underdevelopment, and "economic take-off" to the many able economists in the field. *His* contribution—both novel and provocative—would be to educate the discipline, public policy makers, and the informed citizen as to the problem and promise of affluence or "plenty among poverty" in the world's vanguard economy. Once clear on his theme and focus, the writing—in the words of his biographer—"now came swiftly and he never slackened, getting up early every morning to write. By the time the family returned to Cambridge later that summer [of 1956], in his briefcase was a completed first draft" (Parker, 2005: 280).

Thus, the first reason for revisiting *AS* some fifty years after its first publication is simply that it helped set the terms of debate and discord over what became major economic, social, and political concerns in the succeeding half century and beyond. To briefly foreshadow comments offered later in this book, the radical questioning and reforming of the role of government in advanced economies, the importance of environmental issues, the specter of economic insecurity, and the question of inequality loom large at the present time. With respect to these and other issues touched on by Galbraith—even (especially) when his pronouncements proved to be wide of the mark—*AS* offers a lucid benchmark with which to gauge how far we have approached or diverged from the confident, cautiously optimistic condition that Galbraith foresaw.

A second reason is that his analysis may still, in certain areas, offer insights into the current condition and predicaments we face today and in an uncertain future. Fifty years seems a fair distance from which to attempt such an audit. I argue that this is indeed the case. Galbraith's pragmatic, policy-oriented approach prevented him from being overwhelmed by the theoretical extremes of both naïve wings of the economics discipline, hydraulic Keynesianism and neoclassical fundamentalism.

A final reason for a visit of this kind is to explicitly recognize and celebrate the iconic status of "one of those books." In all disciplines there are marque books that signpost their emergence and development. In almost all cases these books are seen to be deeply subversive at the time of publication. In the case of economics, the following spring to mind: Adam Smith's *An Inquiry into the Nature and Causes of the Wealth of Nations* (1961/1776); Karl Marx's *Capital* (1976/1867); Joseph Schumpeter's *Theory of Economic Development* (1934/1912); Maynard Keynes's *General Theory of Employment, Interest and Money* (1973/1936); and—*The Affluent Society*. In each case, such books set themselves against the prevailing winds and steer new courses. They not infrequently raise the hackles of professional peers and proponents of what Galbraith dubbed "the conventional wisdom." They also create waves outside the discipline, tending to be read widely by non-specialists and opinion makers—a sin for which, as Galbraith often observes, their authors are doubly damned.

III

This book is organized as a series of commentaries on each of the key themes of *AS*. In each case I seek to distil what I see as the essence of Galbraith's original argument, then to reflect on how faithfully these arguments capture the current "spirit of the age," how much of what Galbraith proposed in 1958 helps us to understand where we have traveled in the years since. Included in this intellectual tour will be Galbraith's second thoughts and reflections looking back from the vantage point of 2008 (a portentous year for anyone concerned with the state and future of the capitalist societies) when the fortieth anniversary edition of *AS* was republished. Inevitably, this means that my chapters bear little comparison with the length of or relative importance placed by Galbraith in his explication.

As always, *AS* was a book of its time, reflecting contemporary concerns, priorities, prejudices, and silences. For example, the text is conventionally gendered and little attention is paid to gender issues and perspectives, something Galbraith noted with regret in his 1998 "Introduction" to the revised edition, following his increasing interest in such matters reflected in his writings of the 1970s and 1980s.

Several chapters open with twin quotes from Galbraith and the British economist, John Maynard Keynes. The reason for this will become obvious. However, it is worth signaling here that both economists saw themselves as economic "heretics," taking on the established economics profession of their times. During the writing of what would become *The General Theory of Employment, Interest and Money*, Keynes famously prophesied to George Bernard Shaw that "...I believe myself to be writing a book on economic theory which will largely revolutionize not I suppose at once but in the course of the next ten years the way the world thinks about economic problems" (Keynes 1973/1936: 492). Keynes sought to demonstrate theoretically that an economic system of laissez-faire did not automatically ensure full employment and (thus) a truly efficient allocation of a society's scarce resources. Galbraith too sought to radically redirect the focus of economists, in his case to the novel, emerging problem of affluence in the post-Second World War period. In addition, Keynes's speculative essay "Economic possibilities for our grand-children" (1973/1930), published a few years before the *General Theory*, antici-pated some of the key themes of *AS*.

I in no way intend to "rewrite" the original; such an attempt would be pre-sumptuous and well beyond the slender talents of this author. Nor do I attempt a "biography" of the book or its famous author; there are many valuable bio-graphical and thematic accounts already existing, some of which I note in passing. Rather, this exercise is conducted more in the guise of an exploratory (and personal) foray into the increasingly perplexing present and an increas-ingly uncertain future, resting on a sturdy, if ageing guide. I hope that the outcome does provide the reader with an appreciation of Galbraith's famous book. But my primary aim is to cast light on what is happening now, on the threats to affluence that have become increasingly obvious since the out-break of the global financial crisis in 2008, almost fifty years to the day after publication of *AS*.

The format is the traditional essay form, in the original sense intended by Montaigne—"let us take this subject and see where it leads us." In this spirit the number of references and notes are kept within reasonable limits, a scholarly sin for which I will be criticized. I see no good reason to deprive my critics of this pleasure. I do, however, provide full bibliographic references to sources mentioned in the text in the accepted scholarly manner and, in addition, have appended a note at the end to guide the interested reader towards relevant sources. Quotes appearing in the text by writers other than Galbraith are referenced to the bibliography. Quotes by Galbraith throughout and (others appearing at the head of individual chapters) are not so referenced, in order not to disturb the flow of the argument. The interested reader is invited to track them down. I have used Galbraith's words in places because they help to demonstrate, as no other person could, the highly individualistic style and delicious phrasing that made him, along with Keynes, a great writer.

2

The Power of Ideas: Reflections on the Conventional Wisdom

…the ideas of economists and political philosophers, both when they are right and when they are wrong, are more powerful than is commonly understood.

(J.M. Keynes)

The first requirement for an understanding of contemporary economic and social life is a clear view of the relations between events and the ideas which interpret them.

(J.K. Galbraith)

*   *   *

Galbraith follows Keynes in attributing to ideas an abiding, pervasive, and powerful role in directing human affairs in society in general, and the economy in particular. It was very important for both to understand why and how this influence manifests. If as social actors and economic agents we "are ruled by economic ideas and by very little else" then much else follows, especially if we desire collectively to move governments in ways we believe are beneficial to our communities. Both Galbraith and Keynes were, of course, inveterate participants in the formation and implementation of public policy in their respective countries. Both strove in self-conscious ways to identify and rid themselves and others of ideas they considered harmful and dangerous to the public interest and likely to lead governments in wrong directions in attempting to pursue the latter.

In his famous early chapter on "the conventional wisdom" Galbraith observed that the ideas that predominate at any time are those that are generally acceptable; "(i)t will be convenient to have a name for the ideas that are esteemed for their acceptability and it should be a term that emphasizes their predictability. I shall refer to these ideas henceforth as the conventional wisdom." He argued that acceptability implied both stability and predictability; dominant ideas or ways of thinking changed slowly. In a jump Galbraith also implies that truth or what people believe to be true is largely determined by what they find acceptable. He adduces "numerous factors" that affect acceptability. Ideas are acceptable that one finds "convenient," that contribute to one's self-esteem and further one's self-interests.

In this latter context he points to the unfailing practice of employer representatives who equate the good of society with the rule of unfettered markets in the face of the equally insistent arguments of trade union leaders who tie economic and social progress to collective action and laws that protect worker wages and conditions. "But perhaps most important of all, people approve most of what they best understand." In an uncertain and complex world people cling to "a raft of ideas" that helps us make sense of that world. Just as people adrift in the sea cling tenaciously to a life raft, so people hold fast to their acceptable truths. This construction is reminiscent of Keynes's arguments in Chapter 12 of *General Theory* about the necessity of economic actors to rely on rough rules of thumb to deal with the everyday uncertainties of the economic environment. It also sounds a preemptive "echo" of the more recent and well-grounded findings of behavioral economics.

The tenacity with which people hold to the conventional wisdom not only tends to account for its persistence, even in the face of overwhelming challenge by "inconvenient truths" but also helps to explain the anger and fury that often greet the purveyors of those truths. Here, Galbraith clearly places himself as bearer of bad news, especially for his academic colleagues. Adherence to the conventional wisdom is a special and peculiarly potent form of "vested interest."

> For a vested interest in understanding is more preciously guarded than any other treasure. It is why men react, not infrequently with something akin to religious passion, to the defense of what they have so laboriously learned. Familiarity may breed contempt in some areas of human behavior, but in the field of social ideas it is the touchstone of acceptability.

The specific nature of the ideas forming the conventional wisdom is somewhat malleable, in Galbraith's view. Conservatives and liberals will differ on precisely what acceptable truths are. In one sense there may be a conventional wisdom for liberals and another for conservatives. Politicians and others who wish to influence social or political outcomes will, consequently, tailor their articulation of proposals to recognize and honor these differences. However, for all actors—influencers and influenced alike—familiarity remains as the true test of acceptability. It is originality that destroys security of understanding, raises hackles, and threatens public order. As long as employers always oppose and unions always support strikes, as long as conservatives excoriate and liberals promote big government, then all's right with the world. The ideas that define the understanding and anchor the lives of people are stable and the world predictable, at least to the degree necessary to operate within it on a day-to-day basis. In short, inconvenient and novel truths are the sworn enemy of the conventional wisdom.

Nevertheless, in spite of certain prevailing cleavages in the store of ideas making up the conventional wisdom, there is also a reservoir of widely shared and more or less unchallenged truths within most societies at most times, even those undergoing revolutionary upheavals and structural change. These common ways of seeing and valuing are often embedded in familial, religious, cultural, and tribal traditions and, more generally, in nationalistic and patriotic garb. Thus, conservatives and liberals alike will evince similar views on defending certain rights and social practices, like standing for the singing of the "Star Spangled Banner" or supporting the armed forces of the nation, though some will oppose the particular uses to which those forces are put.

The conventional wisdom is "articulated on all levels of sophistication," including in the terrain of scholarship. In the field of science—and especially social science—conflicting ideas are welcomed but only up to a point. "Minor heresies are much cherished," Galbraith suggests. What is not cherished, and indeed is positively frowned upon, are ideas and arguments that challenge the basic framework of the discipline, the big ideas that seek to define new problems, reinterpret old ones, and provide radically different answers and policy prescriptions from those that currently prevail—i.e. are familiar and generally accepted. This line of argument has some similarity to Thomas Kuhn's (1962) notion of the (dominant) paradigm defining (confining) "normal science," introduced in his influential book, *The Structure of Scientific Revolutions*, published soon after *AS*. Originality for Galbraith remains alive only at the most abstract level in the conventional wisdom in the social sciences so that its "vigorous advocacy" can substitute for originality itself.

II

The conventional wisdom, as a loosely articulated but persevering framework of taken-for-granted ideas, provides a bulwark against the complexities and uncertainties of social and economic life. By its very nature it screens out unpleasant possibilities and anesthetizes anxieties by confining debate and actions to the well-trodden path. This enables people to go about their everyday lives unburdened by the worrying possibility that unforeseen dangers lurk nearby. Where unexpected shocks to the taken-for-granted world explode into consciousness, their speedy reinterpretation within the reassuring conventional wisdom allows normal transmission to be resumed.

Galbraith here anticipates arguments advanced more radically a few years later by Frankfurt School philosopher, Herbert Marcuse. In *One Dimensional Man* (1964), Marcuse points to the closure of the "political universe" creating a new form of totalitarianism resting in turn on "closing of the universe of discourse." By defining and confining human understanding, by socially constructing the very terms through which people make sense of their world, Marcuse saw the roots of an insidious regime of repression. Powerful vested interests—the modern corporation, owners of wealth in its various forms—and the functionaries who objectively operate to support their interests—middle managers, bureaucrats, professionals, police—impose this order on the majority through the routine operation of the economic and social institutions of liberal democracies like the United States. Coercion takes a back seat (except at rare moments of crisis) to "soft power," the molding of opinions and needs through education, advertising, and mass entertainment. The outcome is, in Marcuse's terms, "the paralysis of criticism, society without opposition."

Galbraith too points to the power of corporations creating the needs that consumers pursue in market exchange. He terms this "the dependence effect," to which we return later. However, in *AS* Galbraith's analysis is more restricted than Marcuse's totalizing critique. Galbraith's target is the economists' commitment to the doctrine of consumer sovereignty, to the view that economics is only concerned with how given consumer wants are satisfied, not with how they eventuate. In a later book—*The New Industrial State*—he extends his earlier analysis by situating the construction of consumer demand in the functional requirements of a corporate economy dominated by the planning imperative to ensure continuous, uninterrupted revenue growth.

Marcuse, on the other hand, is interested in demonstrating how mental closure precludes the very possibility of critical thought that might challenge the existing power structure of a modern corporate capitalist society. Corporate power is effective because it is unconsciously internalized by individuals *en masse*. A decade after Marcuse, the sociologist Steven Lukes (1973) coined the term—"the third dimension of power"—to capture this phenomenon. Galbraith, too, returned to this theme in his 1983 book, *The Anatomy of Power* (discussed in a later chapter).

Economists (and according to Kuhn, all scientists) spend most of their working lives busily engaged in exploring the paths and by-ways of "normal science." In this intellectual and social endeavor they are aided by well-established institutional supports. Systems of peer review have evolved to keep research and publication within the orthodox frame. In order to receive research grants, through to gaining acceptance of research findings for publication, economists must satisfy their peers that they are "worthy" of backing. These institutional barriers are very effective in screening out subversive ideas and findings—"subversive" of the orthodoxies that govern the field.

This means that much of what passes for scholarly activity is not—as loudly and repeatedly claimed—a search for new knowledge but a ritualistic exchange and reinforcement of what is generally accepted as true doctrine. "Scholars gather in scholarly assemblages to hear in elegant statement what all have heard before. Again, it is not a negligible rite, for its purpose is not to convey knowledge but to beautify learning and the learned." Academics are one group especially fitted to expound the conventional wisdom. Other groups also fill this role, most notably politicians and business leaders, although Galbraith also reserves an ancillary position for television and radio commentators in this respect—the peculiarly effective and sinister rise to prominence of right wing "shock jocks" in recent times was, presumably, no surprise to Galbraith. Otherwise anonymous individuals of modest talents once elected to public office are "immediately assumed to be gifted with deep insights." The bosses of large corporations are likewise expected to pronounce "not only on business policy and economics but also on the role of government in society and the nature of a liberal education."

Since Galbraith wrote, it might be argued that the scope for articulating the conventional wisdom has become truly global. New communications media, most importantly the World Wide Web, have brought instantaneous, continuous, and exhaustive exchanges within reach of almost all on the planet. In one sense global homogenization reinforces dominant views of the acceptable and familiar, and the purveyors of those views do so on international stages. Thus, the Davos Global Economic Forum (DGEF) provides one such avenue for political, business, and academic leaders to exchange familiarities. However, the same processes of globalization are posing increasing challenges to the westernized articulation; counter-discourses and political movements are arising, drawing on the same communications technologies to inform and mobilize dissent—witness the protests against international forums like the DGEF over the past twenty years and the rise of social media as a tool for informing and empowering people across the globe.

III

Although adherence to the conventional wisdom allows life to proceed along comfortable and predictable paths, the global changes alluded to above cast light on an important insight offered by Galbraith—"The enemy of the conventional wisdom is not ideas but the march of events." Galbraith gives as examples the era of market liberalism ushered in by Adam Smith's demolition of mercantilism in the *Wealth of Nations*, and the subsequent twentieth-century triumph of the welfare state over classical liberalism. The rise of the welfarist conventional wisdom is seen to result from the increasing dissonance between the entrenched truths of laissez-faire capitalism and the undeniable dark realities of industrial capitalism in the second half of the nineteenth century. But as he presciently observes, "(t)here have never ceased to be warnings that the break with classical liberalism was fatal." Since the late-1970s, following the breakdown of Keynesianism in the form of the neoclassical synthesis, market fundamentalism has reasserted its dominance, both in the academy and the sphere of public policy. Neoliberalism and the "Washington consensus" have infiltrated minds and actions during much of this period, only in turn to come under serious challenge in the wake of "the Great Recession" of 2008 and its lingering aftermath.

Galbraith also suggests that the long-standing commitments of western governments in "the long nineteenth century" to balanced budgets was only overturned by the Great Depression of the 1930s, but not immediately; "(a)lmost everyone called upon for advice in the early years of the depression was impelled by the conventional wisdom to offer proposals designed to make things worse." It was this event above all that pushed Keynes to self-consciously attempt to replace "classical" economic ideas with the new macroeconomic theory of his own. By the time *AS* was published, activist (counter-cyclical) fiscal policy had entered the postwar lexicon of economists and policy makers, so that by the early 1970s an American president could say—"we are all Keynesians now."

This timing is ironic, coming just as events were arising that would shatter the orthodox "Keynesian" model. Stagflation—rising inflation coupled with high and persisting unemployment—could not easily be explained by economists operating within the neoclassical synthesis. Neoclassical economics shorn of its Keynesian tail reasserted itself, first in the guise of Milton Friedman's Monetarism and then more fundamentally as "the new classical economics" in which macroeconomics was securely tied to the microanalysis of general equilibrium theory, established by Kenneth Arrow and Gerard Debreu in the 1950s. This path is retraced in the next chapter.

Purveyors of the conventional wisdom play a useful if fleeting role in society. They help impart a degree of stability to a changing world. They act as a filter, weeding out the extreme, impractical, and dangerous, and making room for the eventual triumph of the useful. But because ideas are "inherently conservative" and the world is in flux, today's wisdom must become tomorrow's folly. Today's wise man (Galbraith's prose is conventionally gendered) is tomorrow's "old fogy," confounded by events that he is singularly unfitted to explain; however, with luck Galbraith suggests, by then he will be dead. It is the remorseless march of reality that eventually undermines today's conventional wisdom; inconvenient truths eventually assert themselves through undeniable facts—but rarely without vigorous rearguard action and the passing of considerable time.

Galbraith's chapter on the conventional wisdom, vague and whimsical as it is, is the foundation upon which he builds much of his substantive analysis in the remainder of the book. It provides a rationale and a language for his attack upon certain dominant ideas in the economics discipline of his day, especially as they are called upon to inform public policy. These ideas form an historical continuum—the central tradition of mainstream economics.

3

The Central Tradition

We are suffering just now from a bad case of economic pessimism.

(J.M. Keynes)

The economic system pictured in the central tradition was a thing of peril for those who participated in it and so, *pro tanto*, was economic life in general.

(J.K. Galbraith)

*   *   *

The opening line of Keynes's famous essay, "Economic possibilities for our grandchildren" (1973/1930), was penned in the early days of the Great Depression. This provocative work was meant to reverse the focus induced by his most famous pronouncement (made in 1923) to the effect that "in the long run we are all dead." In his essay, Keynes pointed away from the natural tendency in 1930 to set one's sight on the awful current predicament (in the interests of immediate survival) in order to look one hundred years hence and speculate on how things might be for our descendants. Would they too be forever battling to survive in conditions of scarcity and insecurity? Or would "the economic problem" of how to secure the permanent material needs of the vast majority be routinely met, opening up radical new opportunities and life experiences?

Both Galbraith and Keynes were clear that the period up to the 1930s Depression was dominated by the imperative of solving the economic problem, of ensuring in an uncertain and often unfriendly world that most of the population was able to reproduce the material means of survival. In this they implicitly focused on the nations of the "civilized" world, in par-ticular, the English-speaking world. Scarcity dominated the real world and, hence, attracted the undivided attention of economists from Adam Smith onwards. For Keynes (quoted in Pecchi and Piga, 2010: 25), this meant that the "money-grubbing nature of people must drive the economy: (a)varice and usury and precaution must be our gods for a little longer still. For only they can lead us out of the tunnel of economic necessity into daylight." Until that happy day, society must focus relentlessly on making ends meet, on grubbing out a living.

Galbraith concurred. The four chapters of *AS* following his interrogation of the conventional wisdom sought to trace the evolution of "the central tradition" in economics. Starting with Adam Smith, economists became fixated on how scarce resources are allocated among competing ends. This view was canonized in 1932 by Lionel Robbins in his influential book, *An Essay on the Nature and Significance of Economic Science*. It is true that for the first time in history, the material lot of the majority of people in western nations had improved during "the long nineteenth century." But this had occurred from a very low base and was beset by the unnerving recurrence of economic crises in which trade was disrupted and large numbers of workers were thrown out of employment, culminating in the disaster of global war and depression. Life was still very precarious for most people, even in the advanced nations. It was, therefore, quite natural for economists to concentrate on the prevalence of poverty, insecurity, and scarcity and the pressing need to understand and resolve the economic problem.

The successors to Adam Smith—Ricardian and Marxist—continued "the tradition of despair." Galbraith comments:

> As between the early Ricardian world and that of Marx, there was no difference. For both, the prospect, given the uninterrupted working out of the underlying forces, combined peril with hopelessness. The difference was that Ricardo and his immediate followers expected the system to survive and Marx did not.

In a further respect they differed. Marx held that the eventual collapse of capitalism would usher in an era of human freedom and emancipation—not unlike Keynes's view of the world of "our grandchildren" in 2030, and John Stuart Mill's benign picture of a coming stationary state. Ricardo, on the other hand, saw a future—a malign "stationary state"—in which a class of landowners appropriated the vast fruits of economic activity while the bulk of the population existed at or close to a fairly sparse subsistence. The subsequent "neo-classical revolution" of the 1870s turned the attention of economists away from speculating on distant futures but fixed their attention even more firmly on the problem of scarcity and the imperative of efficiency—the need to make every resource count, to avoid wasting limited means in a world of insatiable ends.

Neoclassical economics, as the dominant orthodox school came to be known, placed almost total faith in the efficacy of the market, in the capacity of free or unconstrained markets, to allocate available resources to their most pressing ends. The role of the state, in this view, was reduced to maintaining civil order, securing external national security, and establishing and enforcing transparent property rights. This was, in essence, Locke's view of "the night-watchman state." Of course, there were some accepted minor limits to the efficiency of fully-fledged laissez-faire.

Marshall's successor in the economics chair at Cambridge, Arthur Pigou, had powerfully identified the unfortunate tendency of some resource uses to generate external effects that were not fully taken into account by market participants. These externalities, negative and positive, distorted resource allocation and reduced actual economic welfare below its potential. However, Pigou (1932/1920) suggested that these inconveniences—when identified—could be dealt with by imposing an appropriate menu of taxes and subsidies to ensure that the effects were properly taken into account by market actors. Current political debates over pricing carbon in order to address the negative planetary externalities associated with global warming reflect this idea of the long-dead economist. Beyond this and a small list of other market failures (monopoly, public goods, etc.) orthodox economics was content to rely on the market to solve the economic problem within the actually existing world of limited resources and unlimited human wants.

What about that nasty tendency of modern capitalist economies to fall into crisis on a fairly regular basis? The orthodox response, then as now, was that recessions are largely the result of unnecessary government interventions in the economy. As long as government allows natural market processes to work, any downturn in the economy will be temporary. Any attempt by government or other institutions like trade unions to prevent prices, interest rates, and wages from flexibly adjusting to current demand and supply conditions will only heighten distortions and delay recovery. In particular, government attempts to boost private spending indirectly through monetary policy or directly by fiscal stimulus will be self-defeating—in the first instance ushering in inflation and in the second instance by "crowding out" private investment.

Benign government intentions will have malign economic outcomes. Government is the problem not the solution. Markets if allowed to operate freely will eventually and always ensure full employment and maximum economic growth. It was this view—cornerstone of the central tradition—that drew Keynes's (1973/1923) famous comment on the long run (in *A Tract on Monetary Reform*); immediately after this most quoted line in Keynes's prolific writings comes the challenge: "Economists set themselves too easy, too useless a task if in tempestuous seasons they can only tell us that when the storm is long past the ocean is flat again" (Keynes, 1973/1923: 65). Here, as noted earlier, Keynes takes the short over the long run view of the operation of the capitalist economy. And yet this is not simply a case of Keynes holding different and conflicting positions over time. When he wrote "Economic possibilities" he was beginning his search for a theoretical demolition of Say's Law, the central prop to the neoclassical view of the self-correcting force of free markets. Once the *General Theory* had demonstrated this to Keynes's satisfaction he was able to argue—even more strongly than before—for an activist fiscal policy by governments in the near term to keep the national economy at or near full employment.

Furthermore, it is only when the economy grows at full employment that living standards are maximized in the long run. If "an output gap"—the difference between potential GDP at full employment and actual GDP—emerges, the lost potential output can never be recouped and through time this loss will compound, making GDP and living standards at any future date far lower than they would have been. For Keynes's 2030 world of plenty to eventuate, the economy, he believed, would need to grow consistently at near full employment. Writing in 1930 Keynes also believed that this could be achieved as long as humanity refrained from further ruinous wars, continued to embrace the productivity enhancing effects of science, and controlled its population growth. A few years later in the *General Theory* he was much less sanguine, demonstrating that capitalist economies were prone to underperform, to gravitate to unemployment equilibrium unless appropriate fiscal stimulation was applied in timely manner.

II

By the time that Galbraith wrote *AS* in the late-1950s, the Keynesian view on government macroeconomic activism had—as noted earlier—taken firm hold in both academia and government, albeit in the form later termed "the neoclassical synthesis." Less politely, Keynes's younger colleague Joan Robinson preferred to call the uneasy mixture of neoclassical microeconomics and a narrow "hydraulic" version of Keynesian macroeconomics "bastard Keynesianism." This volatile cocktail was decades later to spark a heated and far from finished debate between orthodox and post-Keynesian economists on what Keynes really meant and to open a parallel battle on the "correct" micro-foundations to macroeconomics. We return to these skirmishes later in this chapter.

However, for Galbraith writing in the 1950s, the issue was decided. Governments could and should intervene to reduce economic instability, though not (as we will see) without a careful understanding of the institutional context within which the economy operated. This as we will also see influenced his treatment of the key issue of economic insecurity. His biographer Richard Parker notes that Galbraith's first overseas academic foray in 1937 was to England, hoping to meet and discuss Keynes's ideas with the master himself. Unfortunately, Keynes was seriously ill and away from Cambridge at that time and Galbraith contented himself with vigorously discussing these ideas with the master's apprentices, the famous "circus" of young economists surrounding Keynes during the 1930s.

By the time he wrote *AS*, Galbraith could thus move onto other weaknesses he perceived in the central tradition, weaknesses that arose from the failure of economists to perceive that modern industrial societies were gradually but inevitably moving from the world of scarcity to one of rising affluence. The America of his day was in the vanguard. These themes formed the focus for the latter part of *AS* and will be dealt with in later chapters. However, here we briefly mention them.

First, Galbraith takes issue with the doctrine of "consumer sovereignty" that holds that consumers in market societies come to market with fully formed, exogenously determined preferences and full information on their own desires, resources, and goods on offer. He introduces, in contrast, his doctrine of "the dependence effect," the idea that consumer preferences are in part endogenously determined by the institutional web within which real people live, work, and consume.

Second, he also takes issue with what he terms "the paramount position of production," our fixation with increasing the output of goods and services; any goods and services. Whatever markets deliver is good. Whatever markets don't deliver is irrelevant. Politics and policy focus on maximizing national output, conventionally measured as the Gross Domestic Product, annual production throughout the economy valued (of course) at market prices. The trend in real GDP becomes the single measure of economic success and provides an iron benchmark for how one economy is traveling both over time and by comparison with other countries. This, Galbraith suggests, has blinded us to the increasingly important challenges raised by the rise of affluence, to the approaching "economic possibilities" that past and continuing economic growth has ushered in. Here Galbraith seems to be more optimistic than Keynes, at least with respect to the timeline for realizing those opportunities. He writes as if many were present in 1950s America, the mirror of other developed economies' futures.

Third, the fixation on rising output and consumption is, Galbraith avers, increasingly and dangerously dependent on taking on debt. When Galbraith wrote, the phenomenon of consumer debt was in its early stages, focused on buying a house to live in and fitting it (including the garage) out using the new-fangled mechanism of hire purchase. The dangers of debt-fuelled growth are well known fifty years on in the wake of the 2008 global financial crisis. Institutional changes associated with the rise of neoliberalism, especially deregulation of the financial system, and the pace of global economic integration ensured that the debt-sparked recession, when it came, would be deeper, longer lasting, and more "contagious" than anything since the Great Depression.

Fourth, inflation, like taxes and death, has ever been in attendance. "Next only to the virtues of competition, there is nothing on which the conventional wisdom is more completely agreed than on the importance of stable prices."

However, Galbraith also points to the equally constant fact that "(a)ll branches of the conventional wisdom are equally agreed on the undesirability of remedies that are effective." Markets if left to themselves seem to result inevitably in recurrent bursts of inflation, sometimes dampened, sometimes rampant, but governments have their hands tied in dealing with the fallout.

Fifth, the focus on the volume of production has taken attention away from its composition. This observation allows Galbraith to introduce his most famous and contentious "theory of social balance." Markets operating freely increasingly over-supply privately produced goods and services, while under-supplying goods and services, normally provided by government, that are required to ensure the continuing smooth functioning of the economy and society. To some extent, this reproduces Pigou's emphasis on externalities and subsequent discussions of public and merit goods. To this Galbraith brings a quantitative emphasis on the pervasiveness of the deficiencies and a qualitative critique of the resulting broader environment. In this guise, some later commentators have seen Galbraith as an early proponent of environmentalism.

Finally, Galbraith explicitly follows Keynes in pointing to the capacity of rising affluence to change the way most people will in future work and live. Veblen's leisure class would grow with increasing wealth and affluence. This emphasis brings into sharp relief a theme that runs through not just *AS* but the entire corpus of Galbraith's work—that is, the importance of understanding power, its sources, uses, and consequences in the new, unfolding world of affluence. Also associated with this viewpoint was his commitment to see economics practiced in a way that spoke to an informed citizenry in order to influence public policy and reinforce the underlying moral order of a functioning liberal democracy—as, indeed, was Keynes's lifelong mission.

Galbraith's analysis of the impact of rising affluence in the developed world—he was still deeply pessimistic about the prospects of the underdeveloped world—also blinded him to the continuing salience of the twin evils (market failures) of inequality and insecurity. He explicitly acknowledged this failing in his 1998 revision. Just how far off the mark he was here will be discussed in later chapters.

III

By the early 1970s, the postwar long boom was running out of steam and a phenomenon described as "stagflation" unexpectedly appeared on the scene—unexpected because the neoclassical synthesis dominating economic theory and policy held that inflation and unemployment would not occur together, that Keynesian tools of fiscal policy could fine-tune national economies trading off one for the other until an acceptable balance was reached.

But as unemployment approached and inflation breached double-digit figures, perplexed governments and their economic advisers began to question
the then conventional wisdom. In the United States, now the centre of economic science, international factors intensified the gloomy atmosphere. As an
unpopular Asian war dragged on and the Cold War persisted, international
institutional arrangements that formed the bedrock of postwar prosperity
crumbled. The US exited the Gold Standard and the safety net provisions of
the 1944 Bretton Woods Agreement collapsed. Much of the theoretical basis
on which Galbraith worked in the 1950s that both negatively and positively
supported the construction of his arguments in the *AS* came under question.
A new high tide of high theory was washing in.

The central tradition in economics, having held for almost 200 years, began
to fracture. The first divergence, based in the University of Chicago Economics
Department, reached back beyond Adam Smith to resurrect or re-polish the
"Quantity Theory of Money." In this tradition, full employment would follow
from the free play of market forces in the real economy, while the general level
of prices, inflation, was determined by the quantity of money circulating in the
economy. As long as the quantity of money increased at around the long-term
growth rate, inflation would stay under control. Since developments like output and employment were determined in the real economy, independently
of "the veil of money," an economy could continue to grow without either
involuntary unemployment or inflation—but only if governments avoided the
temptation to intervene by—for example—running budget deficits in the vain
attempt to boost employment. Monetarism's Godfather, Milton Friedman,
even went back and reinterpreted the Great Depression as a case study in government failure; the government is the problem not the solution (Friedman
and Schwartz, 1963; see also Friedman, 1971).

More powerful and effective attempts to discredit Keynesian economics,
one of the key planks on which Galbraith had built the arguments of the *AS*,
followed. Economists trained in the new mathematical tools of the discipline
turned their gaze on what were seen as the inadequate microeconomic foundations of Keynes's *General Theory*. New Classical Economics applied the
results of general equilibrium theory (GET) to the macro field. Analysis of
the economy at large had to reflect the basic assumptions (axioms) of GET,
as laid down by Kenneth Arrow and Gerard Debreu (1954) in the 1950s. This
theory rigorously established the "existence" of a Pareto-optimal allocation of
resources in competitive market economies characterized by a set of highly
unrealistic assumptions. For example, all economic actors were assumed to
have *complete knowledge* of (1) all possible uses to which their resources could
be devoted, now and into the indefinite future and (2) all the consequences
of each of those uses. Moreover, every actor was assumed to be able to attach
meaningful probabilities to the outcome of every consequence of every use.
Each actor was a calculating machine, carefully and exhaustively working out

the expected value or utility of every resource use by multiplying the outcomes and probabilities and aggregating in each case. Once in possession of this information, each actor would rationally choose the set of actions/uses that maximized his or her total utility. Since things change over time, the machine never stops calculating and actors are continually adjusting their choices at the margin.

This approach was formally complemented by the theory of "rational expectations," the whole based on what has been called "the ergodic axiom," the view that the future reflects the past, so that actors can extrapolate from past events in order to calculate an accurate set of probabilities about what will happen in the future. In such a world, as long as no one is stopped from freely exchanging in commodity, labor, and financial markets, it would not be possible for any one actor to be made better off without at least one other actor being made worse off. All resources, including labor, are fully employed and the general price level (as opposed to relative prices which continually vary) is stable.

To the obvious criticism that the assumptions on which GET rested were manifestly, even ludicrously, unrealistic, that real world economic actors operated in a fog of incomplete and inaccurate information, and often in ways that appeared "irrational," orthodox economists had a stock answer; the reality or otherwise of assumptions was irrelevant, all that mattered was the logical coherence and consistency of the model. Indeed, Milton Friedman had long before (in the early 1950s) preempted this line of attack in a much-quoted paper, which argued this case explicitly. For Friedman, a sound economic argument or theory did not require realistic assumptions, only that its logical conclusions adequately predicted the empirically observable outcomes.

What became clear, however, was that GET had a number of limitations, even on its own grounds. The proof of the existence of a welfare maximizing equilibrium was dependent on a negative argument. Using the higher algebra, based on the axiomatic approach, economists were only able to establish that given the (unrealistic) assumption set, it was logically impossible for there *not* to be a Pareto-optimal equilibrium. This result resonated with the sentiments of mathematicians but left an oddly unsatisfactory taste in the mouths of many economists (and others). Even more worryingly, not even the higher mathematics could establish the two other features of what would be seen as a complete vindication of GET—namely, the uniqueness and stability of the resulting competitive equilibrium. General equilibrium theorists could not demonstrate conclusively that the resulting equilibrium would be unique; multiple equilibria could not be ruled out, nor could the possibility that once equilibrium was disturbed the economy would diverge further away rather than snap back. Finally, it was clear that the general equilibrium resulting was dependent on the initial distribution of resources or wealth. There was a different Pareto-optimal equilibrium for *every* initial distribution. Efficiency was one desideratum in a world of scarcity but it didn't answer the question of equity in the distribution of the fruits of economic activity.

What then about the tendency of the macroeconomy to oscillate, to lurch from boom to bust? Once the big guns of GET are brought to bear (as long as the inconvenient truth of the stability problem is overlooked), this observable tendency in actually existing economies can be explained away as either the fault of interventionist governments or the unexpected impact of external or exogenous events, like war or technological innovation. A branch of New Classical Economics called "real business cycle theory" formally established this latter argument in the later 1970s and early 1980s. This approach to macroeconomics developed the ultra-rational assumptions of orthodox microeconomics to its logical extreme, resulting in the "dismal" conclusion that all and any intervention by government in the economy was both unnecessary and self-defeating. Increasingly, this element of the central tradition assumed the character of scholastic arguments reminiscent of the medieval monastery.

But, as Galbraith would have appreciated, the great threat to the conventional wisdom—the march of facts—eventually prevailed. Persistent economic instability and torpid growth during the 1980s, especially in those economies like the United Kingdom that embraced the policy prescriptions of this approach, fatally undermined the grip of New Classical Economics, which only lingered on in university economics departments and in the modified form of general equilibrium analysis that converged with the first stream of new Keynesian analysis noted below. Both approaches were subsequently "blind-sided" or ambushed by the global financial crisis; but as we will later see, some ideas never die; they are in Paul Krugman's words, "undead," zombies ready to resurface and stalk the world when the time is right again.

At the same time as the new orthodoxy was sweeping academic economics departments in the US and elsewhere, other economists were beginning to reread and reinterpret Keynes, to distinguish between Keynesian economics and the economics of Keynes, as one of the members of this "post-Keynesian" ensemble termed it in the late 1960s.

This movement broadly broke into two schools. "New Keynesian" economists largely accepted the contours of the neoclassical synthesis, in particular the centrality of the concept of equilibrium, but drew on one strand of the *General Theory* and relaxed the neoclassical assumption of fully flexible prices and/or wages. They developed a range of "fixed price" models of the economy in which quantities vary to establish equilibrium, which can exist at less than full employment. These models hark back to the arguments of Keynes's Cambridge colleagues, Pigou and Dennis Robertson,* who held that recessions could eventuate from blockages in the operation of markets, real and financial. However, one response of policy makers to new Keynesian analysis

---

* See Pigou (1927) and Robertson (1926).

would be the same as the advice proffered by the new classical school—get rid of the barriers to freely operating markets. If this was not possible, only then would new Keynesian policy sanction interventionist fiscal and monetary actions by government.

The second loose group of "post-Keynesian" economists is closely associated with the University of Cambridge, Keynes's own. These economists differ in their emphases but all in some way deny the validity of the new classical approach, assumptions, and method. For these economists, the reality of assumptions was critical to adequately fathoming what was happening in the real world. Economic actors were seen to be limited and fallible in their knowledge and judgments. Drawing on Chapter 12 of *General Theory*, they recognized that the future was essentially unknowable, full of both "known unknowns" and "unknown unknowns." In a world of Keynesian uncertainty, as opposed to calculable risk, the ergodic axiom is violated. The future cannot be reduced to a "statistical shadow of the past," as one prominent American post-Keynesian has commented (Davison, 2009: 38). The past is not necessarily a good guide to the future. Economic actors are left to deal individually with an essentially unknowable future. Rough and ready strategies, or in Keynes's term, "rules of thumb," are fallen back on to cope with this inconvenient truth. Expect the unexpected and be prepared to adjust, might be one such strategy. Assume the best, prepare for the worst might be another. One thing that an economic actor can do in a developed monetary economy to prepare for unexpected and unpleasant surprises is to stay liquid, that is to hold money or assets readily changeable into money, since only money in its various forms is a resource capable of meeting all liabilities when due—the more uncertain the future, the greater the advantage of staying liquid and the greater the premium payable (i.e. interest forgone) to do so.

This reading of Keynes holds that "money matters." There is no sharp distinction, either in the short or long run, between the real economy and what happens in financial markets. Money is not simply a veil, a means of facilitating market exchange. Critically, it also functions as both a common unit of account and a store of value. It is because the future is so uncertain that money is the ultimate hedge—except against future inflation. Post-Keynesians like Paul Davidson and Hyman Minsky (1975) hold that developments in financial markets associated with movements in financial asset prices ramify through to movements in aggregate demand, output, and employment. When investor and consumer confidence is dented, when "animal spirits" are sagging, aggregate demand in the economy slumps and unemployment begins to climb, reinforcing pessimistic sentiments and sparking a cumulative downturn. Economic actors seek to build their liquid positions, the demand for money and close substitutes increases. In a serious crisis, "cash is king." As prices fall deflation threatens and the real value of existing debts mount, further squeezing spending and reinforcing the downward trajectory. It was this "debt-deflation" theory that America's most famous economist of Keynes's time, Irving Fisher (1933), advanced to explain the severity of the Great Depression—though understanding came too late to prevent the loss of his personal fortune in stock market speculation. (Keynes, on the other hand, was a very successful speculator in stocks and currencies, much to the benefit of his Cambridge college.)

Another post-Keynesian strand, associated in particular with the Nobel Prize winner Joseph Stiglitz,[†] takes head on the assumption of perfect information in the orthodox paradigm. Information, he argues, is inherently costly to procure and decipher. More importantly, it is of uneven quality and unevenly accessible. Informational "asymmetries" pervade economic decision making. This, he suggests, is the most deep-seated and important form of market failure. In his (2010) book account of the global financial crisis (GFC), *Freefall*, he systematically points out the factors leading inexorably to crisis. Most actors were simply unaware of the extent to which the solvency of national financial systems was undermined by a combination of perverse incentives, lax lending standards, weak regulation, loose monetary policy, and the division of interests (and information) between wealth holders and managers. The "agency problem" and systemic interdependence of financial institutions meant that all financial sector managers had a common incentive to act in increasingly risky, because profitable, ways while disregarding the cumulative effects ramifying through the financial system as a whole to eventually spill over into the real economy on a global scale. Why didn't markets discipline actors to stop the slide, as orthodox theory proclaimed? Why didn't the world act in ways consistent with "the efficient markets hypothesis?" The CEO of one of the largest investment mega-banks at the time said words to the effect that—"the music was playing, so we had to keep dancing." Once the music stopped there weren't enough chairs to go around and the feverish rush for liquidity in order to meet escalating and intertwined debts turned a liquidity crisis sparked by mass defaults in the once sleepy corner of the debt market (house mortgages) into a solvency crisis that threatened to bring down the economies of the entire western world.

Several of Keynes's Cambridge colleagues extended the short run analysis of *General Theory* to the long run, creating an alternative theory of economic growth to the neoclassical model initiated by Robert Solow and Trevor Swan two years before publication of *AS*. In particular, Joan Robinson and Nicholas Kaldor built on the pioneering work of the Polish Marxist economist, Michal Kalecki (1939), by integrating income distribution and capital accumulation in ways that accounted for the business cycle. Moreover, Kalecki had developed a theory of price formation—the addition of a margin to average variable costs—that better reflected actually observable practices in industry, especially

---

[†] See Stiglitz (2000, 2010).

those exhibiting a degree of monopoly power. This meant—in the eyes of this approach—that Keynesian macroeconomics now had a firm alternative micro-foundation based on the decisions of individual economic actors, while being able to explain the dynamic instability of actually existing capitalist economies. The price paid was to jettison Keynes's specific focus on establishing the likelihood of short run unemployment equilibrium. The whole concept of equilibrium was redundant.

A similar conclusion was reached for different reasons by the "Austrian school," whose main twentieth-century proponents, Joseph Schumpeter and Friedrich von Hayek,[‡] were sharp critics of Keynes and opponents of government economic intervention. Their focus was on the dynamic capacity of capitalist economies to "spontaneously" improve living standards through time—and in Hayek's case, to guarantee freedom.

Keynes's other Cambridge colleague, Pierro Sraffa (1960), launched a long gestated attack on the neoclassical paradigm, culminating in what was called "the Cambridge capital controversies," referring to the debates between economists at Cambridge in the United Kingdom and those at Harvard and MIT (Cambridge, MA). This attack neatly returned the favor by dismissing the micro-foundations of neoclassical/new classical economics. Sraffa's positive contribution was to present a neo-Richardian model whose adherents see in it an alternative not only to neoclassicism but also Keynesian and Marxist theories.

IV

Further heterodox challenges to the central tradition have emerged over the past three decades. From the early nineteenth century onward mainstream economics has implicitly adopted the approach and mathematical form of classical physics, more specifically the central concept of equilibrium taken from Newtonian mechanics. Within this world view, attention fixes on comparative static and steady state dynamic characteristics of economic systems. There is, however, another tradition that looked not to physics but to biology for its inspiration. The early twentieth-century institutionalist economist, Thorstein Veblen,[§] first laid out this line of argument in an explicit critique of the neoclassical model. But even Alfred Marshall, co-founder of that model,

    [‡] See Horwitz (2007); Boettke and Leeson (2007); Schumpeter, 1962/1942, 1934/1912; Wapshott, 2011.
    [§] See M Rutherford "American institutional economics in the interwar period," in W Samuels, J Biddle and J Davis (eds) 2007 *A Companion to the History of Economic Thought*, Blackwell, Oxford.

opined that perhaps capitalist economies developed through real time rather like a forest, with individual firms emerging, growing, and declining to be replaced in a succession of ever changing industry structures.

More recently a fully-fledged "evolutionary economics" has emerged—one is tempted to say, evolved. In part this has developed from a rediscovery of Joseph Schumpeter's early work on economic dynamics, first published before the First World War in his *Theory of Economic Development* (1934/1912) and later reprised for a wider audience in his influential book *Capitalism, Socialism and Democracy* (1962/1942). Schumpeter's key contribution was to accentuate the dynamic role of innovation, particularly bursts of innovation, to create new paths of development underpinning growth over time but also ensuring instability. It was this notion that implicitly underlay Keynes's confidence in the power of compound interest to radically improve living standards in the coming century.

Modern evolutionary economists take the basic Darwinian algorithm—variation-selection-replication—and apply it to the economy treated as a dynamic complex adaptive system. In this non-linear world, innovation creates ever new "path dependent" trajectories that cannot be captured by, for example, static linear simultaneous equation models, and the computable general equilibrium models of the economy on which economic policy makers normally depend. In the words of two prominent proponents: "General equilibrium analysis does not capture the innovativeness and restlessness of modern economies" (Hodgson and Knudsen, 2010: 3), referring to the pioneering work in evolutionary economics of Richard Nelson and Sidney Winter (1982). Innovations create new variations (new products, new business models, new production processes) which when successful drive existing products, processes, and organizational forms out of existence and are replicated via competition and emulation throughout the industry sector. This in turn changes interlinkages with other sectors, stimulating complementary innovations that when selected feed back into the qualitatively new competitive environment, and so on, continuously.

This innovation-focused approach relaxed one of the key assumptions of the central tradition—namely, the pervasiveness of diminishing returns in production, critical in getting the neoclassical mathematics to work. Dynamic, path-dependent change created the likelihood of *increasing returns* and underscored the competitive advantages of being a "first mover," resulting in "the winner take most" outcome prevalent in tournament play. Like the orthodox GET model, initial conditions were critical in determining the end point of market-mediated resource allocation, but unlike GET, the outcome was not predictable—i.e. it was not possible to logically prove that markets maximized efficient allocation. Instead, actual economic trajectories were open-ended; any number of paths were possible depending on where and how the anarchic process of innovation unwound. Just as evolutionary biologists, if existing 60 million years ago, could not have predicted the subsequent dominance of the planet by an obscure, unimpressive mammal, homo sapiens, so economists in the 1990s failed to foresee the rise and impact a decade later of Google and social networking.

This was not good news for economists and their job prospects. Governments could with reason expect their advisers to offer some light as they plotted the future course of the ship of state. "We have no idea" is not a comforting answer to the query as to whether or not there is a hidden reef up ahead. This is even less useful than Keynes's critique of the advice that the sea will be flat well after the storm has past and casts doubt on his hope that economists would one day become dentists, routinely tending the oral health of the economy; even dentists need reliable drill and chair. Is it surprising that an early contributor to this school (Omerod) called his 1994 book *The Death of Economics*?

The American economist Richard Goodwin was an early convert to the emerging non-linear economics. In 1967 he published a model of "the growth cycle" that demonstrated that innovation was endogenous, undermining a further prop to the new classical project. Two decades later, Paul Romer (1986) introduced "the new growth theory" that also undercut conventional linear growth models and entrenched the subversive reality of increasing returns to production.

A second interdisciplinary attack on orthodoxy, also launched in the 1970s, came from the discipline of psychology, both social and (increasingly) cognitive. In the latter case, the term "neuro-economics" began to appear in the last two decades as the human brain became the focus of attention in interdisciplinary enquiry. Biology once more exerted its sway over the dismal science.

The new field of behavioral economics was initiated by Princeton psychologist, Daniel Kahnemann, and Stanford's Amos Tversy who concentrated their fire on how real people actually make economic decisions, as opposed to how economists assumed they did.** This presented a direct challenge to the "rational economic man" (REM) figure so central a part of the central tradition over two centuries. REMs interacted through voluntary market exchange by each maximizing their independent, exogenously given utility functions in the way specified by GET.

Kanemann and Tversy tested this austere expected utility hypothesis by conducting a range of decision experiments with generations of long-suffering undergraduates and colleagues. What they found radically undermined the orthodox model, though this was hardly news to everyone not practicing as economists. People, it appears, are not, after all, rational calculating machines with no off button. This is not simply because information is scarce, expensive, and unevenly accessible, though these are important limitations. People,

---

** For a collection of key papers in behavioral economics, including the seminal contributions of Kahneman and Tversy, see Cammerer et al. (2003).

it seems, have a veritable closet full of semi-conscious and unconscious filters and biases that determine how they'll act in common choice situations. Increasingly, neuroscience is discovering that these tendencies are hard wired into the very structure of our brains. Real economic actors may not be irrational, in the literal sense of the term, but "differently rational." During the 1950s and 1960s Herbert Simon developed his theories of "bounded rationality" to reflect aspects of this condition; however, the later psychological perspective moved beyond considerations of limited information and calculating capacity to explore systematic behavioral biases and proclivities.

For example, we dislike losing more than we like winning—a "loss aversion" bias. We particularly hate having something we have taken away from us. We also are strongly biased to the present, including but going beyond orthodox theories of discounting the future. This too is no news to anyone who has tried, repeatedly, to give up smoking or lose weight; it's always a case of "I'll start tomorrow," but then today becomes tomorrow, so "I'll start the next day," and so and on. When people who are not sociopaths or suffering mental illness make choices they will usually do so with deeply embedded feelings of what is right or fair, modifying the extreme calculus of selfish advantage. This bias is, of course, largely dependent on culture and social milieu and so varies across and between countries and eras.

We have, as Keynes suggested, a proclivity for economizing on mental effort to avoid the pain and anxiety of having to make well-informed decisions, thereby falling back on helpful rules of thumb. Projecting the past into the future, a psychological not logical commitment to the ergodic axiom is one such prop. Even more reassuring are biases that advance one's own interest in the guise of a broader good. Self-serving bias ensures, without exception, that (as already noted), employer organizations oppose any wage increase as an invitation to uncontrollable inflation, if not a threat to public morals, while trade unions strongly support such claims as well within the capacity of the economy to pay. The wealthy will always oppose tax increases on the wealthy as undermining future growth and employment, while also opposing increasing welfare expenditure as inimical to work incentives— and thus future growth and employment. Galbraith a number of times commented on the dualistic theory of human nature held by the wealthy; they need the spur of expected gain to work hard, the poor need the whip of starvation to induce effort.

Finally, behavioral economists point to the tendency of people to overestimate their grasp of the situation, to make decisions on the basic of sketchy or irrelevant information, to rely on long-held prejudices and taken-for-granted truths. People go with what they have. Disconfirming or inconvenient truths are ignored or denied, especially if they conflict with immediate self-interest. Those scraps of information or opinion that confirm already held positions are gratefully received. The unfolding debate on climate change illustrates these biases in abundance. In part, this apparent need to know is probably related to our biological nature as "pattern-seeking animals."

Behavioral economists and some politicians are using these insights to steer or "nudge" public policy in desired directions. How a choice or policy situation is "framed" can affect the outcome for good or ill. It has been found that we as a species are not naturally skilled at making absolute judgments in isolation from context—but we are preeminent at making comparative judgments and fine distinctions. Thus, in any novel situation, people look for a benchmark or anchor point to compare the new developments. When deciding on whether to buy a particular car, we want to know we are getting a good or at least fair deal (remember loss aversion) so we look around for comparisons; what did a similar car sell for yesterday? Experiments have shown that people make widely different judgments of value (utility) depending on their anchor point.

V

In our view, economic theory should be derived not from the minimal deviations from the system of Adam Smith but rather from the deviations that actually do occur and can be observed.

(G. Akerloff and R. Shiller, 2009: 5)

All this, as noted, is bad news for orthodox economics, now under attack on a number of fronts, evolutionarily, behaviorally, and institutionally. Of course, Galbraith didn't and couldn't have known the multifarious ways in which the central tradition was going to break down over the fifty years after he wrote *AS*. However, his work over a long lifetime did express many of the criticisms, explicit and implied, of the dominant tradition. He was particularly concerned, from his earliest publications, to develop explanations based on the actual structure of the developed economy of which America represented the paradigmatic case. It was this tendency that caused most commentators to see Galbraith as continuing the American school of institutionalist economics, following Veblen, Commons, J.M. Bates, and Mitchell and acting as a bridge to recent developments in both evolutionary and "new institutional" economics.

Galbraith's first book (*Modern Competition and Business Policy*, published in 1934) written with a progressive businessman, stressed the emergence of what he later called two sectors in the economy, the competitive realm of small producers in areas like agriculture and the corporate sector dominated by large oligopolists able to set prices and plan over the long term. These sectors operated on uneven playing fields and government could and should intervene in order to bring about more efficient and equitable outcomes. The reality of uneven market power undermined the effective operation of market economies and justified an interventionist state operating at the industry and sector levels, not merely at the macroeconomic level. These views, rising out of his early observations of the problems faced by North American farmers, were never relinquished, resurfacing time and again throughout his extensive oeuvre. They formed part of what Schumpeter (1954) called "the pre-analytic vision" and Myrdal (1953) "the beam in our eyes."

This vision was powerfully evident in *AS*. It colored his treatment of economic insecurity, inflation, and, in particular, the relative imbalance between publicly and privately provided goods and services. Galbraith maintained his position that economic power and vested interests materially influenced both what actually happened in the economy and how economists sought to explain what happened. He remained committed to a realist methodology, insisting on the need for economists to analyze the world as it is, not as they would like it to be—for normative, interested, or analytically convenient reasons. Writing in his 1998 foreword to the revised edition of *AS*, he regretfully comments, "…I still adhere to one of the book's main conclusions—that, sadly, economic writing and teaching instill attitudes and beliefs that resist accommodation to a changing world." Keynes's parting comment on the long-lasting shadow of long-dead economists resonates here, as does his (claimed) response to a critic who queried his tendency to change his theoretical framework—"When circumstances change, I change my mind. What, sir, do you do?"

Understandably, the changing world over the past fifty years has left many of Galbraith's themes and argued conclusions in need of radical repair or replacement. Neither he nor anyone else could have foreseen the degree to which the linked processes of globalization and "financialisation" have altered the face of the globe over the past fifty years. In that world, increasingly witnessing the urban–industrial revolution in China and the rapid growth of other large emerging nations, India, Brazil, and others, it is no longer possible (as it was in the 1950s) to treat the United States unilaterally as the undisputed economic hegemon and simple mirror of other countries' futures. This truth is particularly compelling in the continually confused and uncertain world ushered in by the global financial crisis, stormy seas that we are still, at the time of writing, attempting to navigate. The remainder of this book seeks to place key themes of *AS* in the eye of this storm.

4

Inequality

Few things have been more productive of controversy over the ages than the suggestion that the rich should, by one device or another, share their wealth with those who are not.

(J.K. Galbraith)

In essence, the social pathology of a highly unequal society consists in the destructive effect that inequality has on social solidarity: in the sense that those who live together share a common fate and should work together.

(Brian Barry)

* * *

Inequality, Galbraith avers, has been a constant and continuing concern of economics as practiced in the central tradition. However, its status has remained secondary to the untrammeled pursuit of efficiency. In a world of scarcity, maximum attention is paid to squeezing the most output out of limited resources; the distribution of the fruits of this never-ending battle with nature, inanimate and human, is an embedded by-product. The first line of defense of economic and social inequalities resulting from the efficiency imperative—both thematically and historically—was located in John Locke's moral philosophy of an individual's natural right to the fruits of his or her labor. This position conveniently resonates with the idea, naturally attractive to the wealthy, that freedom or liberty of the citizen is intimately connected to allowing the wealthy to keep what they own. However, this proved to be a dangerously insecure defense. Radicals of all denominations, in the early phase of capitalist development, quickly picked up on the point that real freedom required the provision of a decent basic standard of living for the impoverished masses. In a scarcity defined world posited by the central tradition, in which growth lagged and the specter of "the stationary state" loomed, this could only be achieved through redistributing some of the wealth of the old landed elite and the new industrial entrepreneurs.

A second and more secure line of defense was opened when the fruits of industrialization began to become evident in the second half of the nineteenth century in Britain, Germany, and the United States. Economic growth, rather than stagnation, characterized these vanguard economies. Growth, in turn, was predicated on ensuring that incentives to save, invest, and work were not undermined by reckless projects of redistribution. A degree of inequality was seen as both an inevitable outcome of the new dynamic economy and as a necessary condition for building and maintaining the dynamic. Inequality, in short, attained a *functional* rationale. The wealthy as a group also served a critical function as financiers of growth. Since they couldn't—even in the gilded age of conspicuous consumption—consume all they "earned," their "forced" savings would be the font from which future investment was drawn to fuel continuing growth. True, they would continue to receive a large and perhaps growing share of the growing economic dividend—but in their wake all boats would lift on the rising tide. Inequality could then coexist with rising living standards for a majority of the working population and their families. Although other, elitist arguments in favor of a wealthy class have been advanced—such as their readiness to support high culture and charitable purposes—"... in the conventional wisdom, the defense of inequality does rest primarily on its functional role as an incentive and as a source of capital."

The beneficent functions of inequality have also been used more aggressively to preempt governments from lifting taxes—and to reduce them wherever possible—on the wealthy and high income earners generally. Progressive income taxes have been consistently held in contempt by wealthy interests and their promoters, since they are held to reduce incentives to work, save, innovate, and invest. Galbraith points out here the problematic nature of this claim, problematic for the haves, that is, since "not many businessmen wish to concede that they are putting forth less than their best efforts because of insufficient pecuniary incentive." The argument regarding the incentive to save is particularly unconvincing; the wealthy save by default since there are limits to their consumption space and time. How many designer handbags and private jets can one buy in a year? Finally, Galbraith argues, comparative empirical research offers little support for the claim that rapid capital formation is associated with, still less driven by, a pronounced degree of inequality; growth in egalitarian Scandinavia, for example, greatly outpaced that in Latin America in the immediate postwar period—and, one may add, long after this.

The success of this defense has, Galbraith argues in his original statement, been all but total; "... few things are more evident in modern social history than the decline of interest in inequality as an economic issue." This unexpected outcome can be put down to three main reasons. First, the dire predictions of Ricardo and Marx have not eventuated. Inequality has not increased, indeed, quite the reverse; since the Second World War the share of lower income households has risen and the share of the richest fifth of the population declined, albeit slightly—looking backward from the standpoint of 1958.

Second, the rich were becoming less important and visible in the United States. The super-rich leaders of industry were pioneer owner-managers of their industrial empires, highly visible and influential in political circles. They were "celebrities" in the modern sense, their every action and lavish lifestyles the common currency of mass observation, aspiration, and envy. The three benefits of wealth were power, the possession of physical things, and status. The first of these, Galbraith suggests, has waned. Government has independently increased its scale and scope of operations. The division between ownership and management of "the modern corporation" has reduced the direct day-to-day influence of rich owners in favor of the rise of a new managerial class, offering avenues to affluence to aspiring talented members of the wider society. At the same time, the rich had become more circumspect about the wisdom of conspicuous consumption, confining their activities to elite clubs, private estates, and exclusive neighborhoods. Moreover, other forms of what Galbraith had earlier termed "countervailing power" were in play. Trade unions and a bevy of community-based interest groups pursued different agendas that often cut across or limited the prerogatives of the economic and social elite, in both industrial and political spheres; here Galbraith seems to be embracing the highly influential impact of "pluralism" ascendant in 1950s US academic political science. The status accorded to wealth was also diminished somewhat by the disappearance of "the servile class," that impoverished mass of servants and providers of personal services to the rich; this comment was made before the boom in illegal migrants from Latin America and elsewhere.

Third, the traditional concern with entrenched inequality was overwhelmed by the triumph of capitalist growth, the cascading increase in the production of material commodities. The mass production of affordable consumer goods, cars, television sets, refrigerators, etc., as well as increased access to traditional sporting and leisure attractions distracted mass attention from the continuing truth that some were more equal than others. "Thanks to its tendency to spread its benefits wide, production had a dramatic effect on even the most vocal opponents of inequality." The fact that postwar growth also coincided with or was expressed in rampant suburbanization meant that the social distance between rich and poor was reproduced in physical separation. Rich and poor no longer lived cheek by jowl in large cities. The better off working and growing middle classes moved to the expanding suburbs to live in houses purchased on credit, along with the new items of domestic consumption and mobility. Only the remnant poor—racial and ethnic minorities—were left, forgotten and trapped in urban ghettos or rural isolation.

In the United States, individual aspiration and achievement had always been a powerful cultural force, an enduring characteristic of American exceptionalism. The triumph of production in the US economy underpinned a general faith in the possibility, slim to be sure, that anyone could succeed, with talent, hard work, and a little luck, the fruits of success apparent in abundant consumption of material wealth.

> Modern mass communications, especially the movies and television, ensure that the populace at large will see the most lavish caparisoning on the bodies of not only the daughters of the rich but also on daughters of coal miners and commercial travelers who have struck it rich by their own talents or some facsimile thereof.

The populace at large, Galbraith suggests, may therefore be less inclined to give up their chance at becoming rich by worrying too much about currently being poor. Social mobility predicated on the primacy of production rather than economic redistribution energizes the affluent society. Increased production has become "the great solvent of the tensions associated with inequality."

> . . . we need only notice that, as an economic and social concern, inequality has declined in urgency, and this has had its reflection in the conventional wisdom. The decline has been for a variety of reasons but, in one way or another, these are all related to the fact of increasing production . . . The oldest and most agitated of social issues, if not resolved, is at least in abeyance, and the disputants have concentrated their attention, instead, on the goal of increased productivity.

The overwhelmingly modern emphasis on economic growth—resting Galbraith suggests, on the "paramount position of production"—is, as we will see, a strong thread running throughout *AS*.

II

Galbraith's analysis of the declining salience of inequality in the growing capitalist economy implicitly echoed the general tendency of social scientists and policy makers in the 1950s to focus on the "growing middle," to see society as rapidly becoming "middle class," thereby taking attention away from those at both the top and bottom of the class structure. It is only in a short chapter toward the very end of the book that he takes up the issue of poverty. This almost afterthought is surprising since Galbraith gives as one of the reasons he

turned his gaze away from mass poverty in the underdeveloped world to affluence in his own was to grapple with the anomaly of "poverty among plenty" in
that latter domain.

Galbraith rightly points to the remarkable change during the twentieth century as real, grinding, absolute poverty ceased to be the fate of the unskilled
working majority in countries like the US, to be concentrated in minority
groups and regions bypassed by the opportunities emanating from continuous growth. However, it is clear that he foresaw, in the not too distant future,
a situation where at least some of these unfortunate citizens would be swept
up and embraced by the growth machine. In part, this will occur because of
the inner dynamic governing that machine, in part by wise policies of liberal
government administrations informed by the wise advice of pragmatic economists like himself.

On the latter score, "the war on poverty," unleashed by the Johnson administration in the decade following the original publication of *AS*, might be seen as
an example of what he had in mind, though he himself fell out with President
Johnson over foreign policy. The failure of this attack on deep-seated poverty
in the US is evident in hindsight. Not only was poverty not defeated, it intensified over subsequent decades, a point that Galbraith readily conceded in the
revised edition and elsewhere in his writings. In 1958, however, he regarded
the problem of poverty as marginal, primarily important as "a buttress to the
conventional wisdom" in support of the production imperative—if poverty
remains, let us produce more in order to lift their boats too!

Nevertheless, Galbraith pragmatically accepts that the poor will always be
with us. He identifies two categories. The *case poor* are individuals and their
families who display some personal failing that prevents their "participating
in the general wellbeing." His examples include: "...mental deficiency, bad
health, inability to adapt to the discipline of industrial life, uncontrollable pro-
creation, alcohol, discrimination involving a very limited minority (sic), some
educational handicap unrelated to community shortcomings, or perhaps a
combination of several of these handicaps." This quasi-Malthusian characteri-
zation comes very close to repeating, chapter and verse, the view of poverty
enshrined in the conservative conventional wisdom, the bare bones of which
he outlined early in *AS*.

Insular poverty, on the other hand, arises when individuals are locked within
communities "frustrated by some factor common to their environment," such
as poor local job and educational opportunities, high crime, immobility,
and physical isolation. These people are poor not because of their individual
pathologies but because of their common environmental and cultural location. This view largely echoes the then prevalent "culture of poverty" thesis
influential in American sociology and anthropology; it is a view that has not
traveled well over the past 50 years.

Not surprisingly, in spite of his hope, expressed above, that some poor people would escape their fate, he is relatively sanguine about the near certainty that most will not. The case poor deserve their fate; their exclusion and degradation is their own fault. In social policy terms, they are the undeserving poor. "Since this poverty is the result of the deficiencies, including the moral shortcomings, of the persons concerned, it is possible to shift the responsibility to them. They are worthless and, as a simple manifestation of social justice, they suffer for it." Such views would make a moderate libertarian blush! Galbraith does allow—reluctantly, it seems—that natural human compassion in an increasingly affluent society may share responsibility through private and public charity.

The insular poor, on the other hand, are more deserving of society's assistance, since they are not individually to blame for their predicament. Ameliorative attempts could focus on removing some barriers through educational, social welfare, and employment programs, allowing some to escape their wretched circumstances. However, in both cases the poor, as a disintegrated set of minorities are unlikely to attract significant, if any, political support: "...the modern liberal politician regularly aligns himself not with the poverty-ridden members of the community but with the far more numerous people who enjoy the far more affluent income of (say) the modern trade union member or the intellectual."

In the end, Galbraith gives up on the poor. "It is our misfortune that when inequality declined as an issue, the slate was not left clean. A residual and in some ways rather more hopeless problem remained." He admits that in an increasingly affluent America, remnant poverty is a "disgrace." He notes that although providing a minimum income to the poor was not possible when they were in the majority, the economic means to do so are increasingly present in the affluent society. He therefore seems to be endorsing some form of guaranteed minimum income scheme, at least for the insular poor—a policy direction also supported in time by Milton Friedman. Nevertheless, such action by government is not a moral imperative: "(n)othing requires such a society to be compassionate. But it no longer has a high philosophical justification for callousness."

If there is neither a political constituency for poverty relief through income support nor a moral imperative to help, poverty is further entrenched by a further key structural feature of the affluent society—viz. the reality of "social imbalance," the tendency for private provision of goods and services to swamp public provision. Many of the key services necessary to reduce the barriers that exclude the poor from mainstream society are not supplied by the private market and are undersupplied by revenue-constrained government agencies. Galbraith's theory of social imbalance is one of the most discussed and controversial themes of *AS*, and forms the focus of a later chapter.

III

How does Galbraith's analysis of inequality look fifty years on? Perhaps it is best to let him speak on the matter. After reaffirming, in the late 1980s, his belief in the increase in economic security overall:

> I would now, however, more strongly emphasize, and especially as to the United States, the inequality in income and that it is getting worse—that the poor remain poor and the command of income by those in the top income brackets is increasing egregiously. So is the political eloquence and power by which that income is defended. This I did not foresee.

He was hardly alone here. Western social science long embraced the "embourgeoisement" thesis through and beyond the long postwar boom. In many advanced western economies a mixture of a nascent welfare state and economic policies aimed at ensuring full employment promised that robust economic growth would "trickle down" to all (or at least, almost all) members of their fortunate citizenry. The actual outcome over the last fifty years has been very different and far more problematic. On all three of his key arguments, the march of history has proved unkind. The trend to greater equality, as he later recognized, has reversed. The power of the wealthy too has immeasurably increased, and their hold on government policy tightened, especially since 1980. Finally, the postwar growth machine has stalled, first in Japan, then in other advanced nations, ushering in what the OECD called "The Great Recession" and, looking forward from 2008, the possibility of a decade-long period of economic stagnation.

IV

In the two decades leading to the global financial crisis of 2008 the distribution of household disposable income became more unequal in seventeen of the twenty-two OECD countries for which data exist. Although economic growth in that period averaged a little under 2 percent, the lion's share was appropriated by upper income groups. According to the OECD (2011) in its report, *Divided We Stand: Why Inequality Keeps Rising*, the share of the top 10 percent of income earners is now nine times that of the bottom 10 percent—on average. In fact, this ratio varies greatly, from well under that for the Scandinavian countries to over ten for Japan and the United Kingdom, fourteen for the United States and over twenty for Chile and Mexico.

The Gini Coefficient—a common summary measure of inequality—increased from an average of 0.29 in 1986 to 0.316 in 2008, up by 10 percent. The percentage increase was much greater in some countries, notably the already unequal United States, Germany, New Zealand, and Israel, as well as "low inequality" Sweden and Finland.

These and similar measures indicate a general increase in income inequality across the developed nations. But they do not tell the whole picture. The comfortable picture of all households rising, albeit some on the fast and some on the slow track, ignores several important facts.

First, the picture becomes radically more extreme when we look at the relative fate of the top *one percent* of income recipients. This select group received 18 percent of total income in the United States in 2007 (up from 13 percent in 1990), 14 percent in the United Kingdom (up from 10 percent), and 13 percent in Canada (up from 9 percent). In the case of the US, when capital gains and other forms of unearned income are included, the share of the top one percent rises to 23 percent, almost reaching the level last seen on the eve of the Great Depression. The average income, *after* income tax and transfers, of the top one percent in the US rose by 256 percent between 1979 and 2006, compared to a miserly 11 percent by the bottom 20 percent, according to data quoted by Hacker and Pierson (2010) in their book, *Winner-Take-All Politics*. The concentration at the very top is even more startling. The top 0.1 percent in the US increased its share of total income from 2.7 to 12.3 percent between 1974 and 2007; over that period the top 0.1 percent received more than 20 percent of all after-income-tax income gains, compared to 14 percent trickling to the bottom 60 percent. Corporate CEOs account for about two-thirds of these super-rich elite. In 1965, the average CEO remuneration was about twenty-four times that of the average full-time worker; by 2007 this multiple approached three hundred. Much of the high-flying CEO's remuneration was conveniently delivered in the form of tax-friendly share options.

What this data suggest is a twofold pattern of divergence. The rich are rapidly distancing themselves from the middle, who are leaving behind the bottom. At the same time, the super rich are outpacing the "merely rich."

Second, the average hours worked in many countries has declined—but not, it seems, in line with the prediction of Galbraith (and Keynes) that people would progressively *choose* more leisure as their material wants were more fully met. The decline is much more prevalent in lower income groups than among the highest income recipients and may reflect worsening opportunities in regular full-time employment. The prevalence of multiple income households has increased as the participation of women in the labor market increased, offsetting the decline in male participation rates. These developments track changes in the structure of labor markets that reflect technological changes and increasing casualization of jobs based on the rise of part-time employment and self-employment, especially in the burgeoning service sector where low wages are concentrated. Outsourcing, sub-contracting, and "runaway factories" have intensified downward pressure on wages at the bottom of the income distribution. At the other end, professional services generate extremely high incomes, notably in the financial services sector that (in the United States) now accounts for over 40 percent of corporate profits. The income distribution is being squeezed, with most of the movement down-ward—a case of "the disappearing middle." The phenomenon of the "work-ing poor"—full-time workers and those with multiple part-time jobs who are unable to meet rising living costs—has added another category of poverty ignored in *AS*.

Not surprisingly, across OECD countries the degree of measured inequality sharply increases when part-time and self-employed earnings are accounted for, and further heightened when unemployed households are also included. When non-earned capital income is included, inequality increases across OECD countries and accounts for a growing share of income of the top 20 per-cent in most of them. US inequality for example, has been driven by the large and continuing dispersion of wages and salaries (but only when financial sec-tor incomes and bonuses are included), as well as the impact of capital gains. Unlike a number of other advanced countries, however, *full-time pay* in most sectors and regions of the US economy did not become more unequally dis-tributed during the last two decades of the twentieth century. "What drove rising incomes in the United States in this period and through the 2000s was largely the behaviour of the capital markets, and the incomes of people most closely associated with them" (James Galbraith, 2012: 13). The impact of income tax and government tax payments over the past two decades has only slightly reduced income inequality in the United States; the equalizing effect was much greater in the Nordic countries, Germany, and Belgium. In the for-mer, trickle down has shrunk while gushing up has prospered.

Following the outbreak of the GFC, public attention and angst has been increasingly exercised by the unseemly size of remuneration packages in the nation's financial sector, the locus of the storm that threatened to bring down the industrial economies of the West. How, it is asked, can the very people who caused the crisis benefit from it? Anger at the absence of a persuasive answer has led to largely unsuccessful attempts by western governments to reign in such perceived excesses and, consequently, a rash of uncoordinated outbreaks of public protest, such as the "Occupy" movements that emerged in a number of cities during 2011, the first, unsurprisingly, in Wall Street. Increasingly, the large payments to corporate CEOs are being seen for what they are—massive cases of rent-seeking, rather than the necessary and deserved rewards for ini-tiative, talent, and productive contribution to the general good.

Much of the available data miss, of course, the flourishing informal econ-omy, supported by the growth in illegal migrants to countries like the United States. Many of these people are eminently exploitable, without rights, invis-ible, forming a new servile class to clean the offices and houses of the wealthy, look after their children, wash their Mercedes and Ferraris, and run their errands. Migrants and indigenous minorities legally resident in the advanced economies also experience discrimination and unfair employment practices. While the super rich benefit from the application of new technologies, the majority struggles to maintain their customary levels of comfort and "affluence" and the poor and marginalized struggle to merely survive.

The emergence of a growing underclass in America underscores the inadequacy of Galbraith's original analysis of poverty. The nature and scale of poverty cannot be put down to the personal failings of individuals. Poverty as a profession is deep-structured into a society that continues to generate undreamed of affluence for a powerful few, while threatening a growing majority with declining living standards and, as we will see, rising insecurity. Galbraith, like Alfred Marshall, pointed to poverty as a central problem but assumed that it would "wither away" as economic growth increasingly brought acceptable living standards to all willing to participate in the modern economy. Hence, both economists marginalized poverty in their respective analyses—Galbraith explicitly, Marshall implicitly. Contemporary events suggest that the death of poverty is much exaggerated. Chronic, long-term unemployment, homelessness, ill-health, and the black economy paint a picture familiar to those with an eye to history; those without an historical imagination are poised to repeat it.

Clearly, these structural changes in labor and financial markets have been driven by rapid technological change focused, in particular, on innovations in information and communications technologies that have created an increasing demand for highly educated and skilled workers, and at the same time reduced the demand for a range of unskilled workers across the economy. The first mover advantage has rewarded innovators in a "winner-take-all" world, further enhancing the remuneration of "stars" in all high-reward occupations.

What underlies and conditions these trends and forces are complex patterns of "Globalization." Trade liberalization, capital mobility, labor mobility, and manufacturing relocation have changed the face of capitalism in both the developed and "emerging" (previously called "developing") nations. The new digital technologies have underpinned the rapid globalization process, allowing for the radical disarticulation of production over space and time, while feeding off the pools of low-wage labor in the underdeveloped economies. The demand for and low wages of low-skilled labor in the advanced economies is under a double threat from both the outsourcing of jobs to low-wage countries and the influx of migrant workers at home. "Technology has interacted with globalization to exacerbate the trend towards greater inequality, contributing to income inequality within countries through the move of low and medium skilled jobs overseas, and creating a rich global elite" (Diane Coyle, 2011: 134). Existing government policies have actively assisted these developments. A range of policies, variously termed neoliberalism, economic liberalism, market fundamentalism, and the Washington Consensus, has characterized recent attempts to respond to and guide economic developments at both the national and global scales. Inequality has progressed most in those societies that have most enthusiastically embraced the market—and most effectively reduced the direct and regulatory interventions of government. To understand why this has occurred we need to see why Galbraith's second argument—his confident analysis of declining corporate power—was so far off the mark.

V

In the face of strident claims to the contrary, markets and governments have become increasingly intertwined over recent decades. In the words of Hacker and Pierson (2010: 55)—"The libertarian vision of a nightwatchman state gently policing an unfettered free market is a philosophical conceit, not a description of reality." Government policy *and* inaction are increasingly being conditioned by the direct and indirect interests of the corporate world and other wealthy elites. This, they have managed to do, by both obvious and devious means, in particular, by "rewriting the rules" to favor the already well off.

Taxation has proved to be a major and continuing terrain of struggle, a very uneven struggle with predictable outcomes. Income taxation rates on high incomes in the US have fallen precipitously since the 1970s—with the average rate paid by the top one percent now around 30 percent, compared to around 50 percent in 1974. However, the super rich—the top 0.1 percent—have been even more favored, substantially increasing their capacity to hang on to the bloated gains from their commanding labor market positions. The wealthy have also benefited from a burgeoning cornucopia of tax exclusions, allowances, deductions, and credits, effectively reducing their liability to give up part of their incomes to fund government programs and support payments to the less fortunate. (The wealthy Republican Party candidate for the 2012 Presidential election was reputed to have paid an income tax rate of only 15 percent; unsurprisingly, he made most of his wealth in investment banking.) Where government subsidies are paid, a large share finds its way to well-endowed corporate and other business interests.

This is no accident. Corporate lobbying has mushroomed, focused on the federal legislature in Washington. Robert Reich (2008) in his book *Supercapitalism* shows that the number of registered lobbyists in Washington DC increased from 3400 in the mid-1970s to almost 33,000 by 2005. In that latter year, the total amount spent on lobbying exceeded two billion dollars. Lobbying is an entrenched democratic pastime, embraced by both major parties; Democrats and the Republicans are equally entranced by its attractions. Independent lobbyists form only part of the phalanx of influence peddlers importuning elected officials. Large corporations have their own internal "political action committees" that liaise with external lobbyists, lawyers, and public relations specialists, ensuring that their views and interests are uppermost in the minds of the lawmakers. In addition, the Political Action Committees (PACs) are surrounded by a growing army of think tanks, trade organizations, foundations, special issue groups, and the like. Together, these organizations also aggregate and make substantial campaign contributions—or, on occasion, withhold such—from candidates seeking election or re-election. Their ability to so indulge this pastime was helpfully enhanced by a 2010 decision of the Supreme Court to effectively allow unlimited campaign contributions by non-party organizations. Their remit covers far more than the obvious contested terrain of taxation, though this is, indeed, a critical one for the continuing contentment of the wealthy.

Blocking or shaping legislation as it passes into or through the Congress and the White House consumes an inordinate share of the nation's scarce resources. The free and frequent movement of senior people between the corporate and government spheres ensures that common views on the proper role of government—in the recent era this means minimal interference with the prerogatives of the market—prevail. Nowhere has this been more evident than in the tendency of presidents of both parties to appoint the leaders of Wall Street to cabinet positions and international bodies such as the World Bank. The largest investment bank, Goldman Sachs, has provided several secretaries of the treasury and retiring or defeated officials and representatives have beaten a well-worn path to the boards and senior executive positions of large financial services firms. It is hardly surprising that legislation conducive to the long-term interest of this "carry trade" consistently passes; or that measures threatening that lucrative roundabout are shunted off into legislative oblivion. The dominant conventional wisdom has faithfully and solemnly pronounced on the virtue of the market and ennobled its leading voices.

The situation in the United States is further characterized by the "politics of drift." The US political system is marked by a pronounced division of powers, constitutionally based, that provides almost insurmountable barriers to far-reaching reforms that would challenge the status quo, particularly where the interest of powerful groupings are in play.

> The main reason for this recurrent pattern is straightforward: In American politics it is hard to get things done and easy to block them. With its multiple branches and hurdles, the institutional structure of American government allows organizations and intense interests—even quite narrow ones—to create gridlock and stalemate. (Hacker and Pierson, 2010: 83)

Once imposed, policy settings tend to persist, a political version of Newton's first law. At base, the separation of powers between executive, legislature, and judiciary are overlaid by vertical divisions—federal, state, and local—and the practical impact of ruling protocols and procedures, such as super majority requirements, veto powers, and the Senate Filibuster. There are plentiful opportunities for well organized, connected and funded interests to deflect or block change.

Clearly, as someone intimately involved in federal politics and sporadically active as a Washington insider from the 1930s onward, Galbraith was cognizant of these facts of American politics. Indeed, he wrote thoughtfully on these issues in many works published after *AS*. However, in that famous book his political experience and savvy was overwhelmed by the need to establish the key point that inequality and the economics of scarcity—the driving themes of the central tradition—were in the process of being overturned by the unstoppable tide of events.

Galbraith's analysis of the equalizing force of countervailing power—the political version of Newton's third law—has worn thin to the point of collapse in the neoliberal era. The policies of the Thatcher regime in the United Kingdom and the Reagan Administration (and all subsequent presidencies) in the US have deliberately and successfully dismantled many of the bulwarks enhancing such powers in the past. Trade union membership has sunk to historic lows in those countries. This has followed in part from government action but also from the remorseless march of technology, resulting in the deskilling of a large section of the indigenous labor force and the deindustrialization of large regions of the country in favor of manufacturing production in other parts of the world, coupled with both the growth in low skilled service sector employment and the flood of migrants from poor countries and regions. These workers have proved very difficult to organize industrially and understandably are wary of risking their precarious employment by any form of industrial action against their employers, especially in countries where punitive laws exist. In cultures that emphasize the rights and opportunities of individuals, "aspirational societies," such organized opposition faces further ideological barriers, even in the face of clear evidence that social mobility has stalled and inequality intensified. Mainstream academic economics, as argued earlier, has provided legitimation of these views so palatable to the wealthy and powerful.

The evidence on falling social mobility is persuasive. For example, in a Brookings Institution publication, *Creating an Opportunity Society*, Haskins and Sawhill (2009) found that the sons of fathers in the lowest 20 percent of income distribution in the US were twice as likely to fall into that category, compared to a world where equal opportunity ruled. Increasingly, unequal access to good schools hampers the educational and employment opportunities of children from lower socioeconomic backgrounds and some minority groups. This appears to be occurring at all schooling levels, including universities in countries that have recently reintroduced or hiked student fees.

The effectiveness of other countervailing forces has also been blunted by the rise of the neoliberal state and economy. Pluralism as a positive rather than normative theory of American politics is increasingly untenable. Austere budgetary politics designed to cut taxes and services, allied to deregulation and a litigious corporate culture, has effectively removed much of the infra-structure needed to support a thriving community-based political culture. In the United States, the lurch to the right of the Republican Party and the rise within of "the Tea Party" has sharply polarized political debate and driven the federal system into legislative gridlock, reinforcing developments intro-duced in the early 1990s in the Republican dominated Congress's "Contract with America."

Deregulation and falling international trade barriers have further weakened the bargaining power of labor and enhanced the prerogatives of multinational corporations. In fact, the term "deregulation" is too broad and vague when used to describe what went on. For "deregulation" we could read "asymmetrical re-regulation in favor of capital income over labor income." But the situation is more complicated than this suggests. The politics of inequality in the devel-oped economies is intimately bound up with the reordering of deep-seated institutional structures that systematically favor those who appropriate their incomes from *both* accumulated wealth and their dominant position in the higher reaches of the (executive) labor market. Finally, whereas Galbraith was writing in a postwar world dominated by nation states, with the United States "first among unequals," the complex interlocking processes of globalization have undercut the power of any single national government, even America's, to successfully challenge the rule of markets, especially financial markets; this is a painful lesson now being learnt by the nations of the Eurozone.*

In short, *real politic* in the United States in an increasingly anarchic global economy has removed government from its liberal cast as the guarantor of a level playing field for balancing competing interests and views. The "shrink-ing of the state" has, instead helped to entrench the interests and views of the wealthy, who have used this congenial vacuum to further those interests and impose those views. The case against a strong, interventionist state was summed up and anticipated more than 200 years ago by the radical English libertarian Tom Paine: "Society is created by our needs, government by our wickedness." Ideology and political power matter in understanding how America's affluent society has developed over the past fifty years. "Inequality is fundamentally a political and moral choice, although the politics involved is as much a mat-ter of the acceptable long-term norms of the society as of short-term election

---

* The power of so-called "bond vigilantes," however, should not be overstated. In the United States, at least, the size and dynamism of the economy, the reserve status of the US dollar, and the relatively moderate burden of government indebtedness (by comparison to smaller economies like Greece and Ireland) has not limited the federal government's ability to finance its operations nor driven domestic interest rates up. Rather, the reverse has occurred since the GFC, with his-toric low rates prevailing; when the government's AAA credit rating was cut, the bond markets gave a collective shrug and carried on as normal. The constraints on government financial and economic policy in the US are purely ideological and political, witness the continuing drama of the federal "debt ceiling." This point is made by Paul Krugman (2012) in his book, *End the Depression Now*.

issues such as top tax rates and welfare spending" (Coyle, 2011: 116). However, the norms that matter are themselves the evolving product of the society and economy of which they form part. Increasingly these norms have been defined by the politically powerful beneficiaries of an unequal society unconstrained by countervailing forces that once exerted a degree of balance.

VI

The final prop Galbraith advanced for the declining salience of inequality as a frontline economic and social concern depended on his confident assertion that the ever-increasing production of material wealth would lift the majority into agreeable comfort. For much of the period after the 1950s this fortunate state of affairs appeared to be the permanent inheritance of those living in the most advanced nations. Generally, those economies experienced high employment and economic growth throughout the 1960s, with low inflation, continuing the trends laid down during the long boom. However, as noted in the next chapter, troubles began in the early 1970s and this decade proved to be a watershed, both in economic developments and economic theory. Stagflation posed new problems for governments that the old Keynesian prescriptions appeared incapable of resolving. Economic policy in the era of neoliberalism had arrived, along with a new story that would comfort the well off and anesthetize the rest.

Over the past 30 years, proponents of neoliberalism collectively wrote an historical narrative of postwar development in the advanced economies of the West. The kernel of the story is that the "long boom" of the 1950s and 1960s resulted unintentionally in an over-reliance on government regulation and direction, entrenching a comfortable, complacent, "sclerotic" capitalism, sheltered behind trade union barricades and tariff protection, resulting in the 1970s in falling productivity growth and eventual stagflation. After a difficult period of austerity and deregulation (tough love), inflation was squeezed out of the system, competition reignited, and innovation unleashed, resulting in a sharp increase in productivity growth. "The roaring 90s," in this story, is a period of dynamic rebirth in which the "end of history" signals the permanent triumph of western liberal democracy and American capitalism. The alternatives fell by the wayside with the collapse of the Soviet Union and communism in Eastern Europe, the lost decade of the Japanese economy, and the apparent embrace of the market—though not accompanied by any increase in personal freedom—by Communist China. Deregulation of domestic industries, freely floating exchange rates, reduction of trade barriers (except where this hurt US producers), and above all, the global integration of financial markets underpinned a new aggressive triumphalism.

Economic growth did endure during the 1990s and up to 2007. Likewise, volatility in aggregate output and employment did seem to moderate after the late 1980s recession. Neoliberals put this down to the policies they had been espousing vocally and to the light regulatory touch of the US Federal Reserve under its long-time chairman, Alan Greenspan, who argued that "this time it was different." The productivity genie unleashed by the dot.com revolution and competitive forces, he argued, were sufficient to push back the supply-side constraints on growth; a regime of low interest rates and minimum interference with markets—especially financial markets—would generate rapid and sustainable growth with little risk of inflation. Like earlier episodes, neoliberals and their academic colleagues celebrated the end of the business cycle—right up to the eve of the global financial crisis! One is here reminded of the preeminent US economist Irving Fisher's confident assertion on the eve of the 1929 stock market collapse, that US "stock prices have reached what looked like a permanently high plateau" (quoted in Quiggin, 2010: 5).

What is wrong with all this? Looking backward from now (post-2008), the story of the great moderation appears fanciful, a huge exercise in collective self-deception wrought by forces pursuing obvious interests. Yes, when looking solely at trends in aggregate output, the macroeconomic performance of major economies as conventionally measured did pick up after 1985. However, as the Australian economist John Quiggin persuasively asserts, closer scrutiny reveals a more complex and ambiguous picture. Most of the twenty years leading up to the GFC did see these economies experiencing long upswings in real GDP and short downturns. However, the story on unemployment is more somber. Employment levels grew little for years after the early 1990s and early 2000s recessions, so much so that economists took to referring to the first half of both decades as "jobless recoveries." Moreover, productivity growth, though picking up, like unemployment rates, nowhere approached the heady days of the Keynesian-era long boom forty years before.

We can now see, post GFC, that the recent booms were artificially stimulated and kept going by a combination of low central bank engineered interest rates, falling lending standards, lax-to-non-existent regulation, rampant consumer borrowing, faulty credit ratings systems, and unsustainable housing bubbles, all interacting in an increasingly internationalized financial system that barely avoided the complete meltdown that almost dragged the economies of the West into a 1930s-style Great Depression (and may yet do so). We leave the sad story of the GFC—and its lingering aftermath—until the next chapter. What is quite clear, looking backward, is that economic growth in the developed economies, measured by rising GDP, has not been the solvent guaranteeing an easing of social tensions and a declining concern about the sharpening inequalities of everyday life. Looking forward to the second decade of the twenty-first century, the prospect is distinctly gloomy, on this and other fronts. If a growing economic dividend is not sufficient to ease tensions, then what prospects will arise in a zero sum world where economic activity stagnates for a decade or more?

At this point it is worth clarifying an apparent confusion in contemporary debates over inequality trends. It is beyond dispute that economic interdependence has substantially increased over recent decades and that inequality *within* most countries, both developed and fast-developing, has likewise increased. However, looked at globally the world has become a *more equal* place, an outcome much trumpeted by the proponents of neoliberalism. How can this be? The answer lies in the rapid increase in *average* living standards in a few very populous countries—the BRICs or emerging economies of Brazil, Russia, India and (above all) China. Thus, although, as in the West, inequality is increasing within these countries, the growth in their middle and upper classes has reduced the proportion of very low income people on a global basis. Extreme poverty is being concentrated more and more in areas of sub-Saharan Africa, the so-called "bottom billion." The fact that the other six billion people no longer exist on the edge of physical annihilation is no small achievement, when compared to life before the rise of industrial capitalism, but this is likely to be little appreciated now by the majority of people in each country increasingly being left behind. As so often occurs, averages hide more than they illuminate.

This last point is made forcefully by Galbraith's son James K. Galbraith (2012) in his book *Inequality and Instability*. Using grouped rather than traditional survey data, the latter has been able to explore changes in income inequality through time, at different geographic scales, from local, through regional to national, cross-border, and, ultimately, global. He is also able to discern patterns of and trends in inequality within and between specific occupational groups at each scale. Although the measures are often crude, they are high in information content and rely on readily accessible data sources across time periods and regions. In the case of the United States, Galbraith *fils* is able to demonstrate that virtually all the rise in inequality between counties in the period 1994 to 2000 was concentrated in fifteen counties, five of which—New York, three associated with Silicon Valley and King County Washington—accounted for half the rise—with income gains appropriated "...above all by workers in Silicon Valley and Seattle and their bankers in Manhattan" (Galbraith, 2012: 16); the technology-weighted NASDAQ stock index provided a fairly accurate barometer of developments in this period. After the collapse of the technology boom and during the presidency of George W. Bush, the major gains in incomes at the top end were concentrated around Washington DC in sectors associated with government and (after nine-eleven) the burgeoning national security state. As always, the view depends on where one is standing and the direction one is facing.

VII

Why, it might be asked, was Galbraith concerned about the issue of inequality? Why does the subject continue to exert a fascination for scholars, politicians, and popular commentators in the mass media? Recent advances in behavioral economics, discussed earlier, offer some hints. Human beings, it turns out, are, as has been noted, not human calculating machines. This is no surprise, except perhaps to those trained exclusively in orthodox economics. We have seen that widely held and deeply embedded notions of fairness seem to underlie much social and economic interaction. Where some people are believed to gain rewards beyond their due or fail to appropriately reciprocate when receiving benefits from others, rationalities differing from the axioms of rational choice theory emerge. The extent to which such behaviors are "hard wired" as a result of long evolutionary pathways is a matter for lively debate among social and life scientists. Regardless of the outcome of these debates, it appears that most people really do care about the moral rightness of the distribution of incomes and wealth in their societies; a finding that seems to be genuinely universal, to cut across widely divergent cultures and timescales. This is complemented by experimental work that demonstrates how people search for "anchors" or comparison points when making judgments about a wide range of valuations—as the cases cited by William Poundstone (2010) in his book *Priceless* amply illustrate.

Moreover, as the headline quote to this chapter implies, social cohesion and a sense of community is strained when inequalities are too pronounced. Societies in which individualism runs rampant risk a breakdown in the values and norms that sustain the very operation of market exchange. Trust—the mutual belief among economic participants that agreements will be honored when the time comes for settling accounts—underlies the very possibility of markets and thus of economies organized by their ubiquity. Social capital is a term now widely used to summarize the various overlapping sets of social relationships between people—mediated both through markets and beyond them—that build trust within groups. Highly individualized or atomized societies, those guided primarily by the selfish pursuit of personal gain, regardless of the welfare of others, are unlikely to maintain the degree of social cohesion necessary in the long run to support a happy and prosperous populace. "A society that offends its members' sense of fairness is, in important ways, unsustainable" (Coyle, 2011: 114).

What is not clear is where the tipping point exists; what is too much inequality? Presumably, the social precipice will differ between cultures. The picture is further muddied by the imprecise nature of the concept of social capital. The best that can be said is that unsustainable inequality is best glimpsed in particular cases by looking at key indicators of the absence of trust and contentment in the broad mass of the population. For an extended and insightful summary of recent work along this line the reader should consult the previously quoted book of Diane Coyle.

Wilkinson and Pickett (2010) in their book, *The Spirit Level*, offer an influential recent account linking inequality to various indictors of unhappiness and dysfunction. Their work consists of collecting together a range of data suggesting strong positive correlations between a society's level of inequality and factors such as the rate of suicide, levels of infant mortality, the incidence of various diseases, crime, and obesity. Moreover, they show data that display a high negative correlation between the degree of inequality and social mobility. These linkages, they and others have suggested, undercut trust in society and depreciate social capital. For the United States, Wilkinson and Pickett claim that mobility, measured by the extent to which current income can be explained by the father's income, declined until 1980 after which it climbed to more than double the level it had been in 1950.

The Spirit Level has been justly criticized for conflating correlation with causality. It is also unpersuasive to claim that "everyone" will be better off in a more equal society. In particular, the super rich can effectively seal themselves off from the dysfunctional effects of an increasingly uncivil society—albeit at a cost in defensive expenses like private security guards and higher taxes to pay for increasing incarceration rates. Galbraith makes a similar point.

> It would be idle to suggest that the man of wealth has no special advantages in our [unequal] society. Such propositions are the one-day wonder of the conventional wisdom, and those who offer them have a brief but breathtaking reputation as social prophets.

Nevertheless, the patterns identified by Wilkinson and Pickett are suggestive and plausible explanatory analyses are evident in at least some cases presented by these authors, especially cases relating to the health of people trapped in low income jobs offering little control over their lives. This conclusion can be extended to cover other social groups similarly experiencing powerlessness in everyday life.

The recent experience of global crisis and financial travails suggests a further somber consideration. As James Galbraith has pointed out (Galbraith, 2012: 3):

> In the late 1990s, standard measures of income inequality in the United States—and especially of the income shares held by the top echelon—rose to levels not seen since 1929. It is not strange that this should give rise (and not for the first time) to the suggestion that there might be a link, under capitalism, between radical inequality and financial crisis. The link, of course, runs through debt.

We return to the central problematic of debt in the next chapter and head-on in Chapter 9.

A final charge that can be levied against excessive inequality is that it may undercut continuing economic growth, the very engine on which Galbraith depends for the triumph of production over material want. The jury, it seems, is still out on this charge. The correlation between inequality and growth as conventionally measured is fairly weak, at least for the developed nations. The evidence seems to point both ways. Plausible reasons can be advanced for both positions—namely, that inequality provides incentives to save and work (noted earlier) and, conversely, that the lack of opportunity and incentive to invest in education and training may harm continuing growth. As Coyle (2011: 136) concludes: "(g)iven these conflicting theories, and the inconclusive empirical research, the evidence is on balance suggestive of inequality harming growth in the long term, but it is hard to stake a lot on these results." Quiggin (2010: 158) draws a similar conclusion. "The relationship between inequality and economic growth has been the subject of a vast number of econometric studies, which have, as so often with econometric studies, yielded conflicting results." Quiggin also makes the telling point that those studies that find a positive relationship between the *increase* in inequality and growth in the short run are quite compatible with results showing a negative relationship over the long term. The deleterious effects of high inequality on economic growth take time to manifest.

Bowles (2012) has offered a number of reasons why reducing existing pronounced inequalities could result in enhanced productivity, growth, and incomes by removing institutional constraints on economic innovation and activity. Drawing on recent work on incomplete contracts and asymmetric information, he traces how the engineering of "productivity-enhancing governance structures" that increase the asset base of the poor can increase the productivity and incomes of many without lowering that of others—in other words, can result in what economists call "a Pareto-efficient improvement." In particular, relaxing the credit constraints on poorer people (by increasing their collateral) means that they are able to borrow, take more risks, and pursue entrepreneurial opportunities previously denied them, while also giving them the incentive to invest more in their own skills development. The arguments Bowles offer are technical but intuitively simple to grasp—give people an opportunity to improve their lives—that is to control their endeavors and reap the rewards—and they will work harder without the costly and inefficient spur of managerial supervision and the threat of dismissal.

And does it matter, anyway? The attempt to quantify the extent to which growth—even if more widely defined—and inequality interact may be misplaced. Measures like the United Nations *Human Development Index* or the *Gross National Happiness Index*, the latter originally introduced by the King of Bhutan, attempt to create a single index representing human well-being. The Human Development Index (HDI) combines indicators of health, education, and living standards (life expectancy at birth, years of schooling, and national income) in order to, in the words of the United Nations Development Program, "serve as a frame of reference for both social and economic development." The fact that the United States figures at the top end of this index, as in the case of the single dimensional GDP rankings, cannot be taken as an unambiguous endorsement of the level of inequality and its increase in that country. In his recent book, *Obliquity*, the economic and financial writer John Kay (2010: 71) comments:

> The intentions are admirable. But why should we measure human development in this particular way? Some people might suggest that a measure of human development should include personal freedom, or the strength of religious belief (or its absence), or environmental awareness. Why? Or why not? Even if we agree that health, education and income are the relevant criteria, should we measure them in this way? Why? Or why not? The problem is not just that these are questions on which people might disagree. The problem is that it is difficult to see any criteria by which their disagreements might be resolved. The supposed objectivity of the measure of human development—which is calculated to three places of decimals—is spurious.

It is not only the case that comparisons of growth or development, however defined, can reasonably be said to express "the fallacy of misplaced concreteness," a point missed by much of the recent work on "the economics of happiness." Might not a reasonable case be made for including the absence of extreme inequality in any definition of human happiness or flourishing?

*   *   *

In summary, it appears that fifty years on, Galbraith's original take on the declining significance of economic inequality as an issue worthy of attention is untenable, a judgment with which he subsequently readily concurred, at least with respect to the persistence of serious poverty in the United States. In hindsight, we can see that his original view reflected the optimism and complacency of a society, the United States, enjoying a brief period of unchallenged global supremacy—before the travails of the War on Poverty, race riots, and the Vietnam War; before the collapse of the postwar international monetary system; before the oil crises and the gathering complexities of Middle Eastern politics and Cold War; and, of course, before the deterioration after the turn of the century in the domestic and international security situation. This leads us naturally to the next key theme in *AS*—the concern with economic security.

5

Economic Security[*]

Few matters having to do with economic life have been so much misun-
derstood as the problem of economic security.

(J.K. Galbraith)

The outstanding faults of the economic society in which we live are its
failure to provide for full employment and its arbitrary and inequitable
distribution of wealth and incomes.

(J.M. Keynes)

* * *

Galbraith, in *AS*, and Keynes, twenty-two years earlier in *The General Theory*,
both coupled inequality and insecurity as the age-old failures of capitalism.
Both also believed in the capacity, indeed inevitability, of internal change
that would ameliorate these twin faults and resolve the social tensions that
Marxists and other radicals expected would speed the demise of the system
and its replacement by a society based on satisfying the wants and needs of all.
They only differed on emphasis and timescale. Whereas Keynes (in "Economic
possibilities for our grandchildren" [1973/1930]) looked to the twenty-first
century for the solution of "mankind's economic problem," Galbraith claimed
to observe the clear signs of this happy day in the middle of the twentieth. We
have already, in the previous chapter, commented on his treatment of inequality; this chapter focuses on the linked issue of economic (in)security.

---

[*] This chapter focuses on the area where, perhaps, Galbraith's optimistic prognosis has proved
most problematic. The outbreak and aftermath of the global financial crisis in the years after his
death has forcibly reminded citizens of the developed world, including his own countrymen and
women, of the extreme volatility and uncertainties of economic life. Consequently, in the latter
part of the chapter, I have discussed in detail the genesis and development of the current crisis.
This will not add anything substantive to the many analyses already provided by economists and
other specialists but is intended to guide students and the general reader through the maze of
claims and counterclaims advanced. The discussion here also links back to the critiques of orthodox economics—which failed totally to anticipate the crisis—in Chapter 3.

Both economists, as social prophets, relied on what Keynes termed the power of compound interest—the continuous, compounding effect of growing aggregate production. The latter believed that, over the span of a hundred years, total output in the advanced economies would grow between four- and eight-fold, ensuring that living standards would rise across the board. This rate of increase implied growth in what (after Keynes) we call gross domestic product (GDP) of a little over 2 percent per annum. In fact, as a number of commentators have pointed out, growth since the mid-1930s has averaged almost 3 percent, ensuring that his bottom limit of a four-fold increase was achieved in fifty years and, if continued, would result in a seventeen-fold increase (double his upper estimate) by 2030. Ominously, however, the worldwide slowdown in growth in Japan before and other Western economies following the GFC may pare back that outcome, though not to the extent that Keynes's upper limit will be threatened.

Keynes believed that future generations will escape the grinding necessity to make their living by uncongenial labor, slaves to avarice and usury, and prone to the "semi-criminal, semi-pathological propensities" that currently motivate economic behavior. However, although this way the future lies, we cannot yet anticipate its arrival. "Avarice and usury and precaution must be our gods for a little longer still. For only they can lead us out of the tunnel of economic necessity into daylight" (Keynes, 1973/1930: 25).

In order for the bright future to arrive Keynes posited three conditions. First, the world must avoid the Malthusian curse and control population growth. Second, devastating wars (Keynes had the First World War and its disastrous aftermath in mind here), global and civil, must also be avoided. Third, the application of science to continuing technological improvements had to be trusted to those best fitted to the task; Keynes is vague here but seems to echo Thorstein Veblen's "engineers" and anticipate Galbraith's "Technostructure." Finally, what he later came to term aggregate demand had to be managed to achieve a correct balance between consumption and investment; this, he thought, would follow easily if the first three conditions were met, though in his fully worked out arguments in *The General Theory* (1973b/1936), he came to see the state playing a critical mediating role in offsetting the tendency for demand to falter as the "animal spirits" of investors waned—even to the extent of raising the need for "the socialization of investment." In the world of Keynes's figurative grandchildren, the chronic problems of economic insecurity would be forever resolved.

This brief excursion back into Keynes's thought is useful as a base from which to discuss Galbraith's views on the reasons why he thought that the America of his time was already well on Keynes's path to a secure existence, so that attention could pass to other concerns unconstrained by material scarcity—to life, in short, in the affluent society.

II

In the orthodox model of competitive capitalism economic actors are motivated by the spur of individual gain and the fear of loss. No one actor is secure since no one exerts control over markets, labor, product, or financial. All are price takers, at the mercy of the aggregated efforts of everyone seeking their own benefit. All are therefore liable to suffer from unexpected, unplanned, unpredictable changes in the economic environment, most of which they have no direct part in bringing about. In short, the future is unknowable and, thus, uncontrollable at the level of the individual producer or consumer. In this view, we all must deal as best we can with the presence of both known and unknown unknowns. New technologies, new products, new consumer tastes, new discoveries interact to create an economic environment in continual ferment, out of which matures the rising productivity and growth driving continuous improvements in average living standards.

"These unpredictable changes in fortune were both inevitable and useful." Inevitable because this is the way that the economic system responds via market signals to the external drivers of change. Useful because the fear of being left behind concentrated the mind and galvanized the efforts of firms to survive and thrive and the workers to keep their jobs. Insecurity, in the conventional wisdom, is necessary to ensure the efficient utilization of society's scarce resources and the maximum increase in those resources over time.

The firm embedding of these and supporting arguments in the dominant conventional wisdom fulfills the role ascribed to that institution—namely, that once said and reiterated in general, they can be widely ignored in practice. Almost no one, Galbraith argues, actually behaves as the conventional wisdom prescribes or believes that others do. The one exception, Galbraith mischievously notes with an eye to his colleagues, is provided by the academic fraternity. "Their security of tenure is deemed essential for fruitful and unremitting thought." Insecurity is cherished in "the second person or in the abstract." In reality, the history of twentieth-century capitalism was a long attempt by economic actors to exert some degree of control over the unfettered and anarchic operation of market forces. "In large measure, they were successful."

The business firm pioneered this search for security through the introduction of a variety of strategies designed to control supply and boost demand. Monopoly in selling or buying and predatory tactics designed to disable current and potential competitors formed the core of such activities. As many industries assumed the characteristics of imperfect competition, patterns of strategic interaction emerged that significantly dampened the operation of price competition and introduced various routines that rendered the economic environment more predictable and, thus, to a degree, controllable by the new cadre of professional managers that had emerged to govern the modern corporation. Galbraith here as elsewhere (the theme is a constant through all of his work) presents the large corporation—"modern business enterprise"— as focused on the imperative to reduce risk in order to survive and grow over the longer term. He appears to accept Frank Knight's influential distinction between "risk" (amenable to probability judgments) and "uncertainty" (for which no firm basis for such judgments exist). Absolute security is just as chimerical as absolute insecurity, the art of modern management being to reduce the scope for unexpected and unpleasant future outcomes. This was a position Keynes himself reached in the famous Chapter 12 of *The General Theory*.

Galbraith is warm in his account of how successfully modern corporations have rendered their environments less risky, a subject he was to develop at length a decade later in *The New Industrial State* (1967). This they have addressed through the internal differentiation of their operations. Technological leadership is achieved by developing specialized research and development divisions, reducing the risk that management will be blind-sided by competitors introducing new, more efficient processes and products. Fickle consumer tastes are studied and manipulated by marketing specialists, brands are built, and consumer loyalty shored up. In this latter exercise, the modern corporation is ably assisted by the *mad men* of modern advertising. The practice of reinvesting profits from large-scale operations created at least partial independence from capital markets. Finally, the collective nature of modern management meant that the firm was less vulnerable to the bad decisions of any individual manager (the recent fallout, including bankruptcy, caused by the piratical activities of "rogue traders" in the financial sector might have caused Galbraith to partially recant on this point).

However, the imperative to reduce risk and enhance security spreads well beyond the confines of the corporate sector. Small businesses and farmers seek protection through collective organization and self-regulation, a survival of the activities of medieval guilds many centuries before. The professions likewise organized, along with the broad-based trade union movement, in order to close shop and control unwanted and destabilizing competition. Although some of these efforts are voluntary and to a degree self-organizing, the major strides in reducing market risks for workers, farmers, and the ordinary consumer have come from active state involvement. Well beyond their libertarian night-watchman role, the modern state has been the central institutional guarantor of greater economic security in the affluent society.

The dependence of small business, workers, and consumers on active state protection has rendered their efforts visible and thus open to attack by the guardians of the conventional wisdom, particularly conservative business interests. The latter are in the fortunate position of portraying themselves as swash-buckling entrepreneurs enduring and overcoming the vicissitudes of tooth and claw competition, while quietly ensuring that they avoid the fate of failed entrepreneurial endeavor. Their covert position of security also allows for energetic criticism of the overt efforts of non-corporate interests to achieve a similar state of grace. But this has not, Galbraith points out, prevented large corporations from turning to government as a last line of defense when the economic environment turns against them. He notes that no large corporation has been bankrupted in living memory, explicitly noting General Motors in this regard. Although he doesn't mention this fact, US bankruptcy laws have been helpful, a prime example of government regulation offsetting the fallout from the rigors of competition (as General Motors itself later found to their benefit in the post-GFC recession). In summary:

> The riskiness of modern corporate life is, in fact, the harmless conceit of the modern corporate executive, and that is why it is vigorously proclaimed. Precisely because he lives a careful life, the executive is moved to identify himself with the dashing entrepreneur of economic literature. For much the same reason, the commander of an armored division, traveling in a trailer and concerning himself with gasoline supplies, sees himself as leading an old-time cavalry charge.

Galbraith locates the beginning of the general "escape from insecurity" and "retreat from risk" in the economic and legislative upheaval of the 1930s. It was during the period of the New Deal—in which as a young Harvard instructor he participated on the margins—that the federal government first intervened on a large scale to protect individuals from economic threat. Welfare relief followed by social security programs—age pensions, unemployment insurance, etc.— and policies to support farm prices and farmers helped limit the disastrous impact of the collapse in production and employment. Legislation was introduced to protect small business and consumers, encourage union bargaining power, and regulate the banking sector. Subsequent measures strengthened pension entitlements, unemployment benefits, and limited health insurance.

Galbraith's arguments with respect to the first two-thirds of the twentieth century have been echoed and developed by Robert Moss (2002) in his book *When All Else Fails*. Moss details how, over the preceding century, the state gradually spread its security blanket wider, starting first with "security for business" prior to the First World War, extending to "security for workers" in the period between the wars and "finally" to "security for all" after the Second World War. The decades since 1970, as we will see, reversed the tide, and might reasonably be called "security for the few."

These measures focused on the micro-level of individuals, firms, and specific groups. That left the major source of risk to the realm of the economy as a whole. Insufficiency of aggregate demand was the final frontier of insecurity. It was also, according to Galbraith, quantitatively by far the greatest threat. Alongside the microeconomic efforts to reduce insecurity, a new macroeconomic role for government evolved during the 1930s, driven by the need to confront the worst depression in history. Without the capacity to mitigate the business cycle the microeconomic measures would be inadequate. "Then, as since, economic stabilization was regarded as an end in itself, but it will now become clear that it was only part of the broad effort to escape insecurity which was assumed to be inherent in economic life." The federal government from then on assumed a central stabilizing role in the economy; "(t)he notion that they [depressions] should be allowed to run their course was virtually extinct"—virtually, but not entirely, residing, as we saw, in a zombie state deep within the central tradition. The Employment Act passed just after the Second World War signaled the triumph of the revised conventional wisdom; the rise of Keynesian policies based on the neoclassical synthesis had, at the time of writing *AS*, firmly established government as the protector of large and small economic actors, as the macro-manager of a secure economic environment.

It is not surprising, says Galbraith, that workers, small farmers and businesses, and ordinary consumers were the last to demand and receive government protection. Big business led the way because they had so much to lose and therefore so much to gain by securing their stake. Once the living standards and aspirations of ordinary citizens rose, they too had a stake to protect and government was pressured to extend the security mat in response. When one's eyes are fixed firmly on the next sale or meal, there is little to be gained from pondering the luxury of unemployment protection, retirement incomes, or health coverage. Thus, the modern concern for greater security in the course of everyday life did not come from a response to the age-old fact of endemic insecurity. "Rather, it is the result of improving fortune—of moving from a world where people had little to one where they had much more to protect." Economic security proved to be a "normal good;" as incomes increased so too did the demand to secure those gains. In addition, as the periods of insecurity became more episodic, rather than endemic, the possibility and expectation that they could be controlled, or at least minimized, blossomed.

Galbraith falls short of claiming that these forces and trends were the same across all advanced countries, noting that "allowances must be made for differences in national temperament and political development." Countries like Germany, the United Kingdom, and the Scandinavians (one could add New Zealand and Australia) developed significant welfare states well before the laggards, the US and Canada. He also argues, less persuasively, that it was in the latter two countries that the Great Depression struck hardest, unleashing the greatest demands for protection. In fact, the Depression hit with particular force in many of those countries already well on the way to the welfare state; industrialized Germany and Britain and primary commodity producing Australia and New Zealand suffered just as much, if not more, allowing for the relative sizes of their economies.

His final argument for the declining concern with insecurity draws on one of the pillars of (neo)classical economics—namely, the idea of declining marginal utility. "There are more serious hazards and less serious ones; as the more serious are covered, there will be a declining sense of urgency about the less

serious ones and indeed, also about the entire problem of economic insecurity." Once business, government, and the key institutions of civil society could
control the greatest threats—mass unemployment, price volatility, provision
for retirement, and illness—attention could move to other priorities and challenges thrown up by unprecedented affluence. The American economy, he
thought, had reached that happy state of being able to ignore the remaining
less serious sources of insecurity.

> The meaning of this is that elimination of insecurity in economic life can be a
> finished business.... In fact, the major uncertainties of economic life (subject to
> some marked caution concerning the control of depression and inflation) have
> already been eliminated. The ones that remain are of much reduced urgency.

These economic facts of life are reflected in the political realm as parties and
interest groups are less exercised by a continuing need to extend the safety
net further. Once achieved, the props to security assume a taken-for-granted
status; they cease to trouble the political agenda. "Henceforth, in pursuing
the goal of greater economic security, we will be completing and perfecting a
structure that in all its main features now exists." Oh, how those officials and
bankers closeted together in mutual terror in the days before and just after the
collapse of Lehman Brothers would have loved to have been transported to
such a world!

Galbraith's key proviso is that government successfully controls the business
cycle, reducing the frequency and severity of bouts of depression and inflation. If they are unsuccessful in this endeavor, the fragile balance of microeconomic accommodations will break down unleashing the destructive forces of
cutthroat competition and uncertain incomes, a return to the powerlessness
and uncertainties of early capitalism. "Prevention of depression and inflation
remains a *sine qua non* for economic security."

In "the age of security" the traditional tripartite concern about inadequate
security, equality, and production has narrowed to an exclusive fixation with
boosting productivity. Galbraith quotes figures showing the progressive rise in
productivity and GDP in the two decades since the Great Depression, at a time
of increasing economic security. The correlation between rising production
and security, he argues, reflects reciprocal causation; each is necessary for the
other in a virtuous circle of rising affluence. High levels of production ensure,
as we have seen, high and secure employment, sustainable corporate profits,
and reliable farm incomes. The policies introduced to buffer people from the
economic headwinds—unemployment insurance and farm support prices,
for example—moderate the effects of any economic downturn in the economy through the operation of what are called automatic stabilizers. Measures
designed to reduce insecurity have the happy result of also reducing macroeconomic volatility, a major cause of insecurity. "The conflict between security
and progress, once billed as the social conflict of the century, doesn't exist."

III

Looking now at Galbraith's arguments for the declining reality of and concern with economic insecurity, one is tempted to dismiss them as simply one more example of the seductive dangers of social prophecy, and as a nostalgic reminder of the cautious optimism prevalent during an earlier stage of American triumphalism. Although, as I will suggest, these arguments have unraveled at all levels, this would be a mistake. Galbraith was definitely onto something when he wrote *AS*. Average living standards as conventionally measured *had* increased markedly over his century and continue to do so. It's just that this was far from the only development taking place, then and since. The trend to greater security (and equality) *was* apparent from the 1920s or 1930s onward. However, conceived as a simple graph, with inequality and insecurity on the Y-axis and time on the X-axis, both trends traced a U-shaped trajectory into the twenty-first century. Just as modern capitalism has become radically more unequal in recent times, so too has the specter of insecurity returned to threaten general well-being and social harmony.

As the new century unfolds, insecurity has risen in the United States, as in a number of other countries that have followed the neoliberal trajectory, across the whole range from the micro- to the macro-levels. The vast majority of citizens face a loss of security in relation to their jobs, incomes, housing, health care, and retirement. The future for most is assuming a casino-like complexion, as the state—the final line of defense—withdraws under the unremitting attack of right-wing ideologues and organizations. Many of the institutional props supporting greater economic security that Galbraith identified have been or are in the process of being removed. Deregulation of industry and the financial sector, legislation weakening trade unions, liberalization of trade, removal of price, and other industry support schemes, and the gathering attack on the capacity of the state to fund adequate social security programs are all working their effects across the economy. The remainder of this chapter outlines the main dimensions of societies increasingly living on the edge.

IV

The Great Risk Shift is the story of how a myriad of risks that were once managed and pooled by government and private corporations have been shifted onto workers and their families—and how this has created both real hardship for millions and growing anxiety for millions more.

(Hacker, 2008: 21)

Hacker here identifies two key themes in the rise since the 1970s of growing economic insecurity. First, a growing proportion of individuals and families are experiencing both hardship *and* anxiety about the possibility of hardship. Second, the buffers against both hardship and anxiety, previously provided by government and larger employers, are fast fading. On both these fronts developments are precisely the reverse of Galbraith's analysis in *AS*. Galbraith argued that the state and the large corporation led the way in the mid-twentieth century in reducing risk and insecurity for most Americans. He also held that not only was economic insecurity unambiguously declining for the majority, but anxiety or concern over the next pay packet, where the next meal was coming from, or how to meet incoming bills was confined to irreducibly small groups on the margin.

The increasingly insecure nature of American life is expressed, at base, in the multi-form phenomenon of "precarious income." The income of Americans has become increasingly volatile, both up and, especially for most, down. "Indeed, the instability of American families' incomes has risen faster than the inequality of families' incomes" (Hacker, 2008: 14). Hacker uses the metaphor of an income ladder to note that as the rungs on the ladder are moving further apart, families are more likely to lose their footing and, when they do, they fall further and harder than in the past.

Precarious income arises, in the first instance, from precarious employment. Increasingly flexible labor markets—the aim and outcome of neoliberalism—have progressively stripped away worker protections against arbitrary dismissal and encouraged the loss of previously enjoyed conditions. The reduced bargaining power of workers—caused by the combined weight of weaker unions, repressive legislation, technological changes, and global capital mobility—has left the ordinary worker and the more highly educated and skilled worker at the mercy of employers in a way not seen since the early and middle stages of the industrial revolution. The growing, pervasive reach of financial markets imposes a disciplining effect on both workers and their employers. Firms that don't seek to retrench or relocate their operations in order to compete more effectively risk losing their access to credit. As the recent (and continuing) turmoil in Europe suggests, national governments are not immune from this risk. As medium sized firms in many traditional industries struggle to survive against large multinational corporations, outsourcing, both at home and abroad, resurfaces. Small scale contracting, boosted by the efforts of previously employed workers forced to become self-employed, is creating a *new petty bourgeoisie* hard pressed to earn a living and poorly placed to insure themselves against the growing economic risks they must face. These disparate and disorganized groupings are particularly prone to blame government for their predicament and to oppose measures that might, objectively, relieve their situation. Such people form the storm troops of the Tea Party, just as the real storm troopers once empowered the National Socialists in Germany during the Great Depression.

Precarious employment is not only confined to those in traditional "old tech" industries; it is *not* a characteristic of the "digital divide." As innovation rips through the digital economy, many jobs are shredded as new ones emerge. Having the "wrong skills" are as terminal as having no skills. The "tech wreck" in 2001 and the GFC demonstrated that the high-flying financial sector is also prone to sharp reversals of employment fortune, even for the few CEOs forced to resign, albeit with golden parachutes—excluding the even fewer caught and punished for fraud. On the last point, what Galbraith in his classic short history of *The Great Crash* called "the bezzle" is pro-cyclical. The bezzle is undetected fraud that flourishes when times are good and malfeasance can be hidden, but recedes as the economy turns down and outside attention focuses on where the money has gone. The world champion bezzler, Bernie Madoff, prospered for many years but came undone when the previously plentiful supply of dupes dried up during the GFC and the sleepy regulators were forced by public outrage to act. This is also a time when the masters of the universe are finally seen to have feet of clay; when asked how he could consistently make profits in hedging, the Nobel Laureate Myron Scholes used to reply— "because of idiots like you." When the hedge fund firm he co-founded, Long Term Capital Management, crashed and burned in the late 1990s, he joined the club of idiots as an ordinary member.

The rise of casual employment in many sectors, particularly those in service industries, further reduces security of employment, as well as entrenching low wages and benefits. This has been associated over recent decades with the rising workforce participation rates of women, who in many industries form the modern equivalent of Marx's "reserve army of unemployment." These workers are the last to be employed and the first to be let go. The ranks of this army are further swelled by the influx of recent migrants and "illegals."

Hacker presents data showing the scale of rising income insecurity. Thus, by 2003 the year-to-year volatility of average before tax family incomes was double that in 1973. Volatility means up as well as down. This means that in the early twenty-first century, most families were far less sure of what next year's income would be compared to this year's. This makes it difficult to plan for the future and to ensure the accumulation of an adequate personal safety net to insure against future downward volatility. This last point is particularly relevant to those families sliding down the income ladder before they fall off it altogether. But, in the absence of adequate safety nets provided by government and employers, almost all families feel the sting. Not surprisingly, recent surveys document a big jump in the proportion of people expressing concern about losing their jobs. In one such survey, quoted by Hacker, the incidence of concern has more than doubled in the twenty years since 1985; this fear is likely to have jumped further in the years since 2005. The critical conclusion to be drawn from the recent research on rising economic insecurity is that it is climbing the income ladder. Middle-class America is fracturing, an outcome driven by the vast inequalities noted in the preceding chapter and expressed in the yawning insecurity of lives created. "Insecurity today reaches across the income spectrum, across the racial divide, across lines of geography and gender. It speaks to the common 'us' rather than to the insular, marginal 'them'" (Hacker, 2008: 6).

V

Job insecurity lies at the heart of a cascading wave that inundates the lives of ordinary Americans, adversely affecting their and their families' access to decent and affordable housing, adequate health care, educational opportunities, and a bearable retirement. Insufficiency in these basic fields of everyday life rebounds on the ability to secure permanent employment in a deadly dance that locks an increasing number of people into a permanent struggle to survive. Moreover, cumulative disadvantage and insecurity traverses the generations.

The case of housing is instructive. As argued below, the implosion of the US housing system had monumental macroeconomic consequences globally. At the level of the family it led to the loss through mortgage default, forced sale, and foreclosure of more than two million homes. This social, personal, and economic disaster fed upon itself. As credit seized up in the economy, businesses laid off workers who joined the growing queue of people unable to pay their mortgages, lengthening the list of defaults, further shredding bank balance sheets, and so on. As unemployment hit double digits consumers cut back further on spending and investors ran for cover, causing further job cuts and rising gloom through the economy. Housing and employment insecurity formed opposite sides of the same coin spinning down the drain.

America's hard won health care programs—Medicare and Medicaid—have also come under increasing strain. Achieved during great domestic reform movements in the 1930s and 1960s, these programs are straining to meet the growing demands by people unable to personally meet their health care needs, as well as the demands created by the ageing of the population. The retreat by employers from the provision of health insurance and associated benefits has thrown the burden back onto families, an increasing number of whom are not in a position to take out expensive private health care. The new "in-betweeners" are middle- to upper-middle-income Americans who can't afford insurance and don't meet the increasingly stringent eligibility conditions for government protection—thereby forming a growing "sandwich class." President Obama's Congress-emasculated scheme to extend coverage—"Obamacare"—meets but a part of the growing problem and, at the time of writing, still faces sharp opposition.

The story is similar in the case of educational opportunity and outcomes. Those who cannot afford to send their children to expensive private schools or move into exclusive neighborhoods with well-resourced public schools must depend on the valiant efforts of hard-pressed and under-resourced local schools. The capacity of middle-income families to save toward the college education of their children is hampered by the ever-present chance of one or both parents losing their jobs and the need to service the rising personal debt burden that has grown as these families seek to cling onto the American dream of house, cars, and the accepted contrivances of a once comfortable middle-class existence.

Growing insecurity in the United States has progressed beyond childhood and working life into retirement. Once upon a time, employers in many industries provided "defined benefit" pension schemes to full-time permanent workers. On retirement, workers would receive a guaranteed retirement income related to their working incomes. Although provided by employers, these schemes were partly funded by federal taxpayers. Starting in the 1970s and gathering pace, these schemes were gradually phased out, to be replaced by "defined contribution" products (called 401k), where retirement benefits were variable, dependent on the future investment performance of the funds invested. This neatly shifted retirement income risk from the employer to the worker.

Retirement for those who chose not or were not allowed or able to take out these products has become a deeply uncertain future. Unless they are able to save through other channels they will be left with grossly inadequate resources to navigate the final stage of their lives; reliance on an eroding government-provided age pension will not serve. The prospect of saving sufficiently to self-finance retirement is receding as the growing sandwich class struggle to live in the present, burdened by rising personal debt and culturally inflated aspirations as to an appropriate life style. The retirement futures of those lower on the income ladder are even grimmer. Dickensian-style poverty awaits this unhappy bunch, assuming they survive to what is assumed in some countries to be the "normal" retirement age. On that latter score, retirement in the advanced countries is receding, both because in countries with a legislated retirement age that age is being pushed back and in other countries people with a job can't afford to stop working. The interlinked phenomenon of growing insecurity and widening inequality is causing a radical shake up to the life plans of many in the affluent society.

VI

Where did all this come from? In the space of less than half a century the confident, comfortable America of *AS* has turned into the worried, anxious state we observe today. Clearly, many of the forces unleashed during this period—culminating in the complex processes of globalization—are poorly understood and reflect the coming together in unintended and unforeseen ways of disparate economic, cultural, and political currents. However, in the case of countries that have actively and consciously embraced the neoliberal project, certain drivers are apparent. The United States provides the paradigmatic case. From the 1970s onward, conservative and self-interested forces have waged an unremitting attack on the principle of *social* insurance—on the very idea that government should provide a basic level of security for people to be able to seek and take opportunities to better their lives. In this latter view pioneered in America during the early Roosevelt administrations, individuals could only hope to follow their dreams and achieve their life's goals if they were confident that they would not be blind-sided by the unforeseen and unknowable common disasters of everyday life.

The principle of personal responsibility emerged on the political right during the 1970s to diametrically oppose the principle of social insurance against unforeseeable risks. Based on the revived neoclassical orthodoxy, rational consumers were assumed to be calculating schemers, hell-bent on over-burdening the public safety net by engaging in rent-seeking behaviors that resulted in over-consumption of government services and inadequate provision to meet personal setbacks. The logic applied here was akin to the worry facing fire insurance companies—caused by the incentive that a policyholder has to burn down the house in order to collect a pay out. It was never explained why sensible people would really have an incentive to deliberately lose their jobs in order to collect modest unemployment benefits. And would you or I really engage in dangerous or suicidal activities just because we were covered by a limited government accident and disability scheme? Does the distant, beguiling prospect of government age pensions spur us to live riotously and beyond our means today? The proponents of behavioral economics would answer "no." This approach to decision making assumes, instead, that we operate with a whole range of biases, including a strong tendency to focus on the present. This suggests that if people are under-insuring themselves for important events like losing a job, their health, or the life of a breadwinner, then it is more likely that the cause (in addition to the tendency to put off hard decisions until tomorrow) is inadequate income and savings rather than a desire to defraud the taxpayer. The predictable outcome of a move to individual risk management is that those who can afford to contribute to a pooled insurance vehicle but are not subject to the risks covered do not contribute. This leaves those who do need cover to collectively fund the diminished pool, raising the cost to take out cover and thereby excluding people who need but cannot afford to do so. The whole rationale of compulsory or universal government schemes was to ensure that the costs were spread widely over the whole population and that all were covered regardless of ability to pay. Privatized insurance designed to match risk and cost does not cover those who opt out or are driven out.

The theory of rational choice has little relevance to what actually happens as people battle to deal with the risks and uncertainties of everyday life. But, although these theories have little positive or descriptive validity, they have provided a powerful normative case for neoliberal policies of privatization and public sector retrenchment. The ideology of personal responsibility, discipline, and self-reliance holds individuals to be the authors of their destinies. They are to be held accountable for the decisions and actions they take. If they don't save adequately, take out appropriate insurance, and generally organize their lives to withstand the challenges life throws up, then so be it; they must suffer the consequences of personal inadequacy. People make their own luck. Misfortune is seen as a result of character failing not a defining characteristic of an uncertain future. This pervasive view fits well with the history of American individualism and exceptionalism. It was soon generalized from a critique of social insurance to indict a whole range of government spending and regulatory policies. "Welfare dependence" was held to encourage sloth, immorality (teenage pregnancies, abortion), domestic desertion, substance abuse, crime, and social disengagement. Public choice theorists joined the crusade, arguing that, however well intentioned the intervention, the primary driver and outcome was to feather the pockets of public officials in charge of the policy and re-election of the politicians legislating it. Thus, policies designed to ensure greater security and growth in fact undermined the efficient allocation of resources resulting in *less* security and growth.

The idea that "rugged individuals" don't need the interfering, mollycoddling embraces of the "nanny state" was, of course, selectively interpreted. As Galbraith had divined, the self-image of the buccaneering entrepreneur was a myth covering a host of special pleading and importuning by an institutionalized system of interest peddlers. Throughout the last forty years, corporate interests have continued to extract massive taxation and subsidy benefits from governments, regardless of which major party has been in power. Where free-wheeling, risk-taking management prevailed—that is, in the large banks and shadow banks of Europe and the US—this was facilitated by lax government regulation and the successful offloading of the underlying risks onto unsuspecting passive investors and to businesses and households unprepared for the financial tsunami that struck them. The move to tax-favored retirement savings accounts prefigured the introduction of similar savings vehicles in the education and health spheres. Together, such privatized innovations were designed to wean people off universal government programs, opening the scope for income and wealth-based tax cuts favoring the wealthy. The success of this dual attack on the public finances in the US—the enhancement of corporate welfare as well as cuts to taxes on the well-off—is evident in the trends on rising inequality noted in the preceding chapter.

To return to the primary focus of this chapter, the levels and layers of economic security built up in mid-twentieth century America have been progressively stripped away by a marriage of the orthodox economics emanating from that period and the subsequent rise of an ideology linking classical liberal/libertarian and conservative thinking to the role of the individual and the state. This dynamic has been aided and abetted by a cultural counterattack across a broader front in the humanities and social sciences in what Daniel Rodgers (2011) has termed *"The Age of Fracture."* By removing or scaling back many of the trends Galbraith identified as increasing the security of life in the affluent society, this project has increased the vulnerability of families to unexpected and debilitating economic misfortune, while doing so under the cover of resurrecting a personally empowered and responsible citizenry and an enterprising "opportunity society." A fuller statement on the political context of this transformation is reserved for a later chapter.

VII

That leaves the last and most significant prop to security identified by Galbraith—namely, the capacity of the national government to manage the aggregate performance of the economy in order to prevent significant and long-lasting depressions and inflations. We have seen how, up until the last moment before the iceberg struck, economists and policy makers steadfastly held to their course, repeating to themselves and a gullible citizenry—"we've never had it so good." The self-serving narrative of the Great Moderation lulled all into the belief that the business cycle had at last been tamed and the sea was calm ahead. The shock was all the greater because it was *so* unexpected. Perhaps the most poignant moment occurred when Alan Greenspan, "world's greatest banker," eventually admitted ruefully before a Congressional hearing that he had wildly overestimated the capacity of unregulated financial markets to efficiently distribute risk. (True to form, a year or so later, Greenspan recanted, once again spruiking the benefits of unregulated markets.) The truth, as it had become abundantly clear, was precisely the opposite. Financial markets had generated and concentrated risk at the level of the system as a whole—and systemic risk almost brought the whole financial sector, and with it the world's leading economies, crashing down. To add insult to injury, the locus of the crisis was found to be in what finance specialists had once called "the sleepy corner of the financial system"—housing loans.

With hindsight, it is possible to see the seeds of crisis sown in the early part of this century as the US Federal Reserve dropped and kept official interest rates low after the collapse of the dot.com boom and the shock of September 11, 2001. In an era of easy money, share markets and property markets, especially housing, boomed through the middle years of the decade, reinforced by expanding credit, buoyant domestic consumption, and the rapid growth of the emerging economies, especially China and India. Financial innovation, notably the explosion of new mortgage products and derivatives, met demands by the US government to extend home ownership more widely to previously under-serviced groups. Regulatory reforms reduced the previously clear distinction between the primary (commercial) banking system and the "shadow banking system" (investment banks, hedge funds, money market, and mutual funds), and competitive pressures pushed all these financial institutions to aggressively compete for a share of the rapidly growing market of new and complex securities. Intense competition from foreign banks, especially European, ratcheted up pressure.

Again with hindsight, the housing boom or bubble in the US burst in 2006, ushering in a prolonged series of increasingly serious signs of spreading crisis and eventual recession. These can be briefly stated as follows.

In mid-2007, two mortgage hedge funds owned by the investment bank Bear Stearns went bankrupt, as did American Home Mortgage Corporation and three investment funds owned by the French bank BNP Paribus. In late 2007 there was a run on the British bank Northern Rock, the first such event there in more than 100 years. Northern Rock was effectively nationalized in February 2008. In March 2008, Bear Stearns itself faced bankruptcy and was taken over by J.P. Morgan, with a guarantee provided by the Federal Reserve.

From mid-2007 to mid-2008, ten US banks declared bankruptcy, including Indymac Bank, at that time the third largest bankruptcy in US history. In July 2008, the two largest mortgage lenders—Fannie Mae and Freddie Mac—guaranteeing 40 percent of residential mortgage-backed securities faced insolvency and were rescued by the US Treasury contributing equity capital in the form of "preference shares"; the US Congress authorized US$300 billion to fund this "bailout" and to assist defaulting homeowners to reschedule their debts in order to avoid foreclosure. The Federal Housing Finance Agency replaced the management of Fannie and Freddie.

Then, in mid-September 2008, the crisis hit with full force. The investment bank Lehman Brothers went bankrupt, and was refused the federal assistance granted earlier to fold Bear Sterns into J.P. Morgan. This marked the true beginning of the credit crunch as confidence in the counterparty compliance of financial institutions collapsed and banks and other financial intermediaries in the US and Europe stopped lending to each other. Even more serious was the threat that American International Group (AIG), the world's largest insurance company and the major trader in credit default swaps, faced insolvency. This time the Federal Reserve provided a US$40 billion loan to stave off bankruptcy. Subsequently another US$40 billion of federal assistance was committed to AIG, effectively ceding 80 percent of AIG ownership to the US government. In October 2008, Wachovia, America's third largest savings and loans institution, declared bankruptcy. In Europe, Fortis in Belgium was nationalized to avoid bankruptcy, as were Iceland's three banks and, in

Britain, the Bradford and Bingley bank. The two remaining large US investment banks—Goldman Sachs and Morgan Stanley, converted themselves into commercial deposit-taking banks in order to gain US government guarantees and restore confidence in their solvency. In the UK, the country's largest mortgage lender, Halifax Bank of Scotland, was forced to merge with Lloyds TSB to avert bankruptcy; Treasury guarantees provided to Royal Bank of Scotland, the world's largest company by market valuation, effectively nationalized it.

In the second half of 2008, the central banks of the developed nations, individually and collectively, intervened to attempt to restore confidence to their financial systems and end the credit freeze. They initially sought to do this by aggressively lowering interest rates and providing liquidity through purchasing government securities. However, it eventually became clear that this was not a crisis of liquidity but one of solvency. Over-leveraged banks were in no position to lend more without threatening their existence, regardless of how much liquidity was injected into the system. It was unclear, because of the unknown value of complex securities held and the uncertain credit-worthiness of their existing borrowers, just how thick their "equity cushion" was. Further uncertainty about the credit-worthiness of other financial institutions and a general decline in the economic prospects of non-financial firms and consumers further militated against new lending. The key aim of the banks was to rebuild their balance sheets—i.e. de-leverage—by building up their holdings of cash and other highly liquid assets.

Consequently, national governments were forced to also intervene in other ways, as the full scale of the crisis became evident. An early example at the beginning of 2008 was the move by the Bush Administration to cut taxes by US$168 billion. This move proved unsuccessful as anxious taxpayers saved an estimated 85 percent of the tax cuts, dampening any real boost to aggregate demand in the face of the gathering recessionary forces. In addition to the measures listed above, involving government loans, equity injections, and guarantees, several other approaches were tried. Blanket guarantees were given by national governments to protect savers' deposits in a range of financial institutions in most European countries, the US, Canada, New Zealand, and Australia (with varying reach and conditionality). In Australia, the government also guaranteed the wholesale borrowings of the major banks. Most of the G20 central banks together pledged a US$600 billion reserve fund to effectively keep the international credit default swap market from failing.

In the US, government rescue attempts went through four stages in 2008, with a fifth stage flagged by the incoming Obama Administration. The centerpiece was the enactment of the Troubled Assets Relief Program (TARP), which provided US$700 billion to unfreeze the lending halt; this amount was in addition to that legislated to rescue Fannie Mae and Freddie Mac. The initial strategy was to selectively buy the "troubled" or "toxic" mortgage-backed assets of banks in order to improve their balance sheets by removing these assets for which there was effectively no market. The problem was that without an active market, no one knew how much they were worth and what governments should pay for them. It became obvious that if they were worth very little then taking them off the banks' hands would only underscore their likely insolvency—a case of "the cure was successful but the patient died."

Hence, the second stage was to direct government bailout funds into directly recapitalizing the largest banks in most distress—e.g. Citigroup—by "purchasing" preference shares. However, this did not noticeably increase lending since the recipients were more concerned to shore up their solvency by hoarding liquid assets. As this situation became clear the government contemplated setting up a "bad bank" to acquire all the toxic assets at current marked-down values from all the affected banks—rather than some assets from some banks, as in stage one. Where these assets had not been marked down (because doing so would disclose insolvency), the government would have insured these assets against default; this effectively would have meant relaxing the regulatory requirement for banks to "mark-to-market."

The third stage of the bailout shifted to the US manufacturing sector. As unemployment rose through 2008 and consumption fell, the automobile industry was particularly hard hit. The three large US auto manufacturers—Ford, GM, and Chrysler—faced bankruptcy. They sought substantial subsidies from government to facilitate an orderly restructuring. However, Congress refused to pass the necessary legislation and in December 2008 the outgoing Bush Administration provided (by regulation) a bridging loan of US$17 billion to prevent a disorderly collapse of GM and Chrysler, which would have put at risk the jobs of up to 3 million workers directly and indirectly dependent on these companies. Further developments on this front awaited the new Administration in 2009.

The fourth stage of government intervention has been through the Federal Reserve. Traditional central bank intervention had, as noted above, failed. As the banks swapped government securities for more liquidity supplied by the Federal Reserve, they hoarded it or bought further government securities, even as the interest rate on that debt fell toward zero. Cash is king when banks seek to de-leverage. The great danger when lending freezes is that consumption and private investment fall further, dragging the economy down and threatening a self-reinforcing deflationary spiral, as occurred in Japan through the 1990s. As prices fall the real burden of debt rises and consumers speculate there will be further price falls, further reducing aggregate demand. In response, the Federal Reserve now moved to buy private securities (such as promissory notes and other corporate debt, as well as credit-card debt) from non-banks by effectively "printing money." This "easy money" policy (officially referred to as "quantitative easing") was aimed at encouraging these institutions to lend more, thereby sparking demand. In November 2008 the Federal Reserve created a fund of US$800 million to pursue this strategy, the first time in history that it had moved beyond the banks to stimulate lending, a clear sign of the perilous state of affairs. The Bank of England later followed this lead in the UK.

The fifth stage of this intervention entailed the largest fiscal stimulus packages ever introduced by a national government. The US stimulus package amounted to US$819 billion; about a third of this total was for further tax cuts with the remainder committed to infrastructure, energy efficiency, and social security programs.

The upshot of what has come to be called GFC1 (now that we face the prospect of GFC2, thanks to the prospect of sovereign debt defaults by some European governments) was a massive write-down in the value of financial assets in the US; millions of forced housing mortgage foreclosures and distressed sales, a situation where a third of US housing mortgages are "under water"—that is, where house owners have negative equity or owe more on the house than they can get by selling it; a wave of bankruptcies cascading through many commercial and industrial businesses; and federal government debt that has ballooned toward a level approaching the GDP. Subsequent efforts by the Obama Administration to aid recovery have had very limited success and the US economy continues to fire on three cylinders. With hindsight, we can see that the stimulus policies were simply not large enough to get the job done and by the time the Obama Administration recognized this fact, the political environment had become so toxic that there was no chance to go back to the well for more—the combination of Congressional deadlock, right-wing ideological attacks, and loss of confidence caused by the failure of stimulus mark I stymied further sensible policies. The unwillingness of the Administration to admit its mistakes and timidity in a period leading to Obama's re-election also played a part.

The modest irony involved in the fact that this convulsion was unleashed in the fiftieth anniversary year of *AS* would have not been lost on Galbraith, who would have also wryly appreciated that its genesis lay in what he regarded as the mumbo-jumbo world of money and banking. He would certainly not have been surprised by the truth belatedly recognized that the vast majority of managers and senior executives in the large financial services firms had no real idea of what the hell was happening in their trading and risk management departments. The fact that J.P. Morgan, one of the few large banks to escape the carnage in 2008, was forced to acknowledge losses of over $3 billion in 2012 as a result of a "rogue trader" employed in their London operations, suggests that they (the senior managers) are still clueless.

Considerable uncertainty and controversy surrounds current discussions of *why* the events described above occurred. Broadly speaking, analysis and commentary fall into four categories. They are not mutually exclusive.

The first explanation highlights greed and malfeasance. In this view, popular in the media, greedy and unscrupulous entrepreneurs misled investors, consumers, and governments—sometimes illegally—in order to profit from rising asset values. Financial markets, in other words, did not track basic fundamental values but reflected and rewarded the risk-taking behavior of financial sector operators. The culture enshrined earlier in the decade by the collapse of Enron, etc. pervaded investment markets and led to a range of business practices that resulted in the breakdown of trust throughout the economy, particularly in the US. These practices ranged from outright illegalities like the breath-taking Ponzi scheme of Bernie Madoff to the pervasive "rent-seeking" behavior of senior finance sector executives in enriching themselves through "outrageous" bonuses and generous compensation schemes.

Such accounts are natural in an environment that is seeking understanding quickly and searching for parties to blame. However, they tend to be exaggerated and offer, at best, only part of the answer. Fraud—the bezzle—for example, tends to be uncovered after (and because) the economy turns down, and hence cannot be seen as a cause; this was certainly the case in the Madoff scandal and others like it. "The principal–agent conflict" represented by the evolution of financial executive compensation packages is certainly relevant. These incentives played a material role in stoking aggressive application of the new financial products; but without the plethora of opaque financial innovations in credit derivatives and their non-regulation, the escalating profits would not have arisen to make the huge payouts. "Greed," after all, is but another name for "profit maximization," and the latter is what drives capitalist development. In that sense, greed is always with us but major economic breakdowns are (fortunately) rare.

Other factors must be present for profit-seeking behavior to lead to economic crisis. That said, we can hardly afford to ignore clear signs of criminality and sharp practice when it is uncovered—less we unintentionally reinforce a culture in which such behavior is normalized. The revelations in 2012 that a number of large banks had systematically rigged the process through which banks signal their inter-bank lending rates, thereby indirectly conveying their risk profiles, has further eroded public confidence in our financial systems— especially as it seems that the banks concerned, previously household names for probity, were unofficially encouraged in their behaviors by high government officials. At the time of writing, one bank, Barclays, had been fined around £250 million; other lenders may experience similar financial and reputational embarrassment.

The second culprit identified is government. Explanations based on the failure of government come in two contradictory forms: too much regulation and too little regulation. In the first view, existing government regulation of the financial sector prevented free markets from working efficiently. In the second view, government regulators failed to properly monitor (or even understand) what was occurring until much too late; even then, bureaucratic delays and fragmentation prevented effective and timely action.

What appears to be a more accurate description is not that too much or too little regulation occurred—but that the wrong regulatory structure was in place and the existing regulatory rules and tools were not well-suited to deal with novel challenges posed by the new world of credit derivatives. In a real sense, it was a case of the generals fighting the last war. The proliferating collection of new financial products, most notably credit default swaps (CDS) and collateralized debt obligations (CDOs), was understood by only a very small number of people within the large banks and brokerages, and as it turned out, even these people did not appreciate the real risk being generated throughout the system as a whole by the increasingly tight interlinkages between the banking and shadow banking systems. Beyond that rarefied minority, financial sector operators, regulators, and politicians alike, all accepted the assurances of key spokesmen like Alan Greenspan and Federal Reserve Chairman Ben Bernanke that risk was being efficiently distributed by these derivatives to those investors best able to manage it. This comfortable position accorded well with the prevailing neoliberal view that markets left to themselves were well placed to deal smoothly with any external shocks.

With hindsight, it is clear that the government's decision to allow Lehman Brothers to fail, rather than be assisted to merge, was the great blunder in creating panic, barely averted two weeks later when a policy about-face resulted in the bailout of AIG. However, this was not a failure of regulation but a near-fatal error of political judgment.

Richard Posner (2009: xii), in this respect, comments:

> Some conservatives believe that the depression is the result of unwise government policies. I believe it is a market failure. The government's myopia, passivity and blunders played a critical role in allowing a recession to balloon into a depression, and so have several fortuitous factors. But without any government regulation of the financial industry, the economy would still, in all likelihood, be in a depression. We are learning from it that we need a more active and intelligent government to keep the economy from running off the rails. The movement to deregulate the financial industry went too far by exaggerating the self-healing powers—of laissez-faire capitalism.

It is true that the US government, like counterparts in some other countries, encouraged the extension of mortgage lending to low- and middle-income earners. However, there is no direct evidence that proves that this factor was decisive in causing the current crisis. After all, as Posner notes, no one forced the banks to lend.

Another version of the "government did it" focuses on the wrong-headed economic policy advice and decisions based on the orthodox macroeconomics of the day. Keynesians such as Krugman and Stiglitz argued throughout and in the aftermath of the crisis that governments had forgotten the lessons of the past and hence risked reaping the bitter fruit of the 1930s. Having fallen into a massive liquidity trap, the only way out was for governments to borrow and spend the economy back to health. Combined with moderate debt relief, moderate (re)inflation, and sensible restructuring of the financial system, prompt and bold government spending would substantially shorten the period of stagnation; this, as noted above, did not happen in the US and many other advanced economies.

A third explanation targets investor and borrower "irrationality." Behavioral economists argue that the current crisis was essentially driven by a self-reinforcing psychology of overconfidence among both mortgage borrowers and lenders. The major proponent of this view, Robert Shiller, whose 2008 book *The Subprime Solution* argues that the housing price bubble in major US metropolitan housing markets was caused by a strong positive feedback loop, characterized by increasing confidence in future housing capital gains, plentiful mortgage credit, low interest rates, and continuing house price rises. Many of the biases identified by behavioral economists in other areas were present, Shiller argues, in the housing sector; notably, over-confidence, selective information gathering, "story-telling," ignoring warning signs, trust in experts, wishful thinking. Lenders were as subject to these biases as were borrowers; so were other institutions like the ratings agencies. Derivatives traders and ratings agencies were used to applying standard quantitative tools for assessing the risk and thus price of all manner of debt products. It now appears that they collectively underestimated the real likelihood of subprime mortgages defaulting in the real, as opposed to abstract, world of the standard models. As Gillian Tett (2009) in her book *Fool's Gold* argues, the data simply weren't there in the case of these loans to accurately assess the correlation of potential defaults. In the information vacuum, analysts relied on past data (and implicitly applied the ergodic axiom). In the event, actual defaults and resulting realization losses (from the forced sale of repossessed houses) vastly exceeded the assumptions of the models. Common reliance on the available quantitative models lulled most lenders, agencies, and mortgage insurers into a false sense of security, the bias of overconfidence or hubris.

The increasing interdependence of national economies reinforces the volatility of the global system. When more and more of the world's economies are linked, the economic movements within countries develop closer connections across jurisdictions and come to reinforce each other. The liberalization of financial transactions seems to have left more scope for the herd to gain momentum in both boom and panic when the herd suddenly changes its course.

The final explanation points to systemic market failure. Posner, for one, explicitly rejects the need for explanations that rely on the irrationality—perhaps "different rationality" would be a better term—of economic actors. He claims, instead, that such factors are likely to have been marginal and that the scale, scope, and timing of the crisis can be explained within the standard economic model of rational maximizing consumers and producers. In his view, economic actors were responding as would be expected (by economists) to market signals.

As far as one can judge, he argues, on the basis of what is known today (obviously an important qualification), the depression is the result of normal business activity in a laissez-faire economic regime—more precisely, it is an event consistent with the normal operation of economic markets. Bankers and consumers alike were, claimed Posner, acting in conformity with their rational self-interest throughout the period that saw the increase in risky banking practices, the swelling and bursting of the housing bubble, and a reduction in the rate of personal savings combined with an increase in the riskiness of those savings. The market participants made plenty of mistakes, but that is par for the course. Whenever has it been different? Economic life is permeated with uncertainty.

As credit constraints were relaxed and interest rates fell, households borrowed more to spend on housing. Market-relevant information emanating from the housing industry and government reinforced the message that housing markets were being driven by underlying fundamentals: buoyant economic growth, rising incomes, falling average household size, and increasing population. Lenders were able to lend more because the value of their loan books kept rising. A range of new intermediaries placed themselves between mortgage borrowers and investors, all responding to the incentives of competitive markets. Mortgage defaults were low and well within the parameters of the risk assessment models. These factors remained true right to the moment the housing bubble burst in 2006, apart from industry pronouncements that stayed bullish into 2007, for obvious self-interested reasons. Even though some actors came to see the bubble-like nature of housing before then—and acted accordingly, to their good fortune—most continued to act as before, to their cost. But, as Posner argues: "that is par for the course." Some win and some lose in the uncertain economic struggle. No one, he suggests, can know for sure when a rising market turns into an unsustainable bubble—until it bursts. Until then everyone will continue to pursue his or her selfish economic interests. To voluntarily pull out of a rising market means forgoing potential profits (utility) and watching other actors increase theirs. As the then CEO of the then largest bank, Citigroup, effectively commented, when the music is playing you have to keep dancing, and the music is still playing.

Moreover, the internal organization of the large lenders and brokers contributed to the expansion of the credit derivatives business. Senior bank executives had little experience or knowledge of what the new credit products were, nor how to ensure that appropriate risk management processes were in place and being complied with. This knowledge was compartmentalized in small specialist teams within the organization. The external competitive pressures to grow market share and post rising quarterly earnings led many (but not all) US and European banks to encourage the growth of their most profitable products, which in the context of a booming housing market, meant precisely those credit derivatives tied to housing. To some extent, everyone's overall compensation within the organization became dependent on the continuing growth of this business. Potential borrowers, on the other hand, were faced with attractive conditions and inducements to borrow in order to become homeowners, even households with few resources and poor credit histories.

What this suggests, and Posner argues, is that micro-efficiency and rationality at the individual actor level can, nevertheless, aggregate to system-wide failure. The metaphor is a fire in a theatre; everyone has a strong individual incentive to flee the building as soon as smoke is observed, but as all rush for the exits at the same time, no one gets out and all die. This logic can be applied to the case in point. The dynamic of a booming housing sector in the US led to an insatiable demand for mortgage-backed bonds. Banks could securitize and pass on mortgages, collecting fees for doing so, and remove risk from their balance sheets, freeing up capital to repeat the transactions many times over. This growing demand for mortgages to securitize brought forth a supply response—banks and mortgage brokers offered more and more loans to borrowers who would never before have been considered. This could be done because the new financial engineering turned the subprime individual mortgages into higher-rated bonds attractive to a range of investors. Everyone along the line gained, but only as long as housing prices kept rising and subprime borrowers kept repaying their loans. When the real risks of default became apparent, all lenders and brokers tried to shore up their solvency at the same time, resulting in the credit crunch and a spiral into recession.

In other words, although individual actors were at all times acting in the rational pursuit of self-interest, macro-efficiency was threatened by the systemic effects. This appears to be partly due to imperfect and asymmetric information and partly to endemic "moral hazard." The manner in which risk was transferred through the securitization process meant that no one had both the incentive and opportunity to properly monitor, assess, and control credit risk; hence, no one did so. Banks thought that they had effectively transferred all the risk to someone else—erroneously as it turned out. Eventually, the banks that had most enthusiastically participated in the CDS and CDO trade were left with an unforeseen, unknown, but huge liability for defaulting housing loans. Financial stability on both national and global scales turns out to be a public good; if left solely to the market it is chronically under-supplied.

When investors cannot appropriately price complex new securities, they cannot properly assess the overall losses faced by financial institutions, and where they cannot know who is holding the risk for the "toxic waste," this turns into generalized uncertainty. The outcome is an excessive increase in risk aversion, lack of trust and confidence in counterparties, and a massive seizure of liquidity in financial markets. Thus, once lack of financial market transparency and increased opacity of these markets became an issue, the seeds were sown for a full-blown systemic crisis.

In reality, all the above explanations have some degree of persuasiveness. Even if we agree with Posner that much of what happened can be sheeted home to the pervasive pursuit of narrow individual self-interest, surely "irrational" behaviors, government failures, and fraud had some role. In particular, Posner's claim that agents were acting rationally because one can't know that a bubble is a bubble until it bursts, places a peculiar meaning on individual rationality. Shiller and other behavioral economists have a point when they claim that people decide on the basis of various rules of thumb ("heuristics") based on persistent human biases—to borrow Posner's words, "that's par for the course." To willfully ignore any disconfirming information that a housing (or any other) market is wildly overvalued and act accordingly, hardly qualifies as rational behavior in any meaningful sense.

The major consequence of the Great Recession of 2008 is that it is still with us four years later and shows little sign of abating. Growth in the US economy has barely poked its head above the parapet, while the official unemployment rate still hovers near 8 percent. The situation is much worse in Europe where Spain, Italy, and Greece have fallen back into recession. The IMF 2012 forecast for growth in Europe overall is −0.5 percent, while growth in the developed countries is expected to be an anemic 1.2 percent. Even the large European nations—the UK, France, and Germany—are barely in the black. Unemployment rates are at near-record levels; in Spain almost one-quarter of the workforce is out of a job, while the youth rate is double that. The basic problem is that those economies ran up structural budget deficits during the faux-boom of the early-2000s, driving up public debt, and then were forced to borrow more to fund bailouts occasioned by the first global financial crisis.

Compounding problems, the governments of the common currency Eurozone can't agree on, still less enforce a solution to, the imminent threat of their weaker economies defaulting on their public debt. International bond markets are reluctant to go on rolling over loans to governments that they believe may not be able to meet their repayment commitments. The PIGS—Portugal, Ireland, Greece, and Spain—are in the firing line and the target of desperate attempts by the stronger northern Eurozone members to ensure that they do not default—or, at least, do so in an orderly manner, which is more politely presented as "restructuring" existing loan arrangements. Herculean efforts are being made to prevent the contagion spreading to the larger economy of Italy. However, little consensus is evident across the region.

The German government presides over Europe's strongest economy and wields immense influence over Eurozone decisions. German taxpayers have to date borne the major weight of bailouts to keep the PIGS afloat but understandably evince some hesitancy in writing an open check. In order to maintain assistance through support from the specially created European Financial

Stability Facility and subsequent arrangements, the miscreant governments must agree to impose austere fiscal discipline aimed at bringing their budgets back toward a sustainable balance within the foreseeable future. The big banks, which are terribly overexposed to the suspect government bonds, are also being required to share the pain, by discounting their value by 50 percent or more. No one is happy. The banks are unhappy. The French government is unhappy, since a number of the unhappy banks are French. The PIGS are unhappy, since their proposed expenditure cuts, tax increases, and measures to extend the retirement age are deeply unpopular with their voters and highly likely to be counterproductive by driving their economies even further into recession, thereby increasing rather than decreasing budget deficits. As I write, Greece cannot elect a stable government and the whiff of social revolution pervades the ancient seat of democracy. In a very real sense *The Great Recession of '08* is still with us and shows no sign of wishing to depart. In short, it's a mess.

* * *

The main lesson from the turbulent events of the years following the fiftieth anniversary of the publication of *AS* is that the business cycle is not dead, that economic security at the macro-level has not been achieved through the forces Galbraith identified in 1958. The endemic prevalence of "Knightian–Keynesian uncertainty" makes liars and fools of all economists. Galbraith is no exception. Like the warriors of "real business cycle theory," he underestimated systemic volatility and, consequently, overestimated the efficacy of the macro-guarantors of economic security in real-world global capitalism. The recurrent pattern of economic life is nicely summed up by George Megalogenis (2012: 42), only the names change to protect the guilty:

> History repeats, first as stagflation then as subprime. The global meltdown of 1974–75 is connected to the Great Recession [of 2008] by the common denominator of American hubris. Just swap Iraq for Vietnam, the credit bubble for the Great Society, and China for OPEC. Each crisis began with US excess and spread to Europe and the British Isles by guilt of association.

However, Galbraith's broader point, expressed in a number of places in the book and in other writings, that politics and economics are intimately connected and to understand one it is necessary to gain a firm grasp of the other, still stands. The complicated, confusing, and uncertain events unfolding in Europe are testament to this enduring truth.

6

The Ambiguities of Production

We regard the production of some of the most frivolous goods with pride. We regard the production of some of the most significant and civilizing services with regret.

(J.K. Galbraith)

*   *   *

The short chapter on "The Paramount Position of Production", placed in the middle of the book, provides a key linchpin between the earlier critique of conventional ways of approaching the nature of modern capitalist society and the lessons for sensible economic policy that Galbraith wishes subsequently to hammer home. Having argued that ever-increasing material production had assumed the mantle of redeemer of the faith—leading a fortunate humanity to a secure station in a sea of plenty—he goes on to point to the peculiar lack of urgency in overcoming the remaining fetters on production.

> By way of summary, then, while production has come to have a goal of preeminent importance in our life, it is not a goal which we pursue either comprehensively or even thoughtfully. We take production as the measure of our achievement, but we do not strive very deliberately to achieve.

One answer to this apparent contradiction was stated by Galbraith in his earlier discussion of economic security. Production, he suggested, was a proxy for gainful employment. As long as producers move themselves sufficiently to adequately employ the hands and heads making themselves available for work, then all is well. This is, in some ways, an unfortunate defense for the conventional wisdom, since it implies that we really don't live in a world of scarcity, driven by the natural and human conditions of a post-Eden reality, to labor away at survival. Perhaps humanity may reach a point where we can rest on days other than the seventh. "Yet production remains central to our thoughts. There is no tendency to take it, like sun or water, for granted; on the contrary, it continues to measure the quality and progress of our civilization."

Galbraith supports his thesis by listing the five ways that production or aggregate output can be increased and then arguing that business, government, and citizen—in the thrall of the central tradition—pay serious and concerted attention to only one, the efficient allocation of available resources. Any interventions, blockages, or incentives that impede the capacity of markets to direct all available resources to their most efficient ends must be eliminated. Idleness is indeed the consort of the devil. Monopoly and any restraint on trade, including go-slow tactics of organized labor, hamper the capacity of output to grow.

The other drivers of growth are not ignored but generally assumed to operate at adequate levels left unattended. In particular, increasing production by increasing the supply of capital and labor will, it is held, follow the efficient operation of the market. Savings and capital formation will faithfully follow the market signals expressed by the coming together in capital markets of savers (each seeking to maximize utility over a lifetime) and investors (each seeking to maximize profits). Galbraith makes the point, however, that it is conceivable that more could be done by government to boost both activities. Governments can provide incentives to save and promote institutions to manage savings; they can also provide incentives to invest. His point is that they can and, from time to time, do but not in a comprehensive manner designed to maximize the impact on total production. The patchwork of incentives and other assistance owes more to earmarks than benchmarks—to the success of lobbyists in tagging individual measures to government legislation than to a full-frontal effort to hit ambitious output targets for the economy.

The labor force can also be increased, for example through immigration and pronatalist investments and exhortation by government. Most importantly, the skills of workers and managers can be enhanced greatly by systematic investment, private and public, increasing productivity accordingly. This leads to the final way in which a society seriously committed to maximizing growth, measured by increasing output, could do so—through technological innovation. In many industries dominated by large corporations, just such a discipline exists. But, Galbraith points out, in the plethora of industries formed by small- and medium-scale enterprises—in farming, retail (before the advent of Wal-Mart, of course), clothing and textiles, house construction, etc.—innovation lags, customary practices persist, and production levels oscillate around a slowly creeping incline.

Governments can do much to improve innovation here, particularly through investing in research and development. Clearly, Galbraith is not arguing that governments make no effort in this regard, merely that those efforts are sporadic and, in the main, modest. Soon after publication of *AS*, Galbraith's position was given theoretical support by two doyens of American neoclassical orthodoxy. In the early 1960s, Robert Solow demonstrated empirically that the lion's share of economic growth in America was determined by technological change. At about the same time, Kenneth Arrow, another subsequent recipient of the Nobel Prize for Economic Science, argued from impeccably orthodox premises that markets if left to themselves systematically underinvested in education and skills enhancement.

Galbraith situates the "partial and indeed eccentric" concern for increased production historically, and sees it as yet another hangover from the nineteenth-century world view dominated by Malthus and Ricardo. In a world characterized by diminishing returns, where existing population pressed on available food resources and little scope for technological improvement beckoned, it made sense to ignore the levers of increasing labor supply and capital formation. All that mattered was making the most of what was available. Those other levers offered the potential to drive growth; "[b]ut they are outside the formal and stylized concern of the conventional wisdom for the problem of production." The Second World War demonstrated the point with force that governments could, when suitably prodded, ramp up production massively. The fact that in normal peace time they choose not to, indicates that production is not the holy grail that the conventional wisdom ordains.

II

The final ambiguity in the modern treatment of production for Galbraith— and the critical one in the light of his broader argument later in the book— is the "curiously unreasonable" distinction drawn between different types of goods and services. He notes that although economists routinely include all goods and services in conventional measures of national income—one is here reminded of Jeremy Bentham's remark that "pushpin is as good as poetry"— there is a peculiar public perception that "some are more equal than others." Anything produced by the private sector is seen to be worthy of respect and ambition; anything provided by government is inherently suspect. "Vacuum cleaners to ensure clean houses are praiseworthy and essential in our standard of living. Street cleaners to ensure clean streets are an unfortunate expense. Partly as a result, our houses are generally clean and our streets are generally filthy."

In fact, the suggestion that the economists' conventional measure of well-being, GDP, avoids completely this popular bias is not strictly true. Because many if not most services provided by governments are not provided through the market, they are included at cost, underestimating the contribution that they make to consumer well-being. The choice of the vacuum cleaner example suggests another bias in national income accounting. Although statisticians make an effort to estimate and include the value to consumers of domestic production—that is, goods and services consumed by those who produce them—it is generally conceded that the estimates fall well short of reality. It is also conceded that the vast bulk of household production is provided by women, though consumed by all household members.

Galbraith again finds this conundrum explicable in historical terms. In the prior world of scarcity attention was almost totally fixed on ensuring the basic life supports of food, clothing, and shelter, material goods acquired by people, either by their own hands or through the market. Publicly provided services came later, both in time and order of urgency. They also came with a distinct flavor of suspicion, especially in the United States, founded on a basis of rebellion against their colonial masters, where individual freedom—to truck and barter—trumped government interference. Overtones of the nineteenth-century liberal state hung heavy over mid-twentieth-century attempts to promote the state as an enabler of growth, a facilitator of the good life. Since publication of *AS*, this earlier view has reasserted itself in the neoliberal guise noted earlier.

This gives one more example of the capacity of the conventional wisdom to confound and deny reality.

> In western countries, in modern times, economic growth and expanding public activity have, with rare exception, gone together. Each has served the other, as indeed they must. Yet the conventional wisdom is far from surrendering on this point. Any growth in public services is a manifestation of an intrinsically evil trend. If the vigor of the race is not in danger, personal liberty is. The structure of the economy may also be at stake. In one branch of the conventional wisdom, the American economy is never far removed from socialism, and the movement toward socialism may be measured by the rise in public spending. Thus even the most commonplace of public services, for one part of the population, fall under the considerable handicap of being identified with social revolution.

These words resonate even more strongly today as America deals with the militant rise of the Tea Party and associated mutterings of the right-wing chattering classes, energized by the exhortations of popular radio and television commentators and orchestrated by the more subtle contributions of conservative institutions and public intellectuals. The career of President Obama's health insurance policy—and the earlier experience of similar initiatives under the Clinton Administration—provide only the most obvious and visible case of the conservative conventional wisdom at work in politics.

III

> ...the time has come for a survey of the vested interests in our present attitudes to production. Who is most dependent on the present illusion?
>
> (J.K. Galbraith)

Having established that, for a variety of reasons, historical, political, and cultural, aggregate production rules in the minds of almost all in the affluent society, Galbraith asks—who has a vested interest in this state of affairs and in its maintenance? His first response: "(w)ithout question, the individual with the greatest stake in the present economic goals is the businessman—more precisely, the important business executive." By "important," presumably he is referring to the senior managers of large corporations. The material rewards of corporate remuneration are clearly relevant to aspirations to lead in the business world. But the desire to excel and enhance one's reputation, even to leave a legacy to history, also motivates the aspiring leader; this argument has echoes of Schumpeter's vision of the entrepreneur. In wartime generals assume prime position in the esteem of their fellow citizens. But in peacetime, it is the leaders of large enterprises that seize this mantle and enjoy the social esteem that is thereby bestowed.

The businessman's lofty position is, however, a tenuous one. There are other claimants on the heights of social approbation, notably, the educator, the artist, the medical professional, the judge, politician, and public official who all jostle for the warm regard of their fellow citizens. However, they are increasingly trumped in this endeavor by the businessman. Why? Because he (women were absent in that space at that time) and he alone "knows production." As a "practical" person the businessman is naturally expected to know his craft, and to perform the central task of maximizing production of goods for public consumption. He is also the first to be called upon when the economic engine appears to be stalling. This is not a fully secure position, it must be said. His exalted position rests on shaky foundations; it depends on the continued primacy of production in the public mind. As modern capitalism settles down to a steadily rising level of affluence, the continued urgency of production is rendered problematic. The essential prop to the prime importance of production and his position of social preeminence rests, as previously noted, on the prerequisites of economic security, the need to keep mass unemployment at bay. The danger that production may recede in urgency in the public mind leads to a redoubled effort to assert its importance.

As government turns attention toward other areas of policy, like education, social welfare, cultural enhancements, and infrastructure provision, the opportunity for competing sources of prestige and influence emerge. Such interventions are unwelcome and stoutly resisted by business interests, not only because they fear that they will bear the bulk of the taxes raised to finance them but also because the leaders in these fields pose a direct challenge to their social position. A tension of long-standing and particularly intense force exists between businessmen and intellectuals. Each portrays the other in a negative light. One is seen as a narrow pragmatist, the other as a hopeless "stargazer"; Gradgrind versus Kepler. This tension has generally been portrayed as arising entirely from opposing material interests and ideologies of social utility. Not so, avers Galbraith. "Scientists, writers, professors, artists are also important competitors of the businessman for public esteem." In this competition businessmen suffer certain disadvantages. Intellectuals are naturally more likely to shine in the public sphere, being in general both more erudite and articulate. The role of social prophet—a position conferring maximum opportunities to acquire prestige—although usually short-lived, falls more easily to the intellectual. The businessman must play the long game, seizing whatever opportunity to reassert the primacy of production, and his indispensability, whenever it arises.

Paradoxically, it is the modern American liberal that is most likely to assist the businessman in the defense of the paramount position of production. Following Keynes, liberals have accepted the critical role of governments ensuring high employment levels, greater economic security, and declining inequality through generating growing levels of national output.

> As a result, production did more than impress the liberal. It became his program, and it established something akin to a monopoly over his mind. Here, perhaps, was the nearest thing to alchemy that had ever been seen in the field of politics. Increased production solved, or seemed to solve, nearly all the social problems of the day.

Just as importantly, a commitment to Keynesian demand management of the economy in pursuit of full employment sharply distinguished liberals from their conservative political opponents in ways that conferred significant electoral advantage. The latter long clung onto the tenets of "sound finance," the need for government to balance its budget at all times, lest the tigers of inflation and moral turpitude escape and wreak social havoc. Post-war Keynesian policies helped win elections, reason enough for liberals to join in the chorus celebrating the central importance of production, even when this involved the creation of a growing stream of goods of dubious and declining urgency.

Nevertheless, Galbraith discerns clear signs that the paramount position of the businessman is slipping, as the universal and uncritical concern for ever more production is queried. This he detects in the increasing reliance of business on the rising profession of public relations. The primary task of the PR expert is to "re-engineer" the businessman's image to show that he is more than a mere general in the army of production. Proficiency in the arts is one such avenue to shore up a waning eminence. "A businessman reading *Business Week* is lost to fame. One who reads Proust is marked for greatness." Prominence in the field of charity may also serve a similar function.

However, try as he might, the businessman is fighting a losing battle. Business leaders who persist in pursuing their self-appointed role as social prophet and wise government counselor face a difficult task in being taken seriously. Particular contempt is increasingly reserved for those who write or speak on intellectual matters. Their books and speeches are not judged as good or bad in themselves but "...good (or on occasions bad) for a businessman." The devastating last phrase underlines their second-class status as social commentators. More importantly, as the urgency of material production subsides in the economy and public mind, other concerns and their promoters are arising. Liberals in particular are embracing a wider range of issues, secure in the knowledge that the worst excesses of early capitalism—mass unemployment and grinding inequality—are under control. Environmental protection, social security, racial inequality, and (intriguingly) artistic and intellectual integrity now compete with the previous focus on the prime position of production. Nevertheless, like water and air, adequate production, although less at the forefront of social concern and status, is basic to the survival of society. "If the vested position of production is no longer completely secure, one can still marvel at the way it has survived the enormous increase in the output of goods in modern times."

IV

Looking back from today's vantage point, one would have to say that in many respects Galbraith misread the signs concerning the declining importance of production and growth. The "limits to growth" debate quickly died in the 1970s only to be resurrected in completely different guise in the new century. For much of the period since the original publication of *AS* growth has dominated economic debate and policy. The main disagreements have been about how to achieve it. Serious trouble for Galbraith's thesis can be traced back to the blow-out in the federal budget during the Vietnam War and the inflationary crisis unleashed, compounded by the unexpected appearance of serious and persistent unemployment in the 1970s. Stagflation focused minds on the importance of production at the most basic level—namely, ensuring that people got and kept a job and so were able to meet their basic material needs as well as the many supernumerary ones to which they had become accustomed.

The new era of scarcity and insecurity, as we have seen, opened the way for the central tradition to reassert its sway over economic thought and policy. The 1980s was a period of substantial economic restructuring in the advanced capitalist economies, ushering in a new phase of globalization marked by widespread deregulation of markets, the increased global reach of large industrial and financial enterprises, falling trade barriers, and the pronounced decline in the countervailing power of institutions like trade unions. Government's role was "re-engineered" as "steering not rowing." These forces were fully unleashed in the following decade, "the roaring nineties." The heroic role of the entrepreneur was rediscovered. Universities created named chairs in "entrepreneurship." The importance of the innovative entrepreneur was lauded to an extent not seen since the 1920s. Once again the opinions of businessmen, and now some businesswomen, were eagerly sought and heeded. Unsurprisingly, they reasserted the primacy of production and the imperative of government retreat from matters economic. Proponents of The Great Moderation lined up to reassure one and all that "markets know best." Alan Greenspan, prominent ex-investment banker and long-term Chairman of the Federal Reserve, satisfied himself that the new environment had permanently burst the supply-side constraints that prevented the economy from growing at a rate well beyond historic trend without reigniting an inflationary conflagration. This time it was different.

Greenspan and other like-minded souls suffered the familiar fate of social prophets, much as Galbraith would have expected. They were dumbfounded by the turn of events unleashed in 2008 and forced to recant. A radical disconnect emerged between the ideology of the "omniscience of the market" and harsh reality. A second, reinforcing narrative uncomfortably arose alongside the critique of neoliberalism—namely, the apparent economic success, measured in conventional terms, of GDP growth of regulated state capitalist societies like China. How could China and other "emerging" economies weather the economic storms battering the developed economies when they spurned the self-evident advantages of free markets and free trade? For Galbraith, this would have presented no difficulties, since he held that markets were never free and those economists and policy makers who held that they were, were insulated from real world outcomes by their self-interested immersion in the conventional wisdom.

More importantly, we can see—with half a century's hindsight—that the large corporation is not the only source of innovation. Evolutionary perspectives stemming from Joseph Schumpeter's earlier work point to the importance of small- and medium-sized firms in bringing new products, processes, and business models successfully to market, often blind-siding established market leaders. One has only to think of the rise of Microsoft, Apple, Facebook, and a host of garage start-ups to get this point. Conversely, many large and previously dominant corporations have been broken up, taken over, or failed completely over the past fifty years. Alfred Marshall's canny metaphor of industry as a forest, with individual trees sprouting, reaching for the sun, growing to maturity, and then dying, neatly expresses the historical trajectory informing economist Paul Omerod's (2005) book—*Why Most Things Fail.* However, as an economist well aware of the importance of the institutional springs of economic behavior and outcomes, we can safely surmise that Galbraith would have embraced much of the recent work on national innovation systems, networks, and clustering.

However, returning to the main theme of this chapter (and paradoxically), the near collapse of the advanced economies and the reputations of those who led the neoliberal chorus reaffirmed the importance of production and growth. When the ship is listing, minds and hands are concentrated on imme-diate survival. But the captain and ships' officers may be replaced. Government assumed again its direct leadership position and the discredited entrepreneur discreetly withdrew, at least until a convincing story could be constructed that diminished his (definitely his) culpability and prepared a path enabling him to again challenge for political influence and social prestige. We are currently watching this drama being enacted as government after government in the developed world battles to right their economies and fund their growing debts, advised again by the very culprits who created the crisis.

7

The Dethroned Consumer

Production cannot be an incidental to the mitigation of inequality or the provision of jobs. It must have a raison d'être of its own.

(J.K. Galbraith)

Among the many models of the good society, no one has urged the squirrel wheel.

(J.K. Galbraith)

* * *

The doctrine of consumer sovereignty has been the ruling metaphor in the central tradition ever since the subjective turn in economics occasioned by what is called "the marginalist revolution." From the latter third of the nineteenth century until Galbraith wrote *AS*—and one can note, until now—economics has started with the wants and needs of independent consumers as a given. Analytic attention has focused on market processes and government interventions best able to maximize the extent to which those needs and wants are or are not met. This position provides, suggests Galbraith, the ultimate defense of the primacy of production. Production of useful things and services occurs in order to satisfy the myriad wants and needs of consumers, each trying to maximize the utility or benefit gained from consuming the resulting output.

Economists seemingly face a difficulty here. The theory of diminishing marginal utility, by which the utility or benefit gained from the consumption of each successive unit of a commodity declines until a point of satiation is reached, suggests that the act of production itself will eventually reach its limit. Why go on producing if no one wants the resulting output? If most people eventually reach satiation in consuming those goods most important for basic survival—sufficient food, clothing, and shelter from the elements—what's the use of continuing to privilege the continued production of things that meet wants of declining urgency?

The answer, Galbraith argues, is for economists to accept the reality of the declining urgency for individual goods but not for goods in general. There may indeed be a hierarchy of need but no limit to what one wants. Once one set of goods is consumed, consumers move seamlessly in pursuit of a never-ending stream of new goods. "When a man has satisfied his physical needs, then psychologically grounded desires take over . . . It is held to be neither useful nor scientific to speculate on the comparative cravings of the stomach and the mind." A second line of defense is provided by the universal acceptance (by economists) of the proposition that wants are an integral part of the consumer's psyche and, as such, given data for the economist. What those wants are and how they get there are not questions that need exercise their minds. This stance enables economics to distinguish itself from the other social or human sciences. It provides a degree of professional "closure," a marking of intellectual territory, the creation of a distinct academic division of labor that legitimates the independent practice of a distinct discipline—in short, the final emancipation of economics from moral philosophy and the other disciplines that emerged from this common trunk.

In the words of the historian and philosopher of science, Thomas Kuhn, it allowed economists to claim that the orthodox model embedded in the central tradition formed a dominant *paradigm*, an analytic structure that privileged particular questions, while ruling others out, and established clear criteria for what was (and was not) "normal science." "Nothing in economics so quickly marks an individual as incompetently trained as a disposition to remark on the legitimacy of the desire for more food and the frivolity of the desire for a more expensive automobile." To distinguish between the urgency of the consumer's wants was seen to be "unscientific," to rely on subjective value judgments not susceptible to independent measurement and verification. This professional disposition to equate qualitatively all goods and services has echoes of both Bentham's pushpin and poetry and Alfred Marshall's "starting point" for the economist, namely that they should not study the "mental states" of individuals but the consequences of these states—in subsequent terms, the *choices* people freely make through markets.

Galbraith notes in passing the importance for economists of the assertion that wants have no limit; it provides yet one more group with a vested interest in the unlimited pursuit of growth, of the primacy of production. Economists join business executives in the small priesthood that "know production." They are among the few who are called on by governments to advise on public policy. Galbraith himself was a prominent example of the public-spirited economist who shuttled back and forth from Cambridge to Washington in order to bestow the benefit of his wisdom on the representatives of the people. The policy presence and role of the economist has massively expanded in the last fifty years and is felt in fields as divergent as transport infrastructure and family welfare policy. In the main liberal democracies, no self-respecting public official would approach his or her political master without a suitably arcane cost–benefit analysis in hand.

Denying the common sense view that some goods are more urgent than others has called forth a sophisticated analytical barrage and a high degree of ingenuity, if not sophistry. Having denied the validity of distinguishing between more and less important wants, economists point to the infinite *variety* of goods on offer. Once satiety is reached in one line of consumption, plenty more lines appear. The fact that some wants are perceived as basic and satisfied first—if you don't eat then the prospect of other consumption becomes irrelevant—presents no insuperable problem to the economist. The goods consumed later, after basic needs have been dealt with, are consumed by a different consumer; a consumer with a full stomach is different from one with an empty hollow feeling. There is no way to compare the satisfaction gained by the two consumption experiences, that is, no way of establishing that the second and subsequent acts of consumption return less by way of satisfaction to the insatiable consumer. In that sense, it is not possible to say that income and wealth—the means of increasing consumption—obey the law of diminishing marginal utility. Since individuals have an insatiable demand for goods in the aggregate, then they also crave without limit the means of satisfying that demand. This, it should be noted, provides a negative defense of inequality. If wealthy people received less satisfaction from the consumption of more and more frivolous goods, then by redistributing some of their wealth to poorer people struggling to feed, clothe, and house themselves would increase the total happiness or welfare in society. By affirming the equal capacity of all goods to satisfy consumers, the privileged affirm their right to satisfy themselves without limit.

Galbraith further notes that subsequent developments in the theory of consumer demand have jettisoned the potentially dangerous reliance on cardinal measures of utility and used, instead, ordinal measures, the sets of indifference curves familiar to every undergraduate economics student. Even this approach has been reinterpreted, following Paul Samuelson's lead, to focus on the "revealed preferences" of consumers. Assuming that consumers are rational— that is that they obey stringent logical requirements of consistency—their utility is expressed by the choices that they actually make between consumption options in the present and across time. The economist only has to observe or model the choices that rational consumers make in the circumstances prevailing (or specified in the model). With insatiable needs the consumer is posited to allocate scarce resources to maximize the benefits to be gained, to reach the highest indifference curve within reach of his or her budget constraint; the proof that this has occurred is implicit in the choices that he or she actually makes. By this somewhat circuitous logical route, economists are able finally to banish the threat posed to the primacy of production and entrust the throne to the sovereign consumer.

II

Galbraith refuses to accept the denial, embedded in the conventional wisdom, that some wants are more important than others. He notes, in support of his defense of common sense on this point, the distinction drawn by Keynes (1973/1930: 365) between human needs that

> ...fall into two classes—those needs which are absolute in the sense that we feel them whatever the situation of our fellow human beings may be, and those which are relative only in that their satisfaction lifts us above, makes us feel superior to, our fellows.

Keynes argues that although the second class of needs, and hence the goods necessary to satisfy them, may be unlimited, the first class of absolute wants are not. This is because Keynes wants to show that at some future time the latter will be universally satisfied and humanity will have real choices about how much to continue chasing the former less urgent wants. Keynes clearly believed, as a good middle class English liberal, that once freed, most people would give up the senseless pursuit of status-driven consumption in order to develop the higher sensibilities and refinements of Bloomsbury.

Galbraith, although less of an Edwardian caste of mind, also believed that once people became aware of the realities and opportunities ushered in by rising affluence, they would question the endless drive to acquire goods of declining importance and instruct their governments accordingly when it came to dealing with the deficiencies of the affluent society that were becoming ever more obvious. In short, he held that the importance, economically and socially, of the second class of goods would recede. This, it can be noted in passing, flies in direct opposition to the analysis and prophecy of another widely influential popular book published at roughly the same time as *AS*—namely, Vance Packard's (1959) *The Status Seekers*. Packard saw American society as riven by the imperative to "keep up with Jones's," and preferably to surpass them. But like Galbraith, he pointed to a crucial economic force underpinning this tendency—the rise of mass advertising, a line of reasoning he developed further in another book, *The Hidden Persuaders* (1957).

The existence of advertising provides Galbraith with the decisive proof of the declining urgency of production in the affluent society.

If the individual's wants are to be urgent, they must be original with himself. They cannot be urgent if they must be contrived by the process of production by which they are satisfied. For this means that the whole case for the urgency of production, based on the urgency of wants, falls to the ground. One cannot defend production as satisfying wants if that production creates the wants.

In an economy where an increasing proportion of goods produced flows to "fill the void" created by the act of production, consumers are condemned to a life on the squirrel wheel, forever chasing their tails.

For then the individual who urges the importance of production to satisfy these wants is precisely in the position of the onlooker who applauds the efforts of the squirrel to keep abreast of the wheel that is propelled by his own efforts.

Galbraith argues that most economists, in their saner moments, concede that many wants are synthesized as an integral part of the production process. Sales and promotion expenses are routinely included in the businessman's calculation of expected gain and realized profits and losses. "Outlays for the manufacturing of a product are not more important in the strategy of modern business enterprise than outlays for the manufacturing of demand for the product." At the level of consumer psychology, emulation, the desire to have what others have, works a powerful spell and guides the marketing strategies of firms and the external consultants they hire. Thus, the obvious and increasingly intense links between the business enterprise and the "institutions of modern advertising and salesmanship" cannot be reconciled with the simple dictates of consumer sovereignty, since the prime function of those institutions is precisely targeted at synthesizing the wants to which consumer choice is directed. He asserts the emergence of a general positive empirical relationship between the scale of production and the size of the marketing spend, a commonplace observation that would be "...regarded as elementary by the most retarded student in the nation's most primitive business school." (The modern reader is here as elsewhere in *AS* reminded that it was written in an earlier age both innocent of the niceties of political correctness—in this case, the sensibilities and rights of the intellectually disabled—and accepting of the established pecking order of American universities. Today, he would get away with the latter but not the former.)

The obvious fact that wants are produced as part of the process by which they are satisfied is denied in principle only by economists because it is they who risk losing the analytical and political purchase they have over the minds of government and lay public alike. The fiction of the sovereign consumer helps make the models of orthodox economics mathematically tractable, so marking the economist as a scientist of repute and relevance.

It is true, Galbraith concedes, that advertising has a number of functions; notably it forms an important part of the firm's competitive strategy as it seeks to differentiate its products from its competitors in the manner stressed by his

Harvard colleague, Edward Chamberlin, and other analysts of imperfect competition. Galbraith himself had earlier written usefully on such matters. One can also concede the claim, put forward by advertising and marketing people themselves, that their activities provide an important informational service to consumers, albeit from an interested perspective. Nevertheless, Galbraith focuses on the basic point that consumers do not need to be persuaded or even informed of the goods that satisfy their most basic needs; they only need such guidance when they "...are so far removed from physical want that they do not already know what they want." This state of reduced urgency is precisely that emerging with rising general affluence.

Galbraith calls the self-fulfilling economic process by which wants depend on the process by which they are satisfied, "the Dependence Effect." Given the critical role rising production plays in ensuring greater equality, security, and social peace, increasing demand must be contrived in the way described in order to keep the whole enterprise socially solvent. The alternative of looking for more sensible ways of securing equality, security, and peace by recognizing the pervasiveness of the Dependence Effect and jettisoning the unbridled commitment to growing the gross domestic product—to raise questions of quality of life—proves inconvenient to economists and threatening to their professional position. "It is far, far better and much safer to have a firm anchor in nonsense than to put out on the troubled seas of thought."

III

Galbraith's sharp attack on the doctrine of consumer sovereignty drew in return some of the sharpest criticism of the book from fellow economists. Friedrich von Hayek, Keynes's most prominent critic—both during his lifetime and long after it—regarded this aspect of *AS* as a simple *non-sequitor*. Many others argued that Galbraith had either overstated the importance of the assumption of independently given consumer tastes or misrepresented its intent. Although, as I argue below, there is much that has happened on the consumption front since Galbraith wrote that he didn't and couldn't have anticipated, one is left with the suspicion that his basic criticism of the economics profession—namely, that its treatment of the independence of consumer tastes hides a deep anxiety about the validity and usefulness of conventional models—still rings true and struck a painful chord in the profession, both then and now.

Galbraith's critique of insatiable consumption implicitly assumed that the goods and services produced were "normal" in both the technical and lay senses. A "normal good" for economists is one for which the quantity demanded by a consumer increases as his or her income increases. It is also a readily reproducible product—that is, if demand increases producers can produce more to satisfy that demand. However, there may be some goods and services that are inherently limited in supply and cannot be increased in volume. In the 1970s the economist Fred Hirsch published a book called *Social Limits to Growth* (1976) in which he argued that in modern developed urban societies some commodities assume the nature of "positional goods." A positional good is one that can *only* be consumed by one or a few consumers. Examples include a breathtaking view from a particular housing site, the best seats at the theatre, a specific vintage wine, a Vermeer painting. In some cases close substitutes may be available but close is not always close enough. The limited supply of "the best" in capitalist societies ensures their price rationing to those most willing and most able to pay the highest price. The existence of positional goods and their closest substitutes provides a strong incentive for some people to maximize their incomes; it is only by doing so that they are able to bid for the fine wines, prestige locations, and limited edition designer handbags so widely desired.

The consideration of positional goods leads naturally to the phenomenon of "brands." Initially the development of distinct branded products, especially in mass product markets like automobiles and kitchen detergents, was aimed at building customer recognition and loyalty. In the contemporary world, branding is more likely to be aimed at the middle-income market, rather than at either the mass end or the very top end of the bespoke market. A brand signifies status or prestige in a subtle and unobtrusive way, often through the means of a discreet logo. No longer does social status depend on the garish display of wealth but on buying the right goods and enjoying the right experiences. At the low-cost end of the market, generic goods are sweeping the field. At the top end, one-off products are demanded and supplied. Wherever possible, producers and their image consultants extend the reach of branding outward to create and capture the rising aspirations of consumers for "coolth."

Pushing back the boundaries of exclusion that true positionality entails, consumers are encouraged to work, save, and borrow in order to project the visible embodiment of prestige, and reap the semblance of exclusivity. The image often passes for the reality. The common pursuit of a brand is a recognizably modern demonstration of the power of emulation in motivating consumption. This process *is* akin to life on the squirrel wheel, since, by definition prestige is a positional good, limited in supply—only some can be truly cool, most will merely be wannabes. In theory there can be no limit to aspiring to be on top *but* the ability to achieve and stay there *is* limited by, among other things, one's income and wealth. Thus, the modern phenomenon of branding, while demonstrating the interdependence of consumer tastes, as Galbraith argued, has also underpinned the insatiability of consumer desires and the endless scramble to satisfy them, in direct opposition to his (and Keynes's) expectations.

One further element of the current branding phenomenon is its increasing dependence on the cult of celebrity. No longer do business or political leaders, still less the leading members of social elites, set the tone for cool consumption. Increasingly, sporting heroes, film stars, and people who are famous for being famous add the luster of their reputations to the marketing of products. New industries devoted to creating and sustaining celebrity have emerged, starting with the traditional print and broadcast media but now increasingly driven by the engine of social media. The emergence of Twitter and Facebook has lifted the game to new levels of intensity; the reach and triviality of content have roughly grown in proportion. The result has been a seemingly never-ending growth in the demand for everything from perfumes to photocopiers, computers to cars, holidays to haversacks, dresses to deodorants. The production of celebrity has itself become an industry producing yet another positional good, a hierarchy of "celebrityness," ranging from the mega star to the minor, differentiating the A-list from the rest.

The script for celebrity status revolves around a now familiar theme, based on the trials and tribulations of "coupledom." A male and a female star (the script is overwhelmingly hetero) are rumored to be "an item" (often implying that one or both is deserting another star). The rumor firms into speculation about the imminent announcement of an engagement, which when confirmed leads to long and detailed disquisitions on the scale, location, and attire to be worn at the wedding. The wedding is held in well publicized privacy, often on the private estate of another celebrity, protected from the public eye by high walls, large dogs, and private security guards. The world's paparazzi—a new profession—cluster around the electronic gates and any area of high ground helpfully supplied by nature, in order to catch glimpses of the happy couple or, failing that, of their family and other guests, for immediate sale to the more sensationalist elements of the mass media. The official photographic record of the ceremony will have been contractually pre-sold to a fortunate media outlet long before, the proceeds often publicly donated by the principals to a worthy charitable cause. Almost as soon as the last guests have departed, attention focuses on the whereabouts of the happy couple's honeymoon. Thanks to the loyal band of paparazzi, the public is treated to a steady diet of fuzzy snaps taken at long range under immense practical difficulty. Not long after, the first signs of marital disharmony are broadcast to a sorrowful world, often accompanied by the suggestion that a third party is complicating relations between the primary players. Happily, this normally proves to be mistaken and amid the joyful celebrations, experienced observers are poised to discern the first signs of "the bump" that announces the eventual arrival of a baby who will, on entering the world, be landed with an obscure name, possibly redolent of an exotic fruit or the mysterious orient. This, however, provides no long-term solution to either the marriage or the insatiable need for publishing grist. Increasing speculation centers on "the divorce," providing as much product but with the added benefit of intense speculation as to what and who is to blame. The suggestion that the culprit might be either the claustrophobic attentions of the media or the voyeuristic proclivities of the public is stoutly ignored. And so, the carnival moves on—to another drama in a world that is increasingly unable to distinguish reality from "reality."

The processes just outlined have been substantially assisted by two key developments in the period since *AS* was published; one technological, one economic. The discovery and rapid development of the internet and, more recently, social media has radically expanded the scope of new consumption experiences in both real and virtual space. Internet shopping and banking have revolutionized the way people manage and spend their money. Electronic games and gaming has added new dimensions to leisure activities. Production has become less dependent on particular spaces, decentered and disaggregated on a global scale; the reverse side of this coin is that some spaces, so-called world cities, have assumed increasing significance as "command and control centers" responsible for directing, to the extent possible, the overall operations of increasingly linked local, regional, and national economies. The emergence of search engines like Google has, in some ways, reversed the dependence effect identified by Galbraith. By counting and cross-referencing the billions of computer clicks generated, Google can build detailed profiles for individual consumers and tailor advertising to best mesh with their particular consumption personalities. These electronic traces instruct producers as to what to produce and for whom. New systems of distribution deliver the goods and services in ways that a consumer's profile suggests. At face value this implies that consumers are regaining the upper hand, making producers more sensitive to their tastes and aspirations. Alternatively, we may see these developments as simply the next stage in mass manipulation by better informed producers.*

Complementing the processes unleashed by the internet, consumption patterns have continued their long-established trend away from material goods toward immaterial services and consumption experiences. It appears that once basic needs are met, most people do desire a range of services and experiences, both as ends in themselves and as the modern signifiers of status. A holiday in the Bahamas serves as well as an expensive automobile for the latter purpose. Dematerializing the economy includes but goes beyond the harnessing of the powers of the internet. It is a postwar process that predates the latter and is reflected in the increasing proportion of the workforce employed in the service

---

* The growth in social media is reinforcing the role of networks in determining new consumption patterns and protocols. Paul Omerod (2012) in his book, *Positive Linking*, argues that current economic models, orthodox and heterodox, that rely on the interaction of individual actors miss the main economic and cultural forces increasingly at work in modern societies. His analysis provides a truly radical critique of the individualist assumptions on which economics has rested since the marginalist turn in the 1870s. This approach harks back to Vance Packard rather than Galbraith.

sector of advanced economies, particularly in the information-intensive industries. The rise of finance and producer services generally is, as noted in earlier discussions on inequality, a pervasive feature of the modern world. The significance of an increasingly service centered economy in this context is the expanded scope provided for the creation of new consumer wants and the simultaneous means of satisfying them, in a self-perpetuating circle of endeavor.

IV

Developments over the past few decades have generally undermined the predictions of Galbraith and Keynes on the declining urgency of consumer wants. This can only be accounted for in part by the decline in economic security and the increasing incidence of poverty and relative deprivation. Economic, technological, and cultural forces seem to be strongly interconnected, working together to continually push back the horizon of satiety, putting off indefinitely the age of "the art of living" to which they and long before them, Mill and Marx, looked forward. This, at least, is the general conclusion of the several prominent economists contributing to the Pecchi and Piga (2010) volume, *Revisiting Keynes*, centered on Keynes's "Economic possibilities" essay.

These commentators are generally agreed that Keynes vastly underestimated the scope for the creation of new wants beyond the basic needs. In particular, the vast advances of technology opened vistas never glimpsed in earlier times. International airlines offered the prospect of global travel to the broad mass of people in the developed and fast-developing economies. Major advances in medicine and medical procedures increased both the demand for new medical services and the need to work hard in order to afford them. Galbraith, in an important sense, was right; the process of production *was* creating the demand—for far-flung tourist experiences and sophisticated medical interventions prolonging and improving life—but wrong in claiming that most people would quickly reach the limit of their desires.

The demand for "leisure" turned out not to be a substitute for other goods but complementary to them. More leisure time requires more goods and services to actively pursue leisure pursuits. These commentators also noted that Keynes underestimated the impact of an increasingly unequal income distribution on the demand for even the most basic of goods. The asset-free unemployed don't even face the onerous task of choosing between more goods of dubious need and more leisure; their only option here is the leisure to starve.

However, another aspect of the Galbraith–Keynes position has been to a degree vindicated in a body of work that can be called "the economics of happiness," mentioned earlier. Implicit in the former's work was both a normative critique of consumerist society and a positive critique of the received theory of consumer sovereignty and the inadequacy of economic models based on the theory of rational choice. In addition to the advances of behavioral economics, already noted, economists are joining other social scientists to systematically explore what consumers—that is, people—really want, what actually makes them happy; hence, Diane Coyle's (2011) aptly titled book, *The Economics of Enough*.

The philosophical roots of modern economics lie in the utilitarian tradition. The ultimate end to which a person's behavior is assumed to be directed is his or her utility or happiness. The good society is one where happiness is maximized. The appropriate public policy is one that assists people to reach their goal of maximum happiness. The challenge here, if one is not to argue in circles, is to define and measure happiness in order to see whether in fact people do attempt to maximize it and, if so, how successful they are in various circumstances. Economics has historically found itself in a fearful mess in this space. It first became clear that interpersonal comparisons of happiness are impossible, if one is attempting to use a simple cardinal scale—even though early economists optimistically talked in terms of "utils," suggesting a measurement of happiness akin to the units of feet and inches used to compute and compare height. What *is* happiness? Economists and psychologists have subsequently developed a range of methods for approaching the thorny subject. Both qualitative and quasi-quantitative scales have been advanced. Unfortunately, little agreement has been reached on what is being measured and, hence, what might increase or reduce happiness in a given society.

For example, results have been produced that suggests a positive empirical relationship between income and happiness; other research has found a negative relationship. Some economists claim to find tipping points—that is, happiness increasing with income up to a point and then flatlining or tailing off after that as income continues to rise. This would provide some support for the position staked out by Galbraith and Keynes. Much of this research is bedeviled by the use of average income, proxied by conventional measures of GDP. Far more persuasive are findings that start with multi-variable definitions of happiness. This approach draws on the idea, as old as Aristotle, that human beings are social animals and that the primary goal is to achieve virtue by aspiring to "the good life." Living well is living ethically. To do this a person needs a degree of freedom, real choice, that in turn depends on a range of resources—some material to be sure but also intangibles like achieving "belongingness" as part of a family and community, developing a sense of duty, developing the natural talents one has, indulging one's natural curiosity, and so on.

More radically, Amartya Sen (2009) has suggested that one needs the spur of "unhappiness" or dissatisfaction with one's current lot to motivate individual and collective human action to improve the world. Negative definitions of happiness can also stress the *absence* of certain conditions that result in negative social and family relationships, lack of control over one's life, and deep feelings of shame and personal worthlessness. Many of these blockages to happiness interact, as when toxic relationships within families lead to loss of control over life and feelings of worthlessness and low self-esteem. These latter handicaps can act back on family dynamics, reproducing toxic relationships from one generation to the next. Happiness in this sense is defined by the absence of constraint, external control, conflict, and the all-pervading feeling of anxiety.

Perhaps most difficult of all for those who wish to posit a simple and direct relationship between means and ends, resources and utility, is the nagging thought that getting to somewhere you want to end up often requires extensive detours. According to the economist John Kay (2010), in his book simply titled *Obliquity*, the oblique often triumphs over the direct. This, as noted, holds true in many areas of life, including the pursuit of happiness. Happiness is best grasped—practically and theoretically—indirectly, as the result of other activities. One does not become happy by striving to be happy but by striving. Happiness sneaks up on one when one is not looking, it occurs when one loses all sense of time. Most people have had the experience of being reminded that it is time to leave the party and *then* realizing what a good time they had had. Consumption, in the most general sense of the term, is a verb not a noun. Consumption is not the end to which limited means are directed but one (and one only) means to the end, human flourishing. The latter is the by-product of human endeavor under conditions of reasonable autonomy and self-direction. Perhaps Galbraith glimpsed this oblique truth in his metaphor of the squirrel wheel. But, then, perhaps happiness is not the prime goal people are shooting for, however obliquely—and if it is, the question remains, do governments have a role in helping to bring it about? If not, is some other goal the end of human striving—like "flow," as in flourishing?

8

Inflation

Next only to the virtues of competition, there is nothing on which the conventional wisdom is more completely agreed than on the importance of stable prices.

(J.K. Galbraith)

*   *   *

Historically, inflation has been associated with the worst excesses of human folly—war, civil unrest, famine, and "cosmic disorder." Maintaining price stability would therefore seem to be of overriding importance in capitalist societies where money is the measure of all things. But it is not. "All branches of the conventional wisdom are equally agreed on the undesirability of remedies that are effective." Why is this so? Galbraith has several answers.

First, some people and organizations reap benefits from inflation, particularly those industries and occupations with enough market power to increase their prices faster than the average. Although, for good forms' sake, they raise their public voice against the evil of inflation, "...their opposition is less than impassioned." Debtors who contract their liabilities in nominal dollars gain, and creditors lose, when general prices rise. This is normal—as we have seen, some win and some lose in the general competitive struggle that is capitalism.

The survival of pre-Keynesian beliefs in the self-correcting nature of the economy provides a more basic reason for the tendency to do nothing about inflation. Historically, prices were observed to follow the rhythm set by the business cycle, rising in general when the economy boomed and falling when the economy receded into recession. Inflation could therefore be dismissed as an annoying but at base, self-correcting phenomenon. For economists influenced by the "Austrian School," inflation was both the punishment for the unwarranted borrowing and spending of government and the necessary purge for a return to economic health. It was a useful reminder to government and citizen that any attempt to inflate the economy in order to boost economic activity and reduce unemployment would inevitably make things worse by unleashing inflation and prolonging the return to normal economic conditions. The best policy for government was no policy. The government should in all circumstances balance its budget and refrain from an active monetary policy, leaving interest rates to be set by the natural mechanism of the market.

Galbraith reiterated that by the postwar period, this older view of the self-correcting economy had been superseded in the conventional wisdom and policy circles by the Keynesian view of demand-management in the context of the ever-present threat of involuntary unemployment. Although it was no longer held that depressions (now called by the more polite term, recessions) would cure themselves, the same dismissal of self-righting tendencies was not extended to inflation. "The notion that, in peace time, prices might as a normal thing rise continuously and persistently has had no Keynes." In the absence of a satisfactory explanation for why inflation might be a structural problem, the hope remained that it might after all be a temporary and self-regulating by-product of a growing economy, especially now that governments had at their disposal the Keynesian tool kit for fine-tuning the economy.

Although neither conservatives nor liberals held this view with conviction, they are nevertheless "tempted to wait and see." Their disposition to do nothing was reinforced by the lingering memories of the 1930s Depression and anxieties about the long-term stagnation of capitalism after the Second World War. The dangers of moderate inflation paled before the prospect of mass unemployment and misery. The attempt to control inflation may unintentionally cause a crash, better to live with it.

Although these factors of vested interest and policy timidity touch on the hands-off treatment of inflation, they are by no means the prime reason. The answer to the riddle has already been provided in earlier discussions. "We are impelled, for reasons of economic security, to operate the economy at a level of output where it is not stable—where persistent advances in prices are not only probable but normal." Policies that would control inflation clash with the preconditions for economic security and growth, thereby threatening the primacy of production. The alternative to addressing uncomfortable trade-offs between growth and price stability is a hope that the conflict might not be too intense and a faith that, if it is, then it can somehow be evaded. Galbraith approaches this conundrum by discussing first the nature and consequences of inflation and second, by questioning the confidence placed in attempts to defuse the conflict.

II

The problem of inflation engaged Galbraith long before he wrote *AS*. During the Second World War he presided over the US government's price control system as (in his words) President Roosevelt's "Price Czar." Before the war he had researched and published on the uneven structure of the US economy, characterized by differential market power and the existence of supply-side bottlenecks that could lead to inflationary tendencies when aggregate demand ramped up. His first major book (*American Capitalism*) published after the war in 1952 developed this theme and located such tendencies in the institutional structure of the economy, a line of argument he further refined in *AS*.

Following his earlier writings Galbraith divides the economy broadly into two sectors. The first is comprised of small farmers and businesses in retail, commerce, and services that individually have no influence on the prices they receive or the cost of inputs to their activities. They are, as earlier noted, the price takers so celebrated in orthodox economics textbooks. The other sector, as also noted, includes the large corporations and service organizations operating in oligopolistic competitive conditions; such enterprises exert varying but considerable independence in determining their prices and the timing of changes in prices, along with the myriad forms of non-price competition and market influence that make up the strategic practices of their managerial mandarins.

Firms in the competitive sector have no room for independent maneuver. When demand for their products falls, the prices they receive fall; when demand rises so too do prices. They are similarly at the mercy of changes in their costs that are quickly passed through to prices. However, the extent to which changes in demand and costs affect prices is mediated through the process of entry to and exit from the industries concerned. As demand increases and prices rise, more firms enter in the hope of reaping prospective profits, limiting the price rise (eventually) to generate "normal profits." Those individual firms with particular advantages—some brand loyalty or accessibility, for example—can earn a little more but by and large, they all get what the market decrees. Inflationary forces are therefore driven in this sector through either buoyant aggregate demand ("demand-pull") or rising labor and other costs ("cost-push").

In the case of the oligopolistic sector, big firms have in certain circumstances the ability to raise their prices. The oldest recognized mechanism, harking back to Adam Smith's comment about the habit of businessmen never congregating "but to commit a conspiracy against the public," relates to the simple expedient of formal or tacit collusion to raise prices. However, Galbraith suggests a more technical and strategic way. As these firms approach full capacity each is able to unilaterally increase its price without fearing losing market share to its large competitors, since the latter cannot quickly increase their outputs because they are already operating near full capacity. The next part of the argument is novel. Large firms may choose *not* to use this power in the near term for strategic reasons. The decision to raise prices may need to be timed carefully to avoid attracting the unwanted attention of anti-trust regulators or alerting trade union leaders to the enhanced prospect of wringing wage rises and other concessions. Raising prices may also spark customer displeasure and galvanize populist politicians to impose unwelcome regulations. For various reasons, considerations of long-term self-interest may trump the short-term gains promised by immediate price rises. This means, Galbraith stresses, that large firms are often sitting on "unliquidated profits" from "unmade price increases," a situation where they could increase prices and profits but choose not to—for the moment. The significance for inflation is that when demand in the economy falls and prices fall elsewhere in the economy, large firms may grasp the opportunity to realize their unliquidated profits by *increasing* prices.

This analysis has within it hints of a structural explanation for stagflation. If the oligopolistic sector is large enough compared to the economy as a whole, then, within limits, falling aggregate demand may in the short term lead to inflation as generally measured by a weighted index of price movements throughout the economy; increasing prices in the industries dominated by large firms will outweigh price falls in the competitive sector. However, Galbraith does not quite make this point. Indeed it would be difficult to do so, since he carefully pulls back from overstressing his argument. He notes that as demand falls and unliquidated profits are realized, excess capacity will rise, at some point encouraging the large firm to drop prices to clear inventories. "The important point is only that in industries characterized by oligopoly, the relation between demand, capacity and price has a degree of play. Prices are not restricted immediately when demand is curbed or excess capacity appears."

Having introduced a new twist on the inflation story, Galbraith now reverts to a familiar theme. "In the inflation drama, it remains only to introduce Hamlet. That, by common consent, is the union." When unions successfully push for higher wages for their members, prices rise in competitive industries. That is self-evident. If they didn't then firms would go out of business, since they are operating on the margin, just paying their way, and earning normal profit. Prices must rise to allow survival on the new margin of competitive existence. However, in the oligopolistic sector prices rise because they can, because the reserve of unliquidated profits exists and the short-term conditions now match the firm's long-term interests. The large firm has no need to curtail rises to avoid attracting union action—it's already occurred. Adverse reaction from the public can be side-stepped by blaming the union for "forcing" the rise. Once started, the process can become self-perpetuating, as unions attempt to protect the living standards of their members by seeking new wage rises to offset the rising living costs set in motion by price rises justified by earlier wage rises. Thus, workers join consumers on the squirrel wheel, running to keep in the same place; but then, of course workers and consumers are one and the same. We finally reach the notion of the "wage–price spiral," a descriptive rather than an explanatory device, since neither unions nor employers alone can be fingered as the primary cause of inflation. (Galbraith here slightly changes the metaphor from the squirrel reference. A painted spoke making up a wheel comprised of firms and consumers represents unions. "One cannot single out a particular spoke in a wheel, paint it black [or red] and say that it shoves all the others.")

The impacts, like the causes of inflation, are diverse. General price rises fall unevenly across social groups. Workers in industries with market power and strong unions tend to be relatively unaffected, as are those offering key services in high demand. Doctors and lawyers fall into that latter category. People who are hurt are those on fixed wages and salaries, such as teachers and essential service workers, low-waged service workers such as cleaners and hospitality workers, and the myriad categories of people dependent on pensions and social security benefits. The plight of retirees living on depreciating past savings are often presented as cases most worthy of concern if not action. "Concern over the problem will be marked by the fortitude with which we are all able to contemplate the sorrows of others." Farmers whose products have low or even negative income elasticities are also adversely affected; for example, as money incomes rise, people tend to consume fewer potatoes in favor of a wider range of foods. Thus, the beef-cattle producer will benefit due to the "statistically quite demonstrable tendency of people who have a pay increase to celebrate with red meat."

III

In summary, Galbraith held that inflation was wired into modern capitalism through the wage–price spiral and could be controlled with difficultly if governments were able to moderate the self-perpetuating spiral or adequately reduce aggregate demand. Taking the latter path, however, would normally require a substantial deflationary push, with the attendant threat to economic security—that is, the level of excess capacity created would need to be substantial in order to dissuade large firms from using the opportunity to liquidate their "unmade profits" by increasing their prices. Opting for the alternative of imposing some kind of incomes policy to break the wage–price spiral—a policy direction that became fashionable a decade or so later in America, Britain, and some other advanced countries—ran up against those forces, sanctioned by the conventional wisdom, opposed to government distortion of markets on the orthodox grounds of maximizing economic efficiency. In the face of this unpalatable situation it was natural for pundits, politicians, and public to look for a way out that avoided the need to go on looking in either direction. Was there a third way?

Historically, Galbraith suggests, the task of stabilizing prices was left to the mysterious and arcane world of central bankers, of which the Bank of England provided the original and persisting model. Up until the First World War, in the period of high Victorianism, *The Bank*, as it was universally known, regulated interest rates and international capital flows by manipulating the "bank rate", that is, the interest rate it charged commercial main street banks as lender of last resort. It also helpfully managed the UK government's public debt. When excessive domestic investment and other spending threatened to bring inflation, The Bank raised the bank rate, causing other interest rates throughout the economy to rise; the total effect was to reduce investor appetite for loans and dissuade banks from lending more; indeed their balance sheet exposure may have required calling in some existing loans. In the then world of free international capital flows, organized to a large degree by intermediaries located in London—globalism is not a post-modern invention—capital would flow into the City of London driving the pound sterling up against other currencies, making British exports less competitive and overseas imports more affordable, both effects further dampening excessive demand in the UK. A precisely reverse set of actions and reactions would follow The Bank's response to declining domestic activity. This, it seemed, offered the perfect escape route. Inflation (and deflation) could be moderated if not abolished by the indirect and independent actions of a small and exclusive band of wise men, the economic equivalent of Plato's Guardians. Emphasis here was placed on the "independence" of the central bankers—independence from the commercial hustle of profit making (even though The Bank was nominally a private institution rather than a public one or quango) and from the interfering pettifogging of elected politicians. Similar functions were performed by other central bankers in other capitalist countries, most notably by the Federal Reserve System in the United States.

Galbraith extracts a good deal of enjoyment from his description of the "great reservoir of mystery" constructed around the black art of central banking, a constant theme that runs through both his earlier and later work. Central bankers form part of an economic freemasonry, covering their activities in arcane language and decisions taken behind closed doors. Although during the 1930s this institution failed like all others to deal with the Depression and accompanying *de*flation, and in hindsight was lumbered by some economists like Milton Friedman, with prime responsibility for turning a financial (stock market) crisis into the worst economic disaster in history, the dominant role of the central bank was quickly re-established after the Second World War, as governments and economists came to accept that properly practiced the neoclassical synthesis could, if handled carefully, fine-tune the economy. Monetary policy, especially in the conventional wisdom of conservatives, assumed the dominant prophylactic role. This was, Galbraith suggested, largely because monetary policy least circumscribed the scope for private enterprise to dominate decisions over where and what to invest. Reducing the emphasis on the alternative, fiscal policy also reduced the likelihood that governments would respond to inflationary tendencies by raising taxes. The dominant position of monetary policy in the discourse of public policy resided in its tendency to present itself in a shroud of mystery, to profess a "...faith that, by essentially occult means, monetary policy will stabilize prices without affecting the volume of producer borrowing, investment and spending." In the end, however, Galbraith saw the dependence on monetary policy as an act of desperation. *Something* had to be done about inflation and this was the least bad option for those in the commanding heights of the economy. "There was nothing else, so it had to work."

Unfortunately, argues Galbraith, monetary policy is as ineffective in controlling inflation as Keynes demonstrated it is in stoking recovery from a recession. In the latter case, it is akin to pushing on a piece of string, in the former to pulling on a piece of elastic. Monetary policy makes no immediate or substantial impact on the wage–price spiral and can only act through cutting spending by aggressively reducing aggregate demand. The monetary policy route is closed because both consumers and major investors in the monopolistic sector have evolved ways of avoiding the repressive impact of rising interest rates. The capital market has become very sophisticated (even by the 1950s), offering a range of financial products designed to keep consumers spending. While interest rates are rising, payments made on goods and services purchased on credit increase; but only by small amounts when considered on a monthly basis. Like the frog that boils to death in the pot whose temperature rises only gradually, the indebted consumer happily goes about his or her normal life without substantially reducing household consumption. Moreover, some loans allow borrowers to spread their repayments out over longer periods when interest rates rise, moderating even the minor increases in monthly commitments. Furthermore, any sign of lagging consumer confidence and declining consumption activity serves as a siren call to the want-creation industry. In response, the loaded weapons of Madison Avenue are leveled on the unsuspecting consumer, exhorting him or her to go out and spend.

The impact of monetary policy on investment is more varied and complicated and, hence, uncertain. Again, the effects are influenced by the bifurcation of the economy. The small business, services, and farming sectors are directly and significantly affected. Operating on small margins, even small increases in their cost of working capital can wreak extensive damage on the prospects of their commercial survival. As the major employers in aggregate in the economy, an increase in small enterprise wind-downs or bankruptcies can jolt unemployment up, both directly and via the multiplier effect on other firms as sacked workers cut back on their spending.

The big firms, however, have the scope to absorb interest rate rises and pass them on like wage rises to customers. In addition, as the economy reaches capacity limits, rising prices signal the prospect of enhanced profits for those enterprises able to invest in expanding their productive capacity before others do. With strong balance sheets and prospective profitable investment projects, commercial banks are likely to flock to their doors, further stoking the inflationary process. Big firms also enjoy access to equity finance both by accessing the stock market and retaining profits, reducing their reliance on the banks and other lenders. Strong trade unions sensing rich pickings will renew and inflate their wage demands further adding to the wages–prices spiral.

Finally, however, investment depends critically on what Keynes termed the "animal spirits" of investors. As the most "mercurial" element of aggregate demand private investment can experience very sharp swings in response to any number of unexpected events, a war, a terrorist atrocity, a financial crisis or fraud somewhere in the world, an ill chosen word by a careless central banker. Given the less than perfectly predictable lead times and lags involved in the investment process, sudden reversals of confidence can render central bank interest rate interventions either ineffective or positively threatening to the economy at large. When this possibility is added to the dire direct impacts on the competitive sector, monetary policy assumes a dangerous cast, best embraced in the breach. This is where the value of a rhetorical reliance on monetary policy delivers the goods; it can be left to the experts and ignored by the rest who don't understand either its irrelevance to the achievement of price stability or its deadly potential for derailing the economy in the pursuit of stability. The further payoff to the politician is that the gnomes of the independent central bank provide a ready-made scapegoat if "fighting inflation first" gets out of hand; the rewards to rich lenders when interest rates are jacked up in that fight are self-evident.

IV

All this leaves government with the tools of fiscal policy, varying their revenue and expenditure streams though the annual budget process in order to prevent excessive demand from spilling over into inflation. This policy direction is, according to Galbraith, the preferred path of liberals, as well as the bane of conservatives. The former have pinned their hopes on manipulating taxes and government spending in order to offset the unequalizing tendencies of modern capitalism. Conservatives sense danger in these attempts to interfere with the market generated distribution of economic rewards.

The logic of fiscal policy is quite transparent; if the government spends less than it taxes total demand in the economy will fall, lessening the pressure of spending on firms operating at or near full capacity. This will occur because, as unused capacity increases, firms hesitate to raise prices, even in the oligopolistic sector (assuming the fall in aggregate demand is sharp enough). Unions will defer wage claims. Small businesses will only be able to sell by reducing their prices, once their inventories build up to unsupportable levels. Overall, the general level of prices will stabilize as firms throughout the economy pause and reassess their immediate future environments. Expansion plans are quietly shelved, belts tightened, and an atmosphere of somber reflection embraced.

Unfortunately for the fight against inflation—Galbraith wrote before the use of the term "war" became fashionable, as in "the war on poverty" and "the war on drugs," both of which have been comprehensively lost—fiscal policy has proved as ineffective as monetary policy. This was not due to its faulty logic but to the fact that fiscal policy has not been promoted and applied, even by its strongest proponents. "It was favored in principle but not in practice." This failure he finds explicable for a number of interrelated reasons. The starting point is to recognize that, due to the systematic bias in favor of private spending against public spending—a claim that is more fully developed in his famous "theory of social balance," discussed later—strong political and ideological forces tend to keep government spending at or near a basic minimum. This fact makes it very difficult to quickly cut spending when impending inflation threatens, without cutting whole functions and running up against entrenched interests and inevitable informational and bureaucratic delays. All agree that total spending should be reduced. All also agree that someone else's spending should be cut, not mine. So, no one's is. "Nothing is ever accomplished of sufficient magnitude to affect appreciably the total spending of the economy. Quite often nothing is accomplished." Indeed, there is a strong bias in the annual budget process that locks in increasing not decreasing expenditure, regardless of the imperatives of sound policy. The lead up and performance in setting the budget assumes a ritualistic cast. "The ceremony is solemnly described to the people by press and television. Thereafter, the seemingly indispensable outlays are voted, and the result is almost invariably to increase the budget."

In consequence, the full weight of fiscal policy to control inflation falls in practice on raising taxes. But this path also uncovers steep barriers. Consumers already facing cost-of-living pressures must now contemplate further imposts on their dwindling disposable incomes. Indirect taxes placed on goods and services directly hit household budgets. Direct taxes on incomes bite deep into middle- and even working-class spending power. Taxes levied on business may in part be passed forward to consumers further squeezing their consumption. All these effects are immediately experienced while the advantageous effects on controlling inflation are long term. Some people will be able to protect themselves, for example if they have jobs where their salaries or fees can be increased, but others on fixed incomes in weakly unionized private industries or in the under-funded public sector and pensioners of all kinds will suffer reduced living standards. Wealthier people with access to competent lawyers and accountants may be able to arrange their affairs in order to minimize the impact of higher taxes. They will also tend to be better placed politically and organizationally to influence the details of the tax measures with a similar outcome. The cost of fighting inflation will, in consequence, be very unevenly spread. Such an outcome threatens to upset the social truce between liberals and conservatives sanctioning growth as the solvent of social tensions.

The deliberate and very visible attempt by government to suppress aggregate demand through fiscal means also threatens the deeply held reverence for the primacy of production. "Having persuaded ourselves that production is of paramount importance, we must now persuade ourselves to sacrifice it in return for price stability." Due to the factors already noted, the scale of sacrifice required to achieve stability may be very high. It is not immediately obvious to policy makers, in advance, just how much to raise taxes in order to be effective. Information on the effects is limited and often comes with a significant lag. There are complex interactions between industries, and between consumption and investment, that are difficult to model with confidence in the forecasts generated. The more that full employment is posited as the norm the closer the economy will be running to full capacity and the greater the risk of inflation breaking out before government recognizes, still less acts, to control it. The more potent is the naïve Keynesian conceit that policy makers armed with the tools of fiscal policy can, finally, manipulate tax and spending settings to run the economy at full steam ("the business cycle is dead"), the more likely that inflation will also become the norm.

Galbraith firmly believed that inflation not mass unemployment is the new economic devil in the world of affluence. In theory, government might square the circle by combining fiscal policy to ensure near full capacity operation of the economy with carefully selected and applied controls over prices and wages. History shows that during wartime that is exactly what successfully occurred, at least on the Allied side. Galbraith should know; he was after all Roosevelt's price Czar. However, he expresses doubt as to whether the same happy result will occur in peacetime. A policy based on controlling prices and wages runs up against entrenched opposition. "Nothing better establishes the good sense and soundness of an economist than a suitably solemn condemnation of such controls." The arguments ranged against controls begin with a blanket all or nothing claim that the controls must apply across the board, raising impossible administrative problems. More worryingly, for conservatives and libertarians, such intrusions into citizens' lives conjure a picture of big brother trampling on the hard-won liberties of a free people. Most challenging of all, controls threaten the efficient allocation of a society's scarce resources, the philosopher's stone on which the central tradition stands. As long as economic and social policy is framed within a discourse dominated by images of limited resources in a world of unlimited wants, any attempts to interfere with the free rein of market forces is stoutly resisted.

Galbraith himself is far from convinced that the case against direct controls is proven. In fact, he suggests that controls need not be blanket in coverage. Selectively and strategically influencing specific prices and wages at particular times may offer much greater chances of success in breaking the wage–price spiral without damaging the growth and employment prospects of the economy. He returns to this point later in the book. At this point he merely summarizes by stating that both monetary and fiscal policies are unlikely in the real world that we inhabit to reliably prevent inflationary forces from recurrently erupting. Such policies challenge the interests of powerful groups and the cherished truths embedded in the dominant conventional wisdom. In the affluent society inflation is emerging as the normal state of affairs. "Thus the way seems open to recurrent inflation."

V

Galbraith's basic conclusion that inflation is *the* problem has been amply demonstrated in the decades since he wrote *AS (though not exactly in the terms he envisaged in the 1950s)*. Economic policy and theory in the decade of the 1970s was dominated by little else. Statistics sometimes lie but not in this instance. Official inflation figures moved well into double figures in countries like the United States. In part, this reflected the impacts of external events like the costs of financing the Vietnam War and the oil shocks early and late in the decade. However, as noted in Chapter 3, the attack on the Keynesian inspired neoclassical synthesis by economists of a monetarist and neoclassical bent carried the day. The economics discipline and governments recognized inflation as public policy enemy number one. This was a natural response given that the level of inflation had moved into the red zone where the prospect of hyperinflation could not be ruled out. Something really had to be done, even if it meant substantially interrupting the growth process and jettisoning the treasured certainties of the Keynesian-era conventional wisdom. As ever, the conventional wisdom was refashioned, not by the force of logic, but by the unexpected impact of changing circumstance. Happily for the economics profession at least, the very ideas that could make some sense of the new situation already existed and could be recycled albeit in new garb provided by the increasingly sophisticated theoretical apparatus of new classical economics. The zombies stalked the earth again.

In the United States, robust action by the Federal Reserve under the leadership of Paul Volcker ushered in a period of austerity that saw growth disappear and unemployment soar and delivered the death-blow to the already shaky administration of President Carter. The new President, Ronald Reagan, pushed through far-reaching measures to deregulate industry, reduce taxes, and wind back government expenditure in many non-defense related areas. Some of his conservative supporters were, however, disappointed by the fact that total federal expenditures and the public debt kept rising. Inflation, though temporarily tamed in the early 1980s by the savage deflationary actions of the

Federal Reserve, made a determined comeback later in Reagan's Presidency, to be again temporarily forestalled by the stock market crash in 1987, until then the worst days on Wall Street since 1929 (in fact, "black Monday" was *the* worst day until that time).

Thereafter, inflation—that is, commodity price inflation—returned from time to time but not at the crippling levels experienced in earlier periods. Significant structural changes were occurring in the economy during the 1980s that subsequently reduced the inflationary tendencies identified by Galbraith. This he explicitly noted in his "Introduction" to the 1998 edition. The growth of service sector and information intensive industries at the expense of heavy manufacturing, along with the conservative ideological political agenda, reduced the role of trade unions and thus dampened the wages–prices spiral that previously entrenched the inflationary dynamic. These changes were reinforced by the changing institutional orientation and policy emphasis on dealing with inflation as the primary target of macroeconomic concern. Central banks adopted first the challenge of targeting the money supply, more accurately its rate of increase. When that proved illusory, thanks in part to the impossibility of deciding on the right monetary aggregate to target, the target became the rate of inflation itself. The central bank now aimed to keep inflation within a publicly announced and monitored band, normally framed by 2 and 3 percent—and the weapon of choice was the official interest rate. This marked an historical return to the territory with which central banks were familiar; not surprising since everything else had failed, short of the nuclear option of forced recession, and the global conditions were now much more conducive to a late-nineteenth-century style approach. The current era of globalization mirrored features of that earlier world—the existence of relatively free trade, an accepted international currency, free capital movements, and flexible exchange rates.

The return to monetary orthodoxy sounded the final bell for monetarism. Inflation was not, after all, a purely monetary phenomenon, as economists Friedman and Hayek held. Money mattered, as Keynes and Galbraith countered. Central banks now operated their monetary policies with an eye firmly cocked on the likely effects on the real economy. Acceptance of the non-neutrality of money by practical policy makers focused on fighting inflation first and also undercut the new classical economics whose proponents argued for an aggressively pure form of the neutrality assumption, nowhere more than in the case of real business cycle theory. It also paved the way for "the return of the master" in the words of his biographer, Robert Skidelsky (2009). Yes, Keynes resurfaced after two decades of neglect. His apparent demise was, after all, much exaggerated. The post-Keynesian economist Paul Davison carefully explained why Keynes had apparently succumbed in the 1970s. It was, he suggested, all a statistical misinterpretation. The inflation–unemployment trade-off of the neoclassical synthesis committed the ergodic fallacy; it relied on time series data that assumed the future could be predicted from the past—that nothing significant changed. When both unemployment and inflation rose in the 1970s it simply meant that the statistical relationship previously observed no longer held because something underlying the relationship had changed. That "something" could easily be explained within a Keynesian analysis. With hindsight, suggests Davison (2009), we can see that the first oil shock in 1973 caused commodity prices to jump, feeding into prices generally. Those price rises automatically triggered the wage rise clauses in the cost-of-living agreements (COLA) introduced by union–employer bargaining, setting off the wages–prices spiral stressed by Galbraith. The econometric analysis supporting the simple trade-off thesis was based on data spanning the period when COLA were not as prominent as in later times. Thus, the breakdown of the trade-off in later times is not a definitive proof that Keynesianism failed—"something" had changed. The triumph of neoliberalism had so weakened the power of trade unions and the bargaining power of ordinary workers that COLA were a rapidly disappearing feature of post-Reagan life.

However, the belated recognition that Keynes lives did little to challenge the opposite view entrenched in the conventional wisdom. In a telling vindication of Galbraith's argument that the conventional wisdom is never challenged by ideas but only by the unarguable march of circumstances, it took the full bull run of a speculative boom and its horrid aftermath in global crisis to shake government and citizens to their senses, perhaps too late if the continuing rumblings in Europe and weak recoveries elsewhere stagger on. Paul Krugman (2012) in his book *End this Depression Now* argues that European economic policy makers have consistently and willfully misread the situation, forcing struggling Euro member states to embrace "austerity" when conventional Keynesian expansionary fiscal policy and moderate inflation in both strong and weak states would snap the region out of its economic malaise. Krugman champions the efficacy of fiscal policy both to prevent recessions turning into depressions (the US and Britain in 2008) and in rescuing economies mired in deep depression (Spain and Ireland in 2012).

The most tragic consequence of the hubristic pre-GFC view that inflation, like the business cycle, is tamed, in this instance by the wise use of monetary policy in the hands of an economic "genius" like Alan Greenspan, is that when genius fails it does so unexpectedly and in a context where no "Plan B" is readily at hand. Greenspan believed and convinced policy makers that the new economy unleashed by the information technology revolution had forever pushed back the supply-side constraints on economic growth, and that the economy could be allowed to grow at rates much in excess of past experience without running the escalating risk of inflation. As we now know, growth did boom but the inflationary tendencies shifted from commodity markets to asset markets and the bubble in the latter was bound to burst. Central banks had no charter or weapons with which to control asset markets directly and were only called upon after the party to clear up the mess as best they could, usually by the means of "printing money" and hoping that someone would spend it. The failure of these hopes came quickly in the years immediately after the GFC broke over us. Governments instead turned to the master and embarked on huge fiscal stimulus policies in an attempt to construct a successful Plan B on the run. Fifty years-plus on from *AS* we anxiously await the results.

*   *   *

What would Galbraith have made of all this? One thing is certain. He would not have been surprised by the abject failure of his fellow economists and the governments they advised to predict or be ready to deal with what occurred. He might be somberly pleased with the fact that the limitations of monetary policy when attempting to deal with inflation that he stressed were clearly evident in the current troubles; like generals fighting the last war, economic policy makers engaged the wrong enemy. He would have recognized that the prime cause lay in the consumption-fuelled boom that was based on the general acceptance of growth as the litmus test of economic success. He would also have expressed in suitably crafted prose his contempt for the self-interested nostrums of the "Austerians," as the purveyors of expenditure cuts and budget surpluses have been dubbed (with a play on the Austrian school of economists for whom such measures are holy writ). Perhaps in his more modest and reflective moments he would also have graciously admitted that he had underestimated the capacity for consumers to desire the experiences made possible by the incredible technological advances made in recent times.

9

Debt

It would be surprising if a society that is prepared to spend thousands of millions of dollars to persuade people of their wants were to fail to take the further step of financing these want.

(J.K. Galbraith)

Can the bill collector or the bankruptcy lawyer be the central figure in the good society.

(J.K. Galbraith)

*   *   *

The penultimate piece in the jig-saw puzzle of the dominant role played by the production of ever less urgent goods and services in the affluent society is provided by Galbraith's analysis of the modern phenomenon of debt. It is the rise of indebtedness that most marks off the America of his day from its earlier puritan past. "Neither a lender nor a borrower be" has been overtaken by the run to the loan broker. In the past, debt has been a luxury, enjoyed by people of wealth and social standing who were able to convince lenders, often concentrated in marginalized, even despised social groups, of their ability and willingness to repay. The largest and most unreliable borrowers were governments, keen to shore up their power and extend it through lavish expenditures and ruinous wars. Throughout the twentieth century debt became democratized and spread widely to consuming households aspiring to own the new goods produced by the wonders of modern mass production. In this, Galbraith argues, advertising and social emulation have been the drivers.

The central role of advertising is to create desire where none previously existed, from which it is a short step to finding the means of making the desire affordable. Assuming, in line with the hierarchical view of human needs, the consumer's demand for food, shelter, clothing, fuel, and other necessities are met first out of available income, this leaves a problem. Too little disposable income will remain to satisfy the new wants synthesized by the ad man. Debt fills the void. Advertisers must do more than create the desire for their product; they must also persuade the consumer of the existence, acceptability, and indeed, the imperative to borrow in order to consummate that desire. "The process of persuading people to incur debt, and the arguments for them to do so, are as much a part of modern production as the making of the goods and the nurturing of the wants." Emulation drives demand in tandem with advertising. People have a strong desire to have what their neighbor is having. The same process arises in the case of debt. In earlier times when few people borrowed to fund their everyday lives and indebtedness was widely feared as one step from the bankruptcy court or debtors' prison, seeing a neighbor in debt was to resonate sentiments of compassion or condemnation, depending on temperament. As debt became a normal and necessary means of organizing one's life, the negative social image of the borrower changed. Yes, there were still people who dived in over their heads and ended up bankrupt and bereft. But for most consumers, a calculated strategy of borrowing to buy materially improved their living standards without beggaring their futures. To borrow responsibly became an acceptable, even respectable pastime. Everyone did it.

Galbraith pointed to the sharp rise in consumer indebtedness during the first half of the 1950s, increasing by more than 50 percent in the areas of consumer loans, installment credit, and, especially, loans to buy automobiles. In his later revision he provides data through to the mid-1970s. These figures three decades later look ludicrously small in view of all that has happened in the intervening period. However, they were sufficiently dramatic to allow him to make the point that modern mass consumption would have been impossible but for the explosive growth of mass borrowing. He is careful to stress that he is emphasizing the growth in household debt unrelated to the purchase of housing—that is to the purchase of consumer durables, such as cars, white goods, furnishings, leisure goods, and so on. In those days, housing figured as the platform or arena for consumption and household life not, as in the new century, an automatic teller machine for the withdrawal of housing wealth to buy still more things.

II

Having established the central importance of debt in the process of want creation and satisfaction, Galbraith wonders about the effects of the increasing scale of this dependence on the overall operation of the economy. What are the dangers or tensions that such dependence sets up? In answer he doubts that the process of persuasion in the face of the declining urgency of the wants created can be sustained indefinitely. "Diminishing returns will have operated to the point where the marginal effect of the outlays for every kind of commercial persuasion will have brought the average effect to zero." As the effectiveness of want creation fades, the impetus to borrow and consume will follow. Household savings rates will consequently rise, signaling to producers the wisdom of scaling back their expectations of future sales, resulting in declining total output and rising unemployment. The dampening of animal spirits cuts further into investment expenditure, further leading toward the unemployment equilibrium that Keynes suggested was the possible and possibly normal fate of capitalism, unless government intervened appropriately and at the right time. The disruption to near full capacity operation of the economy would then tear asunder the link between production and security while opening up political struggles over the existing and increasing inequalities uncovered.

The capacity to keep the system going by finding effective means of increasing sustainable debt levels would, Galbraith suggested, be strictly limited. Existing loans can only be restructured so many times as ways to facilitate repayments. Credit ratings can be liberalized only so much. The loan period cannot be extended indefinitely. More tellingly, in the light of recent developments, he comments on the limits to increasing the loan-to-value ratio. "Down payments can be reduced, but there comes a point when the borrower's equity is so small that he finds it convenient to allow repossession rather than to pay a burdensome debt or declare bankruptcy."

A further systemic problem created in an economy increasingly dependent on credit is that the level of borrowing and lending is pro-cyclical, thereby reinforcing macroeconomic volatility, the ups and downs of the business cycle.

Not only is the business cycle not dead, it survives and debt is its necessary life support system! In keeping with the old joke that a banker is someone who is willing to lend you money when you don't need it and turns you down when you do, lending demand and the supply of loans will be greatest when the economy is booming, employment levels high, and wages increasing, but will drop in line with aggregate activity in the economy. Stable and secure growth requires precisely the opposite; lending cutbacks when the economy is running at full capacity and credit availability when recession looms. Our increasing reliance on consumer debt thus renders us hostage to the underlying ebb and flow of the economy at large; more than that, it increases the amplitude of the flows with attendant implications for the social tensions only just kept under control in a growing economy. Galbraith expresses particular concern about the deflationary effects once consumers perceive that they are over-indebted. Concerted attempts to reduce household debt when aggregated across the economy have a very large direct impact since consumption accounts for about 70 percent of total demand. The indirect affects are, as noted above, also important as private investment spending responds to the more dismal market outlook and as employers seek to reduce their major variable cost, wages, by cutting jobs, wages, or hours in order to ride out the downturn, thereby making it even more difficult for borrowers to meet their monthly loan commitments.

The deflationary effects of reduced private consumption could, in theory, be offset by government fiscal stimulus but Galbraith casts doubt on the practical effectiveness of such measures. Bureaucratic delay and inadequate information hamper timely policy, just—as we have seen—in the opposite case of attempts to control inflation. To the technical and administrative barriers one must add the ingrained tendency of economists, when contemplating their models and advising policy makers, to "wait and see" if things will right themselves. The conventional wisdom is, after all, quite clear on the main lesson of the central tradition—namely, that one can in most cases rely on the self-equilibrating tendencies of the economy, assisted by the automatic stabilizers inherent in the modern taxation and social security systems.

Galbraith is uncharacteristically modest when he councils caution. "In fact, we do not really know the extent of the danger." The continual build-up in consumer debt may be sustainable and may eventually taper off. "But we would do well to keep an alarm signal flying over the consumer-debt creation into which the process of want creation impels us." However, he is pessimistic about the chances of maintaining a sufficient state of alarm. To the natural tendency, alluded to above, to wait and see, material and ideological forces will continually push to broaden, not constrain, the sphere of consumer credit. The imperatives of production and security will trump all.

Galbraith completes his analysis of the role of consumer debt by pointing the way to what will become his final critique of the anatomy of modern capitalism—the imbalance in the flow of resources between publicly and privately produced goods and services, described as "...the most singular feature of the affluent society taking form." Before taking up this theme, we must reflect on how well Galbraith, from the vantage point of fifty years ago, anticipated more recent developments on the convoluted terrain of debt.

III

It is possible—with a stretch—to characterize the massive increase in household debt leading up to the dot.com bust in 2001 as a simple quantitative consequence of the growth and sophistication of the advanced economies. Proponents of the efficient markets hypothesis were able to confidently argue that financial markets were simply playing their essential role of allocating available savings to their most productive uses in the real economy. The reality since then is very different. The efficient markets in all but its weakest form lies in tatters. Global credit markets are still attempting to recover from the financial tsunami that hit in 2008, the waves of which continue to reverberate though the major economies. The alarm bell for which Galbraith counseled us to keep an ear cocked rang almost inaudibly. Galbraith famously professed a skeptical and sardonic view of his fellow human beings, especially those who worked in the financial sector. He rarely underestimated their capacity for venality and righteous denial of wrongdoing. But even he—had he lived beyond the fiftieth anniversary of his book—would have been staggered by the scale and devastation of the Great Recession. The main features of these developments have been outlined in Chapter 5. It remains here to delve a little more into the details of what happened to unleash them, and to highlight the nature of the changes from Galbraith's day in the debt environment.

The subprime crisis is the name given for what was an historic turning point in our economy and our culture. It was, at its core, the result of a speculative bubble in the housing market that began in the United States and burst in 2006 and then caused ruptures across many other countries in the form of financial failures and a global credit crunch.

Traditionally, mortgage lenders in the US and elsewhere (generally banks) originated loans to house purchasers on a face-to-face basis. This meant that the lender generally demanded and received a range of information about the borrower, including his or her income, employment history, level of savings, credit history—particularly whether or not they had defaulted on loans in the past—allowing direct judgments to be made on the credit-worthiness of the borrower. Depending on the loan-to-value ratio (LVR) of the purchase (the relative size of the deposit or down payment), mortgage insurance may have been required, shifting part of the risk of default from both lender and borrower to an insurer for a premium paid by either borrower or lender. Borrowers were charged appropriate fees for the credit and related assessment process, as part of the overall transaction costs of purchase. Individual dwellings were valued by certified valuers. Conservative LVRs tended to further protect the lender. As an overall consequence, mortgage default rates were low. In a real sense, all or almost all mortgage loans were "prime," defined as subject to a very low probability of default.

One disadvantage for the banks, however, was that their assets were tied up in long-term loans. A disadvantage for borrowers *en masse* was that credit for both house purchases and other purchases was constrained by the capital adequacy or reserve requirements of the banks and the savings habits of citizens. Housing loans were rationed as the demand in most markets outpaced supply. The rapid growth of secondary mortgage markets and subsequent innovations, especially those following the wave of deregulation that have swept through global financial markets since the 1980s, has changed the face of residential mortgage lending as traditionally practiced. Increasingly, individual mortgage loans were "bundled" together by investment banks and other financial intermediaries. The resulting bonds—mortgage-backed securities (MBS), part of a larger class of asset-backed securities (ABS)—were sold to a range of investors, notably pension and mutual funds looking to park large tranches of savings aggregated from myriad smaller investors and individual savers. The primary lender, banks, passed the loan through (sold it) to a securitization vehicle in return for the principal and a fee. The lender could then re-lend to another mortgagor (purchaser), pass that on in the secondary mortgage market, collect the fee, and so on and so on.

The explosive growth of funds under management by institutional investors seemed to provide an unending source of demand for liquid securities like MBS (and other ABS), as long as they were appropriately "rated" by one of the long established ratings agencies—notably Moody's, Standard and Poor's, and Fitch's Ratings. Although the details varied among the big three ratings agencies, the basic idea was to distinguish "investment grade" or prime assets from others that had a progressively higher probability of default. This was done on a sliding scale with "triple-A" (AAA) representing the lowest risk, down through a series of grades of A, B, and eventually C (the lower rated securities also termed "junk"). For example, Moody's graded bonds on a twenty-one step scale from AAA to a single C; the top ten grades were investment quality or prime. The bond rating was decisive in determining the interest (or coupon) rate that would have to be offered investors—the lower the rating, the higher the interest rate, supposedly representing the underlying risk of payment default in each case.

The ratings agencies had developed sophisticated tools for factoring in the various conditions that had been shown to bring about mortgage defaults in the past; that is, the rating was based on a statistical analysis of a large number of past transactions and default events. MBS could also be insured against default by specialist "monoline" bond insurers, such as the PMI Group Inc. and MBIA Inc., providing further comfort to investors and reducing required interest rates for borrowers. The agencies also rated the bond insurers giving investors a seemingly solid view on how likely the insurers would be in a position to pay out in the event of the insured bonds going into default. The system seemed foolproof, with risk carefully priced and allocated by efficient financial markets to those best able and willing to bear it in order to maximize the sustainable flow of investment into mortgage-financed housing purchase.

During the long upward swing in US housing markets, this picture certainly seemed to be accurate. Lending volumes, securitization, and housing prices followed each other up in a continuing, self-reinforcing spiral. By early 2008, the total value of housing mortgages outstanding in the US was around US$12 trillion: more than half ($6.8 trillion) was in the form of MBS, in turn representing about a quarter of the total US bond market, making it bigger, for example, than the market for US Treasury bonds, with $1.3 trillion of residential MBS lending categorized as subprime. The volume of mortgage loans advanced in 2006, the high point of the subprime boom, reached a staggering $2.5 trillion.

But—from late 2006—warning bells began ringing, albeit sedately, easily blocked out by the music playing in full party swing. The neat system unraveled at an increasing rate during the second half of 2007 and through 2008 as mortgage defaults escalated. Criticism focused on the role of the ratings agencies, as the comment in 2008 by prominent business commentator Roger Lowenstein (2008: 1) suggests:

> ...the agencies became the defacto watchdog over the mortgage industry. In a practical sense, it was Moody's and Standard and Poors that set the credit standards that determined which loans Wall Street could repackage and, ultimately, which borrowers would qualify. Effectively, they did the job that was expected of banks and government regulators. And today, they are a central culprit in the mortgage bust, in which the total loss has been projected at $250 billion and possibly much more.

Lowenstein's "guestimate" of total losses turned out to be a vast underestimate. The true figure may never be known and is still being reckoned. Conservatively, the total direct losses—to lenders, borrowers, governments, charities, and other organizations will be in the trillions of dollars. The losses coming from recession and stagnation in the most advanced economies are incalculable. In 2012 Europe as a whole experienced "negative growth" and the United States grew anemically.

To understand how the unraveling occurred and the culpability of the agencies and other players we need to see how the well-established MBS market morphed into a more complicated, opaque, and uncertain investment climate in which no one really knew who was holding what risks. How did it all go so wrong? To answer this it is necessary to look at recent innovations in financial products and how the established ratings and insurance processes failed to adequately monitor, still less check, the overextension of mortgage credit to borrowers who were likely to default. We focus on the US experience, the locus of the storm. At base, too many borrowers were enabled to buy houses for which they could not sustain the repayments. In other words, loans were advanced to borrowers who would not normally have passed the credit checks of primary lenders or their brokers and insurers. This occurred largely because the brokers and lenders passed on the credit risk to purchasers of MBS, via structured finance products created by the investment banks, and so had little incentive to ensure credit-worthiness of borrowers. This is a prime example of what economists term, "moral hazard." The new investment mechanisms—notably special purpose vehicles (SPVs) and special investment vehicles (SIVs), engineered through "structured finance" by investment banks—allowed subprime loans to back bond tranches attracting prime ratings, swelling the supply of MBS and creating its own demand in an exuberant market climate. This apparently counterintuitive outcome worked as follows.

An SPV would be established as a legal but empty structure—i.e. having no real assets, just a pool of subprime mortgages purchased from lenders, financed by selling bonds to investors. The "trick" was to create a ladder or hierarchy of bond classes ranging from triple-A down to Bs with each tranche sold to investors with the appropriate risk appetites. Thus, pension funds that by law could only buy triple-A did so. Investors with higher appetites for risk bought the lower rated bonds, but demanded and received higher interest rates. The total interest income received from all house purchasers was pooled and paid out in strict order as follows: the interest due to all triple-A bond holders ("the senior tranche") was paid out of the pool first, then that due to the next highest grade bonds paid in full, and so on down to the lowest grade debt. As long as there were no defaults, every bondholder was paid; the banks financing the SPV would also reap their not inconsiderable fees. But any defaults that did occur would be borne initially and fully by the holders of the lowest rated debt ("the equity tranche"), once a cash-buffer provided by the SPV arranger had been exhausted. Only as defaults rose would bondholders further up the chain be affected. For holders of the highest-grade debt only a financial tsunami would disturb their payments. Lowenstein (2008: 3) provides a suitable metaphor: "(i)magine a sea-side condo beset by flooding: just as the penthouse will not get wet until the lower floors are thoroughly soaked, so the triple-A bonds would not lose a dime until the lower credits were wiped out." Of course, a financial tsunami was precisely what did occur—and its genesis was inherent in the complex web of financial transactions undertaken during the first decade of the new century.

Unfortunately, it became increasingly clear that the historical default data on which the underlying bond tranche ratings were calculated did not take into account—that is, did not foresee—the speculative developments in US residential property markets. Thus, an unsustainable price boom, massive consumer debt, and a sharp downward correction in house prices sparked a run of mortgage delinquencies and escalating foreclosures. As a result, the ratings agencies had to progressively downgrade bond issues of many MBS, resulting in follow-on (and increasingly anticipatory) asset write-downs by investors holding those bonds. By early 2008 the agencies had turned their attention to the bond insurers, threatening to downgrade the claims-paying ability of key insurers like PMI, Radian, and Republic, reinforcing the growing concerns about mis-pricing throughout the bond markets. The largest insurers, in the light of expected payouts on defaulting MBS, announced anticipated losses for the years ahead. This was a further indicator of the potential for credit problems generated in the subprime housing market to spill over to other parts of the financial system.

With hindsight, it is incredible that this outcome was *not* foreseen. Surely, *someone* realized that many of the new borrowers would eventually fail to meet their repayments. No doubt some in the chain did. But that would be someone else's problem. One powerful device for "kicking the can down the road," was the widespread marketing of adjustable rate mortgages with "honeymoon" initial repayment periods. For example, borrowers would be offered a mortgage with a 2 percent interest rate for the first year or two that could then be "re-set" to a higher rate for the remainder of the loan. In effect, this made it possible for borrowers on low incomes to initially pay their way and seemingly meet the normal eligibility criteria of the lender, right up until the crunch when the interest rate was doubled or more. By then the originator would be long gone, having taken the fee and passed on the loan to a securitization vehicle.

But the worst was yet to come. A second order or "derivative" market quickly developed in the products of SPVs selling structured layers of MBS. So-called "collateralized debt obligations" (CDOs) were floated and sold as bonds to investors. These were bonds backed by bonds backed by mortgages:

> Miscalculations that were damaging at the level of [SPVs] were devastating at the C.D.O. level. Just as bad weather will cause more serious delays to travelers with multiple flights, so, if the underlying mortgage bonds were misrated, the trouble was compounded in the case of the C.D.O.s that purchased them. (Lowenstein 2008: 4)

To continue the weather analogy—it never rains but it snows. Third order derivatives were also sold—"CDOs-squared"—which were bonds backed by bonds backed by bonds backed by mortgages, further compounding the impact of mis-pricing and rendering even more opaque the real underlying allocation of risks. For the basic "vanilla" structured product, the percentage share of each tranche was carefully calculated to fire proof the senior (triple-A) debt in light of historic default rates of subprime mortgages. For example, before the subprime crisis, it was thought that 20 percent "over-collateralization" plus subordination would mean that there would always be enough money coming into the pool to fully meet the payments to the 80 percent of triple-A bonds. Even though some of the lower-rated bonds in the pool would default, the average amounts recouped on forced sales added to the priority payment to senior debt holders would fully meet the latter's entitlements. In effect, the investment banks were able to use the rating templates of the agencies to just get the package over the line.

In the event, since delinquency rates for subprime mortgages quickly rose in excess of 25 percent and falling housing prices reduced the average amounts realized from forced sales, the triple-A bonds in structured mortgage-backed vehicles appeared to be riskier than comparatively rated corporate bonds. What was really a double-A (AA) or lower bond was masquerading as AAA. This emerging view of mis-rating in financial markets further eroded investor confidence overall through 2009 and beyond. These developments in the housing market were paralleled in other debt markets. Derivative products of the CDO variety were aggressively developed in the areas of consumer loans and commercial real estate; even student tuition loans did not escape the notice of the wizards of Wall Street.

The escalating growth in this market called for an insatiable supply of new borrowers and ramped up the activities of brokers in luring ever more marginal households into home ownership. This could only be achieved by continuously weakening the lending criteria and integrity of the system. No-doc, low-doc, and liar loans refer to the practices of allowing potential borrowers to state their incomes and credit histories without providing any supporting evidence and without follow-up checks by the lender. Finally, as in all recorded cases of financial booms, simple fraud ensued. Prospective borrowers were deliberately misled and lied to. Procedures mandated by law were flouted. Consumer protections enshrined in law were ignored.

Surely, things couldn't get worse. Wrong. The booming market in CDOs was overtaken by the growth in another financial innovation—credit default swaps, CDS. These products truly qualify for Warren Buffet's epitaph, "financial weapons of mass destruction." At their peak the total face value of these derivatives was around $63 trillion, greater than the global value of all listed company shares or the total value of housing worldwide. In essence, CDS were insurance policies taken out by a lender to cover the risk that the borrower would default on repayment. As such, they could be written on any credit product. However, an investor didn't have to actually own the debt on which insurance cover was provided. CDS became a tradable item, the price of which moved up or down in line with data on expected default rates on the underlying debt. Indices were developed that tracked the default rates and investors speculated according to their expectations of future movements in the index. The index could be traded.

The "synthetic" CDO market developed in a similar fashion. Derivative was piled upon derivative. Banks increased effective leverage significantly by trading in synthetic CDOs, but this meant that they had to assume the extra risk in the form of holding "super senior debt" on their balance sheets. In this increasingly murky and opaque world, no central clearing agency kept track of the exploding volumes and variety of derivatives. They were bought and sold "over the counter." That meant, as noted in Chapter 5, that no one really knew who owned what and who owed what. In a state of profound ignorance the only certainty was that everyone was doing it. As soon as the derivative price indices began heading south, greed turned to fear. How could one know that the bank or insurance company that sold you the CDS would be able to honor the payout if the lender defaulted? What if the former went bankrupt under the weight of the rush of claims against it when lenders defaulted *en masse* throughout the economy? This is the nightmare that loomed in late 2008 when American International Group had to be bailed out by the US government. As fear fed on itself, credit markets seized up worldwide.

The spark, remember, was struck in the housing sector. Too many people were enticed by a mixture of personal aspiration, slick salesmanship, all-around greed, and straight-out fraud to take on mortgage loans that they could not afford. The incentives all along the chain, from the brokers and spruikers who went out and quite literally dragged people in off the streets, through the primary lenders, to the investment banks and securitization specialists, the ratings agencies, insurance companies, lawyers, and financial advisers, conspired to create the largest financial disaster in history.

This time it *was* different, but only in nature and scale. Metaphors of natural disaster are impossible to avoid. It *was* a perfect storm. No one and no institution involved in the financial sector emerge unscathed. With hindsight, repeal of the Glass–Steagall Act (which had since the 1930s mandated the separation of commercial banking from investment banking) during the Clinton Presidency was decisive in allowing the creation of the "supermarket banks," organizations able to offer the full range of financial products, old and new. This virtually forced previously sedate savings deposit-taking institutions to move into the murky underworld of financial innovation described above— to risk their depositor's savings and their shareholders' equity in speculating on successfully navigating the unknown terrain in that underworld. Exercises that were supposedly textbook cases of risk management became poorly understood forays into rank uncertainty. The senior executives who "led" the charge had forgotten, if they ever knew, the basic difference between risk and uncertainty, lucidly described by Keynes and the Chicago economist Frank Knight before the Second World War. Also forgotten was the fact that "a hundred year flood" can occur at *any* time in the next hundred years irrespective of *when* it happened in the last hundred years.

Fraud arose, as noted, as many brokers misled house purchasers. But financial chicanery also extended well beyond the sphere of housing finance. The most spectacular case concerned the unraveling of a Ponzi scheme run for over twenty years by a respected though secretive Wall Street insider, Bernard L. Madoff. Promising and delivering steady returns in the low double digits through rising and falling markets, Madoff attracted a growing number of investors, ranging from large funds and wealthy individuals to university endowment funds, charities, and thousands of small investors whose savings (without their knowledge) were channeled through mutual and hedge funds. Unknown to most of these investors their returns were being paid from the incoming savings of new investors, rather than the results of actual investments in securities and other income-generating assets. The whole exercise depended on the building and maintenance of trust—trust in Bernie Madoff— and on the willingness of the growing number of existing investors to leave most of their savings and paper returns in Bernie's stewardship as they practiced their willing suspension of disbelief. Once investors were spooked by the events described above, the game was soon up. Investors began to line up in order to retrieve their investment balances, most of which were merely paper entries in fabricated accounts. The luckier investors had by then at least withdrawn what they had deposited over the years; in the peculiar terminology of the trade they are referred to as "net winners."

What they didn't get and are unlikely to ever retrieve are the fictional balances outstanding at the time Bernard L. Madoff Securities went into administration. Ahead of them in the queue waiting for the crumbs are the "net losers," those people who have not withdrawn all—in some cases, any—of the money they had actually invested with Madoff. This amounted to around twenty billion dollars. Depending on the outcome of multiple civil and criminal trials, this group may end up receiving as little as twenty cents in the dollar; they too will never see the fictitious returns on their real investments. Although tears may not be shed for the wealthy and famous victims, some would say victims of their own greed and gullibility, pity the thousands of small investors who thought they were investing in well diversified mutual funds that instead served as conduits to funnel money to Madoff. Many of these investors ended up losing not just their savings and self-esteem but their future retirement lifestyles. The difference was between a reasonably comfortable retirement and a continuing struggle to live. Those who unwisely took the advice of self-interested financial advisers to borrow on their homes or retirement accounts to leverage investing in Madoff were doubly cursed. In their cases bankruptcy and homelessness threatened.

The Madoff disaster raises an important point of great social concern. As more and more people seek to privately provide for security in old age, financial markets take over the role previously assumed by government in the immediate postwar period. The move to self-funded retirement pensions and the withdrawal of employers from offering defined benefit schemes leaves the average worker at the mercy of poorly regulated financial intermediaries. This trend promises—in addition to the greater threat of serious recession—intensified economic inequality, both within society as the financial class captures an increasing share of the growing economic pie, and across the life course as ordinary workers unknowingly consume their retirement futures through over-consumption today and inadequate (that is, ineffective) saving for tomorrow. A similar fate awaited those who worked for the many companies taken over by Enron before its spectacular collapse disclosed that the retirement savings of workers invested in the company's pension scheme had evaporated. These developments have demonstrated that the democratization of lending as well as borrowing—that is, of the privatization of saving for retirement as well as mass consumption ahead of income earned—is leading to new sources of insecurity at both the individual and economy-wide levels.

One final development in relation to debt concerns the role of financial markets and investment banks in facilitating the rise of hostile corporate takeover activities. The practice of corporate raiding has a history as old as the stock market. In the neoliberal period it has acquired academic respectability as the centerpiece in the theory of "the market for corporate control." Corporate takeovers or their threat, in this view, provide an ever-present incentive for managers of the firm to maximize returns to shareholders. Those managers who can't or won't do this are replaced in a well organized putsch by those who acquire a controlling ownership in the firm. The new management sets about putting the firm in order, cutting waste, chopping out the dead wood, and taking up profitable opportunities missed by their predecessors. The analogy is a pack of wolves that roam around the edges of a buffalo herd, picking off the stragglers and infirm animals, thereby ensuring the survival of the fittest.

In reality, in its modern form, a consortium usually grabs a controlling share of a large company by borrowing large amounts of money on short term and at high interest rates (in the form of "high yield bonds, more commonly known as "junk bonds"), then ruthlessly cuts up the prey into saleable slices, selling off the best bits and leaving the carcass. The returns of sale are used to pay back debt, leaving the raiders with the residue, often a return that is several hundred-fold greater than the initial equity invested—"skin in the game." A company, often with a household name, that was previously paying its way ceases to exist, along with the large numbers of workers sacked in the process of "rationalization."

This version of financial alchemy started in the late 1970s and in the 1980s rapidly took over the bond markets and the business of investment banking. The leveraged buyouts, or LBOs, often involved a coup perpetuated by the existing management of an undervalued firm. They knew it was undervalued on the stock exchange because they had inside knowledge not available to shareholders. The junk bond financed takeover and merger boom that emerged during this decade was a dress rehearsal for the far more disastrous events of 2001–8. The boom involved super aggressive investment banks raising huge amounts of debt funding for consortia of private investors, often including existing managers of the takeover target. These calculated attacks sucked in finance from banks, savings and loan institutions, private lenders, pension and mutual funds all attracted by high interest rates and persuasive arguments that low-grade bonds were underpriced and not really as prone to default as generally thought.

Lack of transparency, insider trading, fraud, lies, conflicts of interest, and absence of effective regulation—the mix of toxic ingredients that later surfaced during the GFC—all played their part in inflating the LBO boom and ensured its eventual collapse. By 2009 the party had ended but the cost was still being paid in lost jobs, personal and business bankruptcies, and forgone opportunities. The end result was churn and massive rent-seeking by the successful financial alchemists, not the innovation and productivity revolution promised. Returning to the earlier episode, by 1990 the leading spruiker, Drexel Burnham Lambert, had filed for bankruptcy having bitten off more than it could chew—a $31 billion LBO of RJR Nabisco; Drexel's star trader, the "junk bond king", Michael Milkin was fined and forced to repay a total of over $600 million to investors and regulators and would soon start a ten-year jail sentence, pleading guilty to various civil and felonious charges (but not insider trading, which was not pursued). (It is impossible not to comment that Mr. Milkin made a fortune "milkin" sheep.) He served fewer than two years and subsequently reinvented himself as a philanthropist. Having started as Prince John, he hoped to end as Robin Hood. Once bitten twice sly, the Wall Street operators developed ever more intricate and opaque wheezes in the years running up to the GFC. Subsequent sober research has demonstrated that the funds caught up in financing the mergers and acquisitions boom generally underperformed the S&P 500.

Government inadequacies are legion and, again in hindsight, easy to see and hard to forgive. Why did government effectively abrogate its responsibility to protect investors and consumers? Part of the explanation comes down to sheer lack of knowledge on the part of regulators and legislators. If the senior executives of large financial institutions didn't know how much risk their organizations were actually taking on, then how could those far removed from the boardroom know what was going down? At one level this is undoubtedly true. But as a defense, still less full explanation, it reeks of bad faith. There were enough early warning signs and statements by budding "prophets of doom" to at least capture government attention. Moreover, the total lack of anticipation did not occur in an historical, ideological or political vacuum. Decades of reliance on the economics of the central tradition and corresponding attacks on the public sector led to declining capacity and morale in the budget-strapped regulatory agencies supposed to monitor the financial sector and control its excesses. The self-styled "smartest guys in the room" did not work for government or even, it appears, the ratings agencies that assumed a quasi-regulatory role. The masters of the universe were stoking the bonfire of the vanities in Wall Street, Zurich, and "the City." In his illuminating book, *Extreme Money* (2011), the Indian born Australian financial analyst Satyajit Das quotes a CEO of a large bank at the 2007 GFC saying with some satisfaction, "the regulators are finally under control."

One lesson that did emerge from the GFC, along with many others, was the lack of financial literacy among ordinary householders. The highly technical and complex language of the financial markets crowded out the simple message understood by virtually everyone—and ironically lying at the heart of the discipline of modern finance theory—don't put all your eggs in one basket. The tragedy of the GFC was that most people, promoters and punters alike, thought that the financial WMDs *were* diversifying exposure, while hiding the fact that the system as a whole was spinning out of control. In the age of financialization the world's leading economies have entered what Das has termed the liquidity vortex, a qualitatively new development of Keynes's liquidity trap. In the vortex, all parties are swept up and swirled away. The fate of all countries, advanced and emerging, is so interrelated that no one can escape the maw. Debt creation has become detached from real wealth creation. Gambling has replaced enterprise. Income distribution has been turned into a rent-seeking game. Asset values gyrate wildly as speculation replaces sound investment. In the Shakespearian world of *Twelfth Night*, the world is turned upside down; lord becomes servant, servant lord, as money exerts a dominant and directing force in economic life. In one of his most often-quoted statements Keynes said—"When the capital development of a country becomes the by-product of the activities of a casino, the job is likely to be ill-done" (1973/1936: 159).

*   *   *

At base, the functional link Galbraith traced between consumption and debt has come to dominate life in modern capitalism but in a way that undoes the social settlement he foresaw between production and inequality. The causality has reversed. Instead of growth in output and consumption salving the wounds of unequal shares, increasing inequality is forcing the diminishing middle class, the expanding working class, and the growing army of the technologically unemployed to maintain the level of consumption to which they aspire and are urged by making up the increasing gap between income and expenditure though borrowing. In this hopeless task, the middle will not hold. Debt levels must eventually reach unsustainable levels, resulting for the individual in declining living standards and personal bankruptcy and for society as a whole in recurrent economic breakdown such as that we are living through early in the twenty-first century. The growing structural reliance on debt thus accentuates the uncertainty and volatility of economic life; insecurity, inequality, and the ever-present threat of the debt collector march hand-in-hand. The danger that Galbraith sensed in the affluent society's increasing reliance on debt has indeed been realized in our lifetime.

10

The Theory of Social Balance

The final problem of the productive society is what it produces. This manifests itself in an implacable tendency to provide an opulent supply of some things and a niggardly yield of others.

(J.K. Galbraith)

There is an allied problem in the way we commit the resources that are available for investment in the economy.

(J.K. Galbraith)

* * *

Why do we have so many privately produced and marketed goods and services and so few publicly provided ones? Why, in an environment of opulence, is consumption of the former considered a triumph and consumption of the latter a regrettable necessity at best and a case of wicked wastefulness at worst? Galbraith's answer is that we live in a state of collective cognitive dissonance, complaining as to the inadequacy of public services important for our well-being while also complaining about the insupportable burdens of all the ways of paying for them to improve. In the most quoted passage of the whole book Galbraith vividly describes the scene thus:

The family which takes its mauve and cerise, air-conditioned, power-steered and power-braked automobile out for a tour passes through cities that are badly paved, made hideous by litter, blighted buildings, billboards and posts for wires that should long since have been put underground. They pass into a countryside that has been rendered largely invisible by commercial art. (The goods that they advertise have an absolute priority in our value system. Such aesthetic considerations as a view of the countryside accordingly come second. On such matters, we are consistent.) They picnic on exquisitely packaged food from a portable icebox by a polluted stream and go on to spend the night at a park which is a menace to public health and morals. Just before dozing off on an air mattress beneath a nylon tent, amid the stench of decaying refuse, they may reflect vaguely on the curious unevenness of their blessings. Is this, indeed, the American genius?

(I here follow every other commentator on *AS*, being unable to avoid parading this scene before the reader; no other piece of prose so perfectly captures Galbraith's unique wit and style.)

At the time even Galbraith thought that he might have laid it on too thickly. He later tells of his internal battle as to whether or not to leave the passage in, deciding at last to do so. "Never have I more narrowly escaped error." It is difficult to imagine Galbraith (or any writer), having composed such compellingly descriptive prose, killing it in the name of judicious authorship. The purported struggle sounds more like Oscar Wilde's one-liner on the rigors of the writing craft—that he had spent the morning inserting a comma and the afternoon taking it out.

Galbraith begins by noting the generally accepted truth that in a well functioning economy there must be "a tolerably close relationship" between certain products. Steel production requires iron ore and coking coal. Factories producing products of all kinds require adequate electric power—and so on. The list in a modern economy is endless. Input–output analysis can establish the technical coefficients linking the complex patterns of congruence or balance across the economy. If the right balance is not struck between inputs and outputs, then bottlenecks develop and total production stalls. The great advantage of market societies is that, in general, "the hidden hand" manages to evolve a workable approximation to the correct balance in many though far from all cases, as opposed to centrally planned economies in which inadequate information and incentives often lead to major mismatches and bottlenecks. Equally, on the side of consumption, certain complementarities impose themselves. Automobiles need roads to ride on and regulatory regimes to avoid mass carnage. Petrol, car insurance, and emergency wards must be accessible to drivers when needed. "More vacations require more hotels and more fishing rods. And so on."

These complementarities in production and consumption cross the line between private and public provision, though the line shifts between regions and over time. However, in most cases efficient private production calls for adequate public services. At base, the institutional and legal structures guaranteeing public order, the sanctity of contracts, and defense of the realm establish the necessary conditions for the operation of private markets. Beyond that, public provision is still ubiquitous.

> In all cases if these services are not forthcoming, the consequences will be in some degree ill. It will be convenient to have a term which suggests a satisfactory relationship between the supply of privately produced goods and services and those of the state, and we may call it Social Balance.

The automobile—as the quote above amply demonstrates—is, for Galbraith, the paradigmatic case of social imbalance. "The result [of imbalance] has been hideous road congestion, a human massacre of impressive proportions and chronic colitis in the cities." From time to time citizens are forcibly reminded of the perils of imbalance, as when strikes or natural disasters temporarily shut down public transport and hospitals, creating mass colitis, literally and metaphorically.

Galbraith is one of the first economists to directly target the connection between the economy and the environment. Up until the 1990s, most economists had tended to regard the natural environment as a given, a quarry for free resources and a sink for inevitable waste. Not so, opines Galbraith. "The greater the wealth, the thicker will be the dirt." Environmental despoliation rises along with production. Arthur Pigou, as noted, one of the few economists to anticipate this argument, introduced the concept of negative external effect to capture the phenomenon. Los Angeles is offered as the obvious example, where air pollution and traffic congestion are creating the "agony of a city without usable air."

Galbraith generalizes the point, identifying other examples of defensive expenditure necessitated by economic growth. For example, as commerce develops, so too does fraud and theft, requiring appropriate provision of police and judicial services; in the current era of globalization, the latter pastimes have been given full rein. The expansion of production has also colonized youth, creating a range of new consumption desires, some of which are of distinctly dubious nature—here Galbraith sounds the age-old alarm of an anxious parent. The sum total of all the defensive expenditures called forth by the inevitable linkages forged is included in the conventional measures of economic well-being, another sense in which the dependence effect is at work.

The dynamic unleashed also impinges on the basic social structure of society, the family, in ways that further intensify social imbalance. The prime stress placed on expanding debt-fuelled consumption, under the reign of the dependence effect, encourages the growth of the two-income family. "If both parents are engaged in private production, the burden on the public services is further increased." Care of children and the elderly, previously the almost exclusive responsibility of married women, is passed on to the community— but only partly as many women in paid employment are also called upon (put upon?) to perform a double role. If adequate public services lag, anti-social behavior rises, creating an enhanced demand for the services of law and order. Allowing for Galbraith's conventional background image of the 1950s family, as portrayed in popular television series of the day like *Leave it to Beaver*, Galbraith once again identified what became in the decades following a dominant feature of the economy, society, and public policy. The progressive growth in female employment has indeed eventuated, creating the demands for more publicly provided care services, among other impacts. With remorseless demographic change and improving health technologies, emphasis has shifted more towards the end of life. The case of housing is, he suggests, also instructive. Other societies, notably in Northern Europe, have developed housing systems that usefully match public services with private construction. The government contributes though strategic planning, land acquisition, effective zoning, and public financing options, resulting in standard houses of superior quality to those built in the US.

By recognizing the ubiquity of social imbalance it is possible to identify opportunities to substantially increase citizen welfare. That this doesn't happen is partly caused by the process of want creation previously remarked upon. The forces of mass persuasion levied by modern advertising privilege privately produced goods. Consumers are frequently reminded of the urgent need to upgrade to the new model automobile and rarely if ever as to the equally urgent need to fill the deepening pot-holes. Public education suffers: "(t)he engines of mass communication, in their highest stage of development, assail the eyes and ears of the community on behalf of new beverages but not of more schools." In fact, existing schools also perform the task of expanding the consumption of new beverages, as when they are induced to install vending machines in the hallways. Galbraith would have been amused by the counterfactual development decades later when a university in Florida reaped huge financial dividends from discovering and co-developing the world's most popular "sports drink." An engineer or businessman who discovers and successfully sells a new gadget is publicly lauded and richly rewarded but a politician or public official who "...sees need for a new public service may be called a wastrel. Few public offenses are more reprehensible."

II

In short, the first and basic reason for endemic social imbalance in affluent societies is an inherent tendency for public services to fall behind private production. Two further factors reinforce the tendency to imbalance. First, any reliance on increasing the provision of public services necessarily casts light and heat on the truce concerning inequality. Since most public services are not marketed, they are not paid for directly by consumers. The thorny question of *how* they are to be financed is raised. This normally revolves around how to levy a tax sufficient to cover the level of provision required. In effect, all the opposition roused against effective fiscal interventions to control inflation now focuses on the hapless proponent of improved schools, roads, public parks, and the like. Liberals oppose levying indirect taxes because the poor pay more proportionately than the rich. Conservatives oppose income tax, in part as a reflex motion, and at the level of well-worn argument by citing their adverse effect on incentives, growth, and employment. "Since the debate over inequality cannot be resolved, the money is frequently not appropriated and the service not performed."

The gap and lag in public provision is only kept in rough check—not allowed to escalate—by the process of economic growth by which government revenue increases in step. The problem is that although the total quantum of tax revenues increases as the economy grows, there is no automatic tendency to direct that revenue stream to the areas of greatest economic and social need. Public revenue streams are not, in general, tied to specific purposes, at least at the federal level in America. The forces determining the tax take differ from those setting expenditure on public services. Powerful but different influences will act on both sides of the government budget. Well placed interests can direct or derail specific proposals to fund particular services. New roads to nowhere may be the political price to get other roads built to somewhere they are actually of economic use. The squeeze on federal expenditures is made worse by the large call that national defense makes on the federal budget. The voracious appetite of what President Eisenhower called "the military-industrial complex" sharply constrains the capacity of governments to adequately fund other areas of policy. Given that the United States has been engaged (unsuccessfully) in at least four major wars since Eisenhower's parting shot in 1960, this drain on national treasure (and conscripted servicemen and women) has been considerable; Afghanistan and Iraq are simply the most recent cases.

The situation is even more constrained at state and local government levels, where the scope for revenue growth is limited compared to the tendency of demands on services to increase. "Because of this, increased services for states and localities regularly pose the question of more revenues and more taxes. And, here with greater regularity, the question of social balance is lost in the debate over equality and social equity." One consequence of this permanent situation of "vertical fiscal imbalance" between the three levels of government is that the federal government is constantly under pressure to assist lower level fund services and projects that are best delivered closer to the final user, whether household or business.

The final source of social imbalance lies in the impact of inflation on relative wages in the two sectors. Due to fiscal constraints and ideological prejudice, wages in the public sector lag behind those on offer in the private sector. It becomes increasingly difficult to recruit and keep public sector workers, particularly in buoyant economic times of high employment demand and inflation. Lower levels of government, in particular, find it increasingly impossible to meet both the rising materials and overhead costs of providing services, the demand for which is increasing with population and economic growth, and the total wages bill necessary to keep and expand their workforce. The heavy dependence of state and local governments on property taxes that only increase with inflation after a considerable lag (that is, after the next general property re-valuations and/or the political fights leading up to rate increases) further reduces their capacity to operate effectively. In some jurisdictions, Galbraith allows, strong public sector unions may reduce the wages gap, but the unresponsiveness of revenue in inflationary situations remains a major barrier at lower government levels.

In consequence, proponents of the public sector are always on the defensive; they must fight to keep what history has delivered and fight much harder to improve upon that legacy. "Even public services that prevent disorder must be defended. By contrast, the man who successfully devices a nostrum for a nonexistent need and then successfully promotes both remains one of nature's noblemen." The conventional wisdom, as always, applauds efforts to limit public spending by recourse to the ideology of the free market. This reflex enshrines a logic of the "four legs good, two legs bad" kind. On this point Galbraith notes the developed capacity of defenders of the faith to simultaneously hold that taxes to finance public services will hold back investment and that investment is too high to avoid disastrous inflation. This is explicable because "men of high position are allowed, by a special act of grace, to accommodate their reasoning to the answer they need. Logic is only required in those of lesser rank."

III

Social imbalance is associated with imbalance in the allocation of investment resources. Conventional economics is clear on the importance of a society adequately investing in the continual expansion of its capital plant and equipment. Only by accumulating capital can growth accommodate increasing population and rising living standards. This task has both quantitative and qualitative dimensions. An increasing supply of current capital goods is necessary to support a growing workforce and increase its productivity. Productivity is also enhanced by technological improvements; this is the qualitative drive that has increasingly come to underpin economic growth. As capitalism has matured, the necessary spur to qualitative improvements through technological advance has shifted from the gifted entrepreneur to the skilled technician. The former is born but the latter has to be produced. "Investment in human beings is, *prima facie*, as important as investment in material capital." The accumulation and deployment of what economists from the 1950s on came to call "human capital" has taken over as the critical lever of growth. This requires an economy to organize large and growing investments in education, training, scientific, engineering, and managerial capacities in the population. Innovation is now a highly orchestrated process that relies on the steady production of talented individuals. "Without them investment in material capital will still bring growth, but it will be the inefficient growth that is combined with technological stagnation."

This then leads Galbraith to "the nub of the problem." Markets are generally effective in directing material capital investment towards areas of private production holding out the most profitable prospects. However, the same urgency is not evident when it comes to ensuring investment in the human capital necessary for the most productive use of the resulting plant. Thus, investment in oil refineries will be planned without any surety that the engineers to design and operate it will be available. Still less is it clear that scientists will emerge to find new and more efficient ways of refining the plant's products. The high potential return across the economy from investing in the education and training of scientists, engineers, and other specialists will not automatically ensure their supply, that is, will not redirect investment funds from less productive uses. One way this conundrum could be solved—suggests Galbraith with tongue-in-cheek—would be to indenture the talented young to the study of mathematics, science, accounting, and other skilled areas of knowledge and tie each for life to a particular employer. In such a situation, employers could be relied upon to redirect sufficient investment away from material capital into human capital in the right proportions to maximize profits. Of course, there might also be some unfortunate side-effects, like the elimination of personal freedoms such as is only approximated in democratic nations in time of war.

Galbraith explicitly notes that human development is an external economy. No single employer has an incentive to invest in the education and training of its employees beyond a certain level, because they cannot appropriate all the benefits in enhanced productivity that such investments create. The commercial benefits will flow to whomsoever hires the employee who carries in his or her head and hands the skills engendered by the investment. This is a classic case of market failure—the inability of private competition through market exchange to deliver the goods in appropriate amounts. The case is clearest when considering basic scientific research. Not only can individual investors not appropriate *all* the benefits that might flow from such activities, they can't anticipate and price the probability that *anything* of commercial value will eventuate nor *how long* it will take to discover *if* an investment will pay off. There are no accepted guideposts to determining when to pull back or out of an investment.

This insight was subsequently rigorously developed by Kenneth Arrow in the early 1960s and provides the still compelling reason for why governments need to step in and fill the gap when it comes to funding scientific research. The payoff from generations of government funding of public universities and other research institutions is beyond dispute, even by the most vocal proponents of neoliberal ideology. Breakthroughs in new materials, health care, and information technology, culminating in the launch of the internet, provide a crushing retort to those who argue that all government expenditure is inherently sterile. Many of the most important developments, like the internet and the commercial airplane, were unexpected spin-offs from the bias in government investment towards the military. It is simply not possible to comprehend what modern economies today would look like without the emergence of the innovations sparked by these and other advances. On a more somber note, it is also inconceivable that a whole range of deadly and dubious developments would have been possible without the advent of these technologies; one has in mind here the growth of organized crime, military adventurism, pornography, terrorism, and global financial crisis.

One admittedly speculative advantage Galbraith discerns in evening the balance between investment in material and personal capital is that it may reduce our vulnerability to the imbalance between private and public consumption. Much private consumption, as we have seen, is contrived and debt financed. If the dangers in such a process are realized, the recessions resulting from sharp shocks to consumer confidence and capacity will be somewhat muted if consumers *en masse* have previously rebalanced their consumption in favor of greater utilization of public services. The latter are based on wants that are generally not contrived and thus less vulnerable to a breakdown in the debt–want creation process. "Since they are sold on the installment plan, they are not subject to curtailment by any of the factors that make people unwilling or unable to incur debt."

This is, at best, a long stretch. One might equally argue that a greater reliance on tax-funded public services renders the economy more vulnerable to economic shocks. When economic fortunes decline people may respond by more energetically seeking to avoid or evade paying their taxes, saving rather than spending the proceeds. In any event, this "speculation" seems to be an afterthought to Galbraith's main argument. The same can be said for his parting thought that increased investments in education form a double-edged sword, providing the intellectual means for people to apprehend and neutralize the blandishments of advertising. The same critical outcome, if not facility, is more likely to follow the widespread take-up of digital recording machines primed to skip through the advertisements or, for that matter, behavioral routines involving strategically timed trips to kitchen and bathroom.

Galbraith's critique with respect to education and training is mainly targeted at the conventional wisdom's fixation on the primacy of private production. He also reserves a few comments in this case for the non-economic benefits of education, alluding to its time-honored role in improving the mind and character of a people. In this he betrays his values as well, perhaps, as his vested material interest in shoring up the role of the educator. I for one—an educator too—am inclined to indulge him in this conceit.

IV

The development of capitalism in the United States and elsewhere in the West since publication of *AS* has borne proof to Galbraith's instinctive feel for what was in the process of occurring on his watch. Various developments in the discipline of economics underpinned the gathering attack on the size, role, and funding of the public sector. Some of these developments were mentioned in the earlier discussion of "the central tradition." Of particular import to the theory of social balance was the appearance and flowering of *public choice theory*, associated with the economist James Buchanan and what came to be called "the Virginia School" lodged in and around the economics departments at Virginia State University and George Mason University.

Public Choice Theory (PCT) applied the rational choice model to actors (both elected and appointed officials) in the public sector. The politician was assumed to act in ways that maximized his (usually) chances of winning election and re-election to public office. The bureaucrat was assumed to be single-minded in maximizing the scope of public duties and budget spend under his or her control. This hard-headed model contradicted the underlying normative base of orthodox economics promulgated since Alfred Marshall, namely that economics was about improving the welfare of the people. It also contradicted the comfortable conceit among economists that their dis-interested advice on maximizing economic efficiency offered through liberal democratic institutions would be taken at face value by selfless public servants of impeccable integrity. Among the many conclusions of PCT was the claim that unless restrained, government budgets would blow out in a competitive race by public officials to expand their bureaucratic empires, supported by log-rolling politicians shoring up their re-election prospects. The fact that in the US Federal (and many state) legislatures most politicians faced re-election so frequently that they were almost always in election mode made sure that their attention stayed focused on the main game—electoral survival at all costs—and the costs were met by vested interests in return for favors that ulti-mately impacted negatively on the welfare of citizens.

In other words, public choice economists were promoting a version of the theory of social imbalance—but one that was precisely the reverse of Galbraith's. Too much public provision was forthcoming rather than too little. Too many resources were being diverted to finance the activities of the state, most of which were marginal at best and wasteful at worst because their true driver and outcome was not enhanced production and welfare for the masses but enhanced living standards for the providers. Public sector workers in gen-eral were not contributing to overall prosperity but merely "rent-seekers" liv-ing off the labor and ingenuity of workers in the private sector, the real locus of wealth generation. Even in areas of public provision like primary and sec-ondary education, budgets were bloated and empires shored up; how many people does it take to change a light bulb in a school? Answer: one janitor and seventeen bureaucrats.

It is not difficult to see how this line of argument appealed to the deep anti-taxation streak in American society and character. Current rhetoric of the Tea Party and the A-list radio shock-jocks draws (unconsciously) on this austere academic current. It is also easy to trace a line directly from PCT to the subsequent academic and political programs pushing for the privatization of public services, a core component of the neoliberal project.

Proponents of neoliberal policies believe that by relying on market processes, individual welfare will be optimized, in part because the waste endemic in the public sector will be eliminated and resources freed can be put to their most productive uses. This has meant support for policies that outsource or privatize key urban services, such as major roads, telecommunications, hospitals, prisons, airports, railways, electricity, and much else that used to be provided by government or closely regulated quangos. At first glance this approach appears spurious, since private provision is more costly to finance. That is, governments in well-governed jurisdictions can always finance major projects more cheaply than private investors. There is always a risk premium on private equity and loan finance by comparison to government bonds, at least in those countries the bond markets have not dismissed as basket cases.

This means that the weight of the argument in favor of privatization rests on the claim that private ownership will deliver operational and dynamic efficiencies absent in public provision. The capital market, it is argued, will discipline private providers forcing them to reduce waste, innovate, and pay close attention to meeting consumer demands. Public sector provision, on other hand, does not directly feel the heat of demanding consumers and ruthless financial markets. Public sector workers, protected by strong trade unions, can organize service provision to further their own interests and that of the current crop of politicians in power, just as the findings of PCT dictate.

Clearly, there are plentiful examples of chronically inefficient public sector organizations in the US and elsewhere. "Government failure" is an ever-present challenge to democratic government. However, neoliberals treat government failure as an axiom, while ignoring the many cases of market failure (and, more generally, coordination failures), especially in modern urbanized capitalist societies. The GFC, as already noted, provided countless cases of rent seeking among senior financial sector executives. Corrupt dealings between private sector operators and complicit bureaucrats and politicians bedevil the provision of public services. The rapid growth of the lobbying industry in countries committed to neoliberalism is clear. As we have seen, in his book *Supercapitalism* (2008), Robert Reich stresses the role of both "independent" lobbyists based in Washington DC and the in-house lobbying units—political action committees or PACs—of large corporations in bending US government policy to further the commercial interests of those companies. In *Winner-Take-All Politics* (2010), Jacob Hacker and Paul Pierson argue that the "super-rich" have hijacked the political system and used their power to entrench and enhance their economic interests and rewards.

Most prominent in these elite ranks are leading members of the financial services sector. An indication of the degree to which the "financialisation of capitalism" has progressed in the US resides in the fact that the share of this sector in total profits increased from around 15 percent in the 1970s to 40 percent in 2007. The dominance of Wall Street is also aided by the frequent and ready movement of leading investment bankers into senior government positions, most notably in the federal Treasury and the movement in the opposite direction by ex-elected officials. Representatives of each shuttle back and forward between each other's worlds with impressive regularity. These extra-market processes operate at all levels of government and, if left unregulated, bias resource allocation away from the abstract ideals of orthodox economics. Instead of subjecting all systems of public provision to critical scrutiny in terms of actual outcomes on the ground, neoliberals *assume* markets work well enough and governments almost always fail—"four legs good, two legs bad."

The provision of infrastructure—roads, bridges, tunnels, airports, railways, ports, and the like—provided an irresistible target for the financial alchemists. Public–private partnerships (PPPs) could, in theory, be structured to offer investors long-term steady returns, protection against inflation, and liquidity—ideal investment outlets for pension and mutual funds seeking better returns than government bonds but with little more risk. A bit more upside but not too much downside please. Such products were especially attractive in countries where governments, under the watchful eye of bond markets and neoliberals, were pushing their budgets into surplus and paying down debt. The new infrastructure bonds filled a gap in the diversified portfolios of the big funds.

Unfortunately, this avenue was also prone to attract the most aggressive financial buccaneers. One of the most active—Australia's Macquarie Bank— developed hundreds of infrastructure funds based on the debt-driven purchase of assets all over the world; at its peak Macquarie operated in more than one hundred countries. The Macquarie model entailed complex arrangements in which it collected initiating, transacting, and management fees at every stage of the operation. Based on its fee harvesting talents the bank was dubbed "the millionaires factory." Peaking at almost A$100 per share before the GFC, Macquarie's share price fell precipitously thereafter where it lies still, the company a shadow of its former self.

Many of the infrastructure projects built through the efforts of institutions like Macbank staggered on, underperforming the market, while others never got off the ground or sank back into it. Returns to investors turned out to be much more volatile and much less rosy than forecast. The financial asset pricing models failed; betas turned into zetas.

When looked at in a hardheaded way, it is possible to find examples of both successful and failed privatizations in the Anglo-democracies. Railways offer the clearest case of failure. The UK and New Zealand governments privatized track and operator functions in the 1990s only to renationalize them in the new century. Telecommunications and electricity have proved mixed bags. Where greater competition in delivery of final services has been achieved, consumers have benefited. The problems have arisen at the heavy infrastructure end, the point at which natural monopoly exists. In Australia, the federal government has been forced to step in and commit to building a national broadband network open to competing providers, since no one private operator could be trusted to own the network. The US and other countries like Australia have reaped poor returns from experiments in privatizing key welfare state services such as health and education and other sectors such as prisons and mercenary military forces. New Zealand's attempts to privatize their hospitals and public housing sector created massive social problems and were quickly dropped by the incoming Labor government in the late 1990s and subsequently not revived by the recently (re)elected conservative government.

The key lesson of the privatization strategy for modern economies is that there are some public services and assets for which governments can never transfer catastrophic risk. Some level of government *must* take over and ensure adequate performance of, for example, the urban public transport service and major hospitals, *if* private operators fail, in order to avoid systemic *economic* breakdown, just as governments had to and did step in to effectively nationalize the banks and other financial institutions deemed too big to fail.

It is also true that there is a degree of self-fulfilling prophecy about the neoliberal critique of public sector provision. The very arguments that favor private over public provision call for starving the public sector of resources to adequately operate those services. Aggressive political maneuvering to cut taxes and severely limit public borrowing undermines the ability of government agencies to effectively carry out these functions. It's like shooting Usain Bolt in the leg and then complaining that he can't run the 100 meters. This has been the driving political strategy of conservative forces over the past decade, both inside and outside Congress.

The end result of "leaving it to the market" in the provision of much economic and social infrastructure is chronic undersupply, substantially worsening the investment and functional imbalances identified by Galbraith. Governments in countries under the grip of neoliberal policies struggle to maintain standards of service in health, education, and the urban environment. The *Report Card* of The American Society of Civil Engineers (2009) estimated that the extra investment required to bring the country's failing roads, bridges, dams, water, waste, and public transport systems up to acceptable quality would be $2.2 trillion over the next five years. The "grades" given to these assets, critical to the health of the economy and citizenry, all fall in the D minus to D range. The direct and follow-up costs to government budgets of the GFC—and the ruinous cost of the ongoing wars—have effectively precluded investment at the required levels.

State and local governments badly burnt by investing in the toxic financial assets are particularly poorly placed to respond, further reducing local economic prospects and accelerating the continual degradation of infrastructure systems. The lingering political paralysis of the American body politic, culminating in the still perennial problem of the federal government debt limit, sharply underlines both the power of neoliberal forces to regroup after the crisis unleashed in 2008 and the massive negative overhang of the neoliberal policies that led to the GFC. Economists are now openly talking about the ten years to 2017 as America's "decade of debt." Rising interest rates on existing government debt will further undercut necessary investments in social and economic infrastructure over the coming years, if and when the world eventually loses confidence in the greenback.

One unexpected and unfortunate consequence of intensifying social imbalance was the effect on financial markets. Part of the urgent demand by institutions for higher return and supposedly low-risk debt securities was caused by the reduction in the supply of government debt. A lower availability of genuinely AAA government debt, as governments budgeted for surpluses and debt repayment, created the space for financial alchemists to work their magic. As Satyajit Das (2011: 131) so succinctly put it: "The new economics allowed politicians to implement their ideological agendas. The new finance provided the moral and intellectual basis for financial conquest, plunder and pillage."

* * *

Galbraith considered the theory of social balance as one of the enduring contributions of his book. In view of recent developments in global capitalism one can only agree and applaud his foresight and courage in highlighting the gaps in the economics of his day and in the decades to come. As we gaze at the increasingly run-down state of our public infrastructure, the strain on basic services in education and health, the potential costs associated with climate change, the fragility of our financial system, and the increasing hopelessness of a generation of the unemployable and homeless, we might well ponder the alternative path taken since Galbraith and other liberals extolled the necessity and basic integrity of an empowered public sector.

11

Switching Tracks

Social philosophy far more than nature abhors a vacuum.

(J.K. Galbraith)

Philosophers have hitherto only interpreted the world in various ways; the point is to change it.

(Karl Marx)

*   *   *

Having laid out his theory of social balance, Galbraith reached the end of his critique of contemporary ways of seeing the economic world. He saw the destruction of the comfortable and self-serving myths underlying the economic theory and practice of his time as the primary purpose of *AS*. He was confident that the march of circumstance, rather than the direct impact of his arguments, would eventually confirm the accuracy of the latter; "(t)he threat to the conventional wisdom is always its own irrelevance, not the appeal of a relevant alternative." He hoped, however, that his "destructive criticism" would make a modest contribution to unsettling the conventional wisdom in ways that "constructive alternatives" could not. Nevertheless, he was not content to sit back and wait for the current unsatisfactory state of the world to collapse under its own contradictions. Instead, he offered a number of ways that modern economies could and should shift direction—the point is to change it! In aspiring thus, he effectively argued against his often repeated claim that "the enemy of myth is circumstance" not ideas, however subversive. In effect, he was subscribing to Keynes's assertion that the ideas of economists and political philosophers are more powerful than is commonly understood.

The trajectory that the US and like societies was tracking rested on the unchallenged belief that production, especially the private production of goods and services, was an open-ended and self-validating process of meeting the limitless wants and needs of consumers. The likely consequences of remaining in thrall to the tyranny of production he graphically described. They involve, in essence, a mindless enslavement to consuming a stream of goods and services of declining marginal importance to the lives of an increasing proportion of the population. At the aggregate level of the economy, the road currently traveled promises increasing insecurity associated with mounting debt, an imbalance between the public and private sectors of truly impressive proportions, and an endemic tendency to inflation. How might we take, instead, the road less traveled, a pathway to a future where the threats of unemployment, civic impoverishment, and self-defeating striving give way to a more civilized environment in which the basic needs and modest wants of all are routinely met and resources are still left over to cultivate the higher, even spiritual, ambitions of human kind? This alternative pathway is implicit in *AS* but echoes visions explicitly promoted in earlier times by John Stuart Mill, Keynes, and even Marx in his cryptic comments on life under communism crow-barred into a stinging rebuke of German socialists as they formed the Social Democratic Party.

Galbraith points to both a necessary condition for freeing ourselves from the thralldom of production and the barriers, psychological and political, to realizing that freedom. To move towards a saner world characterized by balanced production and consumption, people, including politicians, will need to radically alter their attitudes from a mindset immured in the past. In times past, scarcity in the realm of material want mandated a dominant concern for the efficient allocation of available resources. On that point, economists, policy makers, and the ordinary citizen agreed, and the conventional wisdom decreed. Although scarcity in that sense has receded, the attitudes and beliefs that it inculcated over the millennia have survived like relics from an earlier age. Economic archeologists of the future must scrape away the remnant detritus obscuring an accurate picture of life as it was in order to better understand life as it now is. "What was sound economic behavior before may not be sound economic behavior now. What were the goals of individuals, organizations and, perhaps more especially, of governments before may not be so now." However, the mind recoils from the necessary mental effort and anguish. It is far easier to fall back on long treasured beliefs, a natural tendency enthusiastically endorsed by those with a vested interest in maintaining the benefits they derive from business-as-usual. To call for change is unsettling and seen as dangerous, even "feckless." Galbraith compares the difficulties of changing views and behavior in the affluent society to those facing Keynes twenty-five years earlier in trying to convince policy makers and his economist colleagues of the need for government to intervene by investing heavily in infrastructure during the depths of the Depression.

II

The stakes are high. If the conventional wisdom prevails and the urgency of production upheld, public policy will remain locked within its current cell. In particular, the stalemate surrounding taxation will prevail unchallenged. If a tax or levy is proposed to fund an urgent increase in basic public services, it can be blocked by the familiar cry that such measures would reduce efficiency in the allocation of resources to their highest and best use. If, however, it is widely accepted that the private production forgone is of limited value, then what economists call "the opportunity cost" of public provision falls towards zero. The problem for reformers pushing along this poorly traversed track is that there are only crude techniques for establishing the relative value to consumers of public and private goods. The latter present little trouble, since what consumers are willing to pay in the market provides the benchmark. In the case of non-marketed public services, the tools of cost–benefit analysis can be utilized to estimate what consumers would be willing to pay but the calculations are fraught and contested. Many of the benefits and costs elude even the most diligent analyst and tend to effectively be zero valued by relegating them to the vague category of "intangibles."

The choice of the rate at which to discount future costs and benefits also encounters sharp controversy. To cap it all, the measure of efficiency implicit in the resulting cost–benefit ratio is distributionally weighted in favor of higher income consumers, since a dollar of benefit (or cost) is assumed to be the same for the rich and the poor; a benefit of $100 to a rich man is held to reflect an efficient outcome even if it also results in $10 losses to nine poor people, since the winner could hypothetically fully compensate the losers and still have $10 left. If the losers live in another country, the issue of cross-border impacts must be dealt with. Discounting future net returns effectively disenfranchises future generations, a thorny problem in the case of macro-environmental concerns like climate change and ocean pollution. Various techniques can be used to tweak the calculation but there is no agreed basis on how the tweaks are to be administered. Alternatively, we may simply recognize the presence of incommensurable effects and seek to explicitly trade-off efficiency as conventionally defined and equity impacts across populations. Either way, in the morass of competing values advanced, the focus of the exercise—justifying an adequate supply of public services—is easily lost and practical policy tends to recede into comfortable channels, accepting whatever the market delivers (and ignores). The political cost of relying on the market, buttressed by the conventional wisdom's sanctification of efficiency, is much lower than that engendered by stirring up the opposition of powerful interests to contested programs of public provision. "It is so much simpler than to substitute the other tests—compassion, individual happiness and well-being—which now become relevant."

Galbraith diverts in order to subject the concept of economic efficiency to further insult. The modern corporation, he notes, has received a bad reputation, not always deserved. Large scale allows longer term planning, significant research and development, and a capacity for innovation not open to smaller enterprises busy surviving in a competitive scrum. This argument is similar to that offered by his Harvard colleague, Joseph Schumpeter, and is a theme running throughout Galbraith's long career, most famously aired in his later (1967) book, *The New Industrial State*. He notes further that if efficiency was the overriding goal of public policy, governments should do all in their power to facilitate the free migration of workers between countries and regions and not just rely on free trade and capital mobility. In fact, as we have earlier stated, no popularly elected government would countenance such a policy. Familial and community ties lock people into their local milieux, while darker and deep currents of distrust of newcomers, expressing varying degrees of xenophobia, prevent an open-door immigration policy. Considerations of maximizing efficiency have in the recent past also condemned coal miners to an early, sometimes accidental, death. The conventional wisdom has slowly evolved on the matter of industrial work health and safety with efficiency cost consequences.

If and as the urgency of private production recedes in the public mind, the cry of inefficiency that effectively blocked many economically and socially productive developments will also disappear. Not only will debates over tax policy assume a more rational character, but issues such as health and safety, science and education policy, environmental conservation, and tariff protection will surface from their underworld to demand attention by government, industry, trade unions, and community. "Why should life be intolerable to make things of small urgency?" The grip of scarcity on the mind of the average American is hard to shake precisely because it is buried deep in the national character. This question is, at base, a moral one, a point we return to in Chapter 13.

III

The final defense of the supremacy of production mounted by the conventional wisdom pertains to the link with economic security previously discussed. Maximizing growth and minimizing the downtime of the economy ensures high and rising employment. This is important because only through gainful employment will most adults secure sufficient income to survive in a market society and provide adequate tax revenues for government to ensure a minimum support for those who are not employed. "The income men derive from producing things of slight consequence is of great consequence to them." This truth is revealed in times of economic crisis when the cost is reckoned not in terms of lost output but of lost jobs. Politicians and pundits eagerly devour the latest employment figures as a barometer of the success or failure of policy. "It's the economy, stupid" is more accurately conveyed as "it's the job rate, idiot." In affluent times, the importance of maximizing employment—more precisely, minimizing involuntary unemployment—is reinforced, because unemployment is all the more anomalous; "(s)uch discrimination seems altogether too flagrant."

The solution to stepping off the squirrel wheel cannot be to let the wheel turn more slowly since mass unemployment is hardly a sensible way to even up living standards. Some way must be found to cut the tie between production and income. People must have an alternative manner of deriving at least a basic income that does not depend on permanent full-time employment, especially as overshooting full employment threatens runaway inflation, reducing the living standards of everyone on fixed incomes. One solution would be to build on the system of unemployment compensation. However, as normally constituted, "the dole" was never intended to be a permanent device for supporting people. It is generally time-limited and set at levels much lower than full-time average earnings. These restrictions have always been judged necessary to preserve the incentive to work for a living. Why put oneself to the inconvenience of regularly showing up to work, particularly at onerous, boring, or dangerous jobs, if one can sit back at home and continue to receive the regular check from Social Security? "The tendency to think of idleness as 'a species of fraud upon the community' is not peculiar to the upper income classes, for whom, indeed, it is often considered quite tolerable." No doubt, Galbraith suggests, there will always be idleness and malingering among an unreformed minority but most people do not require minimum support while unemployed to jump at the first opportunity of a job. People could be guaranteed a basic income substantially higher than current unemployment compensation without destroying the will to work. The received opinion to the contrary is grounded in both an Old Testament view of human nature and a continued commitment to wringing every last ounce of energy out of available resources, human as well as inanimate.

If production loses its urgency, then what previously passed for anti-social malingering may as easily be the result of rational choice—"rational" in the broad sense. In this changed world, being without a job would lose the social stigma currently attached to that state. This suggests a "chicken-and-egg" conundrum. We revere production because it provides us with income and freedom from social condemnation; we receive income and self-respect by being productively employed. How can the link between production (employment) and income be severed? Galbraith suggests that the first action is to cut the knot by raising unemployment compensation closer to average earnings, thereby diminishing the inflationary pressures of full employment and undermining the stigma associated with unemployment. Second, he proposes that alternative sources of income be provided to those who can't or shouldn't work—the disabled, infirm, elderly, the uneducated, and unskilled. Many but not all of those falling into this diverse category can be assisted through suitable health, education, and training programs to develop the skills in excess demand in the economy. This has the doubly beneficial effect of improving the life chances of the newly employable and easing the skill bottlenecks that drive inflation. If the increasing productivity gains can be partly diverted from the increased production of increasingly useless goods to righting the social imbalances, further gains are forthcoming at the individual and economy-wide levels.

Galbraith notes in a later edition of his book that he originally had in mind a version of what came to be called a guaranteed minimum income scheme or negative income tax (a policy also favored by Milton Friedman); but at the time he published the original version he thought such ideas were not "within the realm of practical political feasibility." His judgment was sound. Guaranteed income approaches have only very recently been canvassed seriously in a few countries, tried in modest form in even fewer, and remained noticeably absent from his own country.

IV

A critical challenge to business-as-usual is, as we have seen, posed by the growing social imbalance between the private and public sectors. Redressing the balance becomes a matter of urgency in the affluent society. The conjunction of private affluence and public squalor threatens the functional success of the private sector—that is, appropriate and adequate public services are necessary, if nothing else, to support private production and to lessen the vulnerability of the economy to recurrent recession—as well as the social peace of the nation. Having first pointed to the challenge of overcoming vested interests in support of traditional views and values, Galbraith now reverts to a stress on the "technical" factors biasing production towards the private sector: "... to a far greater degree than is commonly supposed, functions accrue to the state because, as a purely technical matter, there is no alternative to public management."

He reiterates a point made earlier. Those goods and services that can be sold at a price will gravitate to the private sector, leaving the state to provide the rest. This oversimplifies the division of labor, even in Galbraith's time when many fee-charging public services, from mass transit and public housing to child-care centers and power utilities, were operated by government agencies. In part, government operation made up for inadequate private supply, either because the service proved too profitable (as in the case of natural monopolies) or too unprofitable, for example, with respect to affordable rental housing. Although genuine public goods like defense and clean air would only be provided if governments took the lead, most goods and services could to some degree be marketed, so undermining Galbraith's focus on this factor. Education can and is privately provided, from kindergarten to doctoral level. Private police (security) services are legion. A few years after publication of *AS*, Chicago University economist Ronald Coase demonstrated that polluted air and water could, in theory, be handled by markets when property rights in these scarce resources were clearly demarcated and enforced.

Ignoring this diversion, Galbraith's main argument is that for the other reasons noted above, proponents of public services must engage in strenuous acts of persuasion in order to get their priorities met, as opposed to the routine delivery of unnecessary goods though the market. To even the balance—of investment and provision—governments must introduce a system "... which automatically makes a pro rata share of increasing income available to public authorities for public purposes." This amounts to a plea for a collective hypothecation of tax revenues to the provision of a set of designated government services. The federal government offers the best prospect for instituting such a regime since their major revenue sources like the income tax tend to grow more quickly than the economy as a whole. Unfortunately, as the US perfects its role as the world's policeman, defense swallows a large and growing share of federal revenues, limiting the scope for domestic social and economic hypothecation in the form he favors. Given this constraint, government must find other ways to raise the necessary revenue. Two avenues suggest themselves. First, government can wind back the complicated web of deductions and allowances enjoyed by wealthier taxpayers—that is, loopholes in the income tax can be closed. Second, indirect taxes must be levied on a large range of goods, perhaps all, in order to broaden the tax base. An expenditure tax of some kind is required, requiring state and local government to join the fray. This tax has the dual advantage of automatically swelling government coffers as the economy expands, while also making privately produced goods on which it is levied more expensive and less attractive to consumers. "We pay more for soap, detergents, and vacuum cleaners in order that we may have cleaner cities and less occasion to use them." A consumption or sales tax cast widely would allow state and local governments to wind back other taxes and charges that raise insufficient revenues and make no direct contribution to improving social balance. The ubiquitous property tax, for example, is a blunt instrument, inflexible, lags changing property values and highly discriminatory. By matching tax take and spend to property values, public services are gold-plated in wealthy neighborhoods and poorly provided in poor areas.

Conservatives are bound to oppose the former approach, while calling for still more concessions. Liberals will oppose the latter, since—as we saw in Chapter 10—it forces the poor to pay more, proportionately speaking. Galbraith counters the retort that indirect taxes hit the poor too hard by arguing that in a rich country many of the items taxed are of no real urgency to most consumers and that any problems of poverty should be directly attacked by governments armed with adequate resources to allocate. Improving social balance will, of itself, be progressive in its impacts. The only hope for advance on this front for Galbraith will come if liberals jettison both their traditional opposition to tax increases and their support of tax cuts that include lower income people in the list of those benefiting. Even though this will break the truce on inequality, it must be done in the interests of restoring balance.

> The rational liberal, in the future, will resist tax reduction, even that which ostensibly favors the poor, if it is at the price of social balance. And, for the same reason, he will not hesitate to accept increases that are neutral as regards the distribution of income.

Galbraith is harsh in his judgment of his fellow liberals. "The American liberal has been, all things considered, the opponent of better schools, better communities, better urban communications, and indeed even greater economic security." They are invited to indulge their egalitarian scruples by flushing out the multitudinous perks and loopholes of the well-to-do. "There is work enough here for any egalitarian crusader."

Galbraith's campaign in support of indirect taxes on consumption goods is radical. He allows no exemptions. "In the affluent society no useful distinction can be made between luxuries and necessities." Food differs not from fripperies in this respect. All are fodder for the taxman. In essence, he is claiming equal time for social balance. Improving balance must itself be in balance with the generally accepted economic goals of economic stability and fair distribution. Even if indirect taxes necessary to lift the share of public investment in public services undercut, to a degree, the pursuit of stability and equity, this is a trade-off worth pursuing. Moreover, if properly managed, the trade-off need not be extreme. Consumption taxes on synthesized wants divert consumption onto more stable paths that will include a range of public services the demand for which will not fluctuate with animal spirits in the economy. Similarly, with respect to improving equity, providing better health and education services to the disadvantaged is likely to lift their incomes and life chances over the long term. Finally, investing in human capital will support the accumulation of material capital, both together increasing the sustainable rate at which the economy can grow, again lifting livings standards over time.

Galbraith notes that liberals—wedded to Keynesian principles—will find it difficult to lessen their reliance on the income tax and embrace the sales tax (though, interestingly, one of Keynes's most illustrious followers, Nicholas Kaldor, was an early champion of a broad-based expenditure tax). But, Galbraith suggests, Keynes did not foresee that widespread acceptance of his ideas would eventually require a shift in emphasis from ensuring adequate aggregate demand driving total output—which ensures a fully employed workforce—to a more nuanced concern for its composition. Had Keynes faced the new world of affluence, glimpsed in his essay, "Economic Possibilities for our Grandchildren", he would have appreciated the point. Too many of his heirs cling onto the letter of the message, "black ink Keynesians," captives of the focus on aggregate demand and output. "Such is the fate of anyone who becomes part of the conventional wisdom"; Galbraith implicitly excludes himself from such company, content to assume the role of lone ranger, an outsider roaming the countryside and taking shots at the bad guys.

There is a final advantage of the sales tax for addressing issues of social balance. Conservatives support it. Indeed, they agitate for it. They bless it. Properly instructed liberals can join forces with conservatives and push through new taxes in this direction. "As a political point this is not negligible." But that it might it be a mixed blessing seemingly eludes Galbraith, so keen is he to buttress his argument. Conservative support for indirect taxes is usually joined, as if welded together, with a demand for compensating reductions in direct taxes, especially those impacting on the wealthy. Perhaps Galbraith is uncomfortable about this particular arrow in his armory, since he tacks it on almost as an afterthought at the end of his chapter.

The concept of "balance" implies a certain precision in observation. At the very least we need to know when something is *not* in balance, or when it is "close enough." The problem with social balance is that there is no unambiguous way of identifying when the economy is "balanced enough." Galbraith freely admits that there is no definitive test, partly because of "...the cardinal error of comparing satisfaction of wants that are synthesized with those that are not." But, he claims, this is not important. An affluent society has a wide margin of error in such matters. Once it is plain to all but the most ideologically blinkered opponent of government provision that serious imbalances exist and are getting worse, then *any* move towards improving public services will be applauded.

> This being so, the direction in which we move to correct matters is utterly plain....When we arrive, the opulence of our private consumption will no longer be in contrast with the poverty of our schools, the unloveliness and congestion of our cities, our inability to get to work without struggle, and the social disorder that is associated with imbalance. But the precise point of balance will never be defined.

V

What are we to make today of Galbraith's attempts to switch tracks, to push citizen and government to reduce their unthinking reliance on production at all costs? An obvious response would be to say that his "destructive criticism," making up the bulk of the book, has fared much better than his constructive contribution. This he would, I think, readily but ruefully accept. After all, he did hold that the former was the more important exercise, both because it comes first in the natural order of argument and it is more likely to weaken the grip of the conventional wisdom on the popular conceptions of people and their governments, assuming that objective conditions in economy and society are suitably present.

It is clear that most of the negative externalities and infelicities of modern life highlighted in *AS* are still with us, many enhanced by developments during the intervening decades. Galbraith himself was clear about this in the foreword to his 1998 edition. Above all, environmental problems demand ever more urgent attention. Some, such as localized air and water pollution—what we might call "micro-environmental" problems—are being addressed with varying degrees of success at local and national levels. But other large macro-environmental problems are much less amenable to effective policy. It is true that concerted international cooperation and strong government regulation leading to the phasing out of chlorofluorocarbons resulted in stabilizing and eventually reversing the hole in the ozone layer of earth's atmosphere. Conversely, limited outcomes from the Kyoto Protocol and the collapse of the Copenhagen Climate Change Conference, 2009, have effectively stalled successful global cooperation in the effort to tackle the many risks identified. The politics of climate change has introduced novel factors and forces, creating new coalitions, both for and against. As part of the new environmental politics, green political interest groups like Greenpeace and organized political parties are emerging across the world. Non-government organizations (NGOs) are assuming a greater political role at national and international levels.

The social imbalance resulting in chronic undersupply of public services has not been improved. The policy directions Galbraith identified have not paid dividends in this respect. Indeed, as we have seen, the attack on the public sector has been concerted and successful, leading to a tendency to chronic budget deficits—as Galbraith had foreseen—and deteriorating public infrastructure in the United States and a number of other western nations. The power of wealthy individual and corporate interests has increased, focused on reducing taxes and regulations that encroach on those interests. An important tactic in shrinking the role and resources of the state has been to force expenditure cuts; by refusing to maintain public expenditure, even in basic areas like health and education, governments dominated by conservatives can justify tax cuts—since the revenue isn't needed. By packaging the cuts carefully, the benefits can be presented as flowing widely to all, while actually being biased heavily to favor their supporters. This is precisely the reverse of Galbraith's proposed political approach in which increasing tax revenues would fund improved public services. The ideology of the central tradition has maintained its grip

on public policy and the public mind. The "transition" of the affluent society
that Galbraith hoped for has never eventuated.

Galbraith himself was one of the most politically active economists of his
era. His early experiences in Washington as a minor player in the New Deal,
his later wartime experiences in the Office of Price Administration, and, above
all, the decade of the 1950s and 1960s advising first Adlai Stevenson and then
Presidents John F. Kennedy and Lyndon Johnson gave him an abiding grasp
of the intricacies of American politics. He was an insider but with a foot in
the wider world of academia and the popular media, a public intellectual of
the first rank who could move between Washington and the wider world. He
was both an habitué of the Capital and a stern critic of what went down there.
In the end he lost political influence in Washington as the Democratic Party
became enmeshed in the bog of war in Vietnam and the country began its long
trek to Republican Administrations. By the 1970s, he had also become marginalized within the economics profession; his presidency of the American
Economics Association a belated ceremonial honor heralding his effective
expulsion from the club. Only through his writings could he continue to reach
a wider audience.

* * *

The next two chapters attempt to explore his political and ethical positions,
which are, admittedly, only hinted at in *AS*. With this aim in mind, I therefore
draw in a limited way on some of his other writings. I am aware that this steps
outside the brief outlined in the introductory chapter and entails a certain
license or liberty-taking on my part. However, I suspect that Galbraith would
have understood if not approved. He, after all, confessed—in the acknowledge-
ments section to his small book of essays called *The Liberal Hour*, published
in 1960, soon after *AS*—that he had taken to heart the publisher's invitation to
revise the original lectures on which the book was based; "...in the matter of
revision I have gone from opportunity to license." Nor should we forget that
originally Galbraith accepted funding from a foundation to write a book on
poverty, not affluence.

12

The Idea of Power

For some forty years, more years than I like to think, I have been involved with the subject of power—with the ideas and, in some degree, the practice.

(J.K. Galbraith)

* * *

Galbraith's direct political involvement during the early and middle years of his career made him acutely aware of the influence government has on the real world economy. This consciousness reinforced the experiences of growing up in a remote farming community in Ontario before and during the First World War. Governments had power over how markets did their job. They were not merely the boundary-setting institutions of orthodox economics, best marked by their unobtrusiveness. Governments had important economic roles to play beyond the traditional areas of defense, customs, and communications. It was clear to Galbraith very early in his career that the economy was an important arena of power and influence.

This was no more evident than in his chosen field of agricultural economics. Agriculture, well into the twentieth century, made up a significant part of the American economy. Farming and the industries linked to it absorbed a large share of the nation's workforce. Agricultural industries, based in villages, service towns, and large cities suffered in the extreme from fluctuations in market conditions, caused by the vagaries of the weather, diseases, herd behavior, and consumer tastes. Although—perhaps because—they met the textbook conditions for competitive industries, their experiences of uncertainty and volatility made farmers, farm laborers, and associated small businesses peculiarly open to calls for government intervention and assistance. Politicians at all levels vied to meet their demands. In part, this reflected widely held views as to the supposedly superior virtues of simple rural life and character, a view embedded in the folk history of the nation, stretching back to its founders. This image was contrasted with the supposed evils of the big city, where significant numbers of recent arrivals were migrants from rural areas of Europe.

The very independence of America had been fought and won by rough and honest farm folk invoking their God-given rights to life, liberty, and the pursuit of happiness. Having invented the federal government, it was understandable that their heirs would feel justified in calling on Washington's help when times demanded.

Like Mr. Smith, Galbraith went to Washington in the 1930s. He first did so from his base at Harvard where he had been employed as one of Professor John Black's stable of bright young assistants. Black was the doyen of American agricultural economics who had talent spotted Galbraith while the latter was still undertaking his doctoral studies at Berkeley. (Galbraith's PhD topic strayed somewhat from the agricultural furrow, indicating an early fascination with public finances.) Under Black's supervision Galbraith completed a number of research projects on matters to do with New Deal farm policy, giving him a close-up view of how the Roosevelt Administration was trying to deal with the devastating impacts of the Depression on that sector of the economy. Agricultural assistance was the major focus of the New Deal, especially during its early phase, meaning that Galbraith was given a front-row seat at the economic policy show of the century. Although he was already in the process of leaving agricultural economics behind, these early experiences must have permanently inoculated him against the impoverished conception of government's economic role as enshrined by the central tradition.

II

From his earliest days Galbraith focused on how markets actually worked, how producers and consumers actually behaved—and why. He was, at base, concerned with *microeconomics*, but within a framework informed by behavioral and institutional factors. He accepted much of the new Keynesian economics but, as we have seen, was prevented from embracing the neoclassical synthesis and its "hydraulic" conception of macroeconomic policy. In effect, Galbraith—as in so many areas—anticipated the later debate over the correct "micro-foundations" of Keynesianism. Power was an inherent feature of the market. Some agents had more and some less. Large corporations were able to build market power, to influence demand for their products, see off competitors, and bend public policy to their purpose. Countervailing loci of power evolved in the rise of trade unions, environmental groups, and consumer organizations. Advertising and want creation biased effective power in the allocation of resources and distribution of incomes in favor of particular well placed and organized groups.

This power-centered view of the economy is apparent in Galbraith's earliest papers on marketing and market structure. His biographer Richard Parker

(2005: 60) commented: "(t)hroughout his major works, Galbraith again and again returned to this central issue of economic structure—of real world relations in tension with, even in opposition to, the blackboard models of economists." Parker suggests that Galbraith's recognition of the importance of power in economics came from his personal exposure to the way that politics, economics, and policy "collided" as Roosevelt unleashed his New Deal. The experiments in agricultural development, into which Galbraith was pitched, highlighted the extremes of market power between large landholders and farming corporations on the one hand and farm laborers and sharecroppers, on the other. The latter were comprehensively done over by a Congress coming down heavily in favor of the former, resulting in the forced exodus of prominent liberals in the Roosevelt Administration. "Galbraith never forgot the battle over the Southern tenants and sharecroppers. Hereafter, power—a concept so uncomfortable to conventional economists because it disrupts the very workings of economic theory—was a central and defining idea for him" (Parker, 2005: 67).

The 1930s was a fertile period for economics. Not only was Keynes working to reconstruct the way governments should intervene in the economy, new theories of imperfect competition and the role of increasing returns to scale were filtering through to the academy. To this literature Galbraith was keenly drawn. *The Modern Corporation and Private Property* (1932), a book written by a lawyer and an economist, had an earlier and more immediate impact on debate and policy. Its authors, Adolph Berle and Gardiner Means, argued that large corporations were increasingly concentrating economic power in a way that, centuries earlier, the church had achieved a monopoly of religious power. The key feature of this structural revolution was the appropriation of power *within* the corporation by its senior mangers. Shareholders were increasingly irrelevant to the decisions taken by the managers; the former were increasingly merely the recipients of the dividends that managers deigned to hand over, they were mere "coupon clippers" (in Marx's words), little different from a corporation's bondholders—in fact worse off, because they stood behind the latter in line for payment. This influential book pointed Galbraith further towards recognizing the new institutional terrain on which modern capitalist economies were tracking.

The fruit of these early insights were not fully realized until thirty years later, though as noted earlier, the bones of this approach were evident in AS. In *The New Industrial State* (1967), Galbraith further developed the idea, introduced in his earlier work, of a radical bifurcation of the US economy into two sectors. The first, to repeat, comprised the myriad small and medium-sized firms in industries such as construction, retail, and consumer services of all kinds reacting to institutional parameters and market signals beyond their control; this sector, "the market system," is made up in number by the vast majority of producers in the economy. The other sector he called "the planning system," comprising the several hundred large corporations operated under market conditions of monopoly or oligopoly. With the increasing separation of ownership and control, and the subordination of the owners to the increasingly specialized managerial class, the planning system rose to an influence well beyond the immediate scope of operations of its members.

Defining power as "the ability of persons or institutions to bend others to their purposes," Galbraith identified the various ways that managers achieve their purposes. The imperatives of corporate success entail an ability to reduce uncertainty by exerting control over all areas of corporate activity. Managers and technical experts—forming what he called "the Technostructure"—thus seek to ensure future prices for and costs of their products in order to reliably calculate expected profits and growth. Strategic actions here include the carefully orchestrated efforts of salesmanship and persuasion leading to the dependence effect identified in *AS*, backward vertical integration or long-term contracting to tie up the supply of key inputs, generation of retained profits to free the corporation from the constraints and vagaries of the capital market, and the concerted effort to influence government policies favorable to their interests.

A crucial development has been the symbiotic development of corporate and public bureaucracies. Leading firms producing weapons and other defense material have become intertwined with military and civilian leaders in the Pentagon and Department of Defense, causing them to cooperate to ensure that the budget for military and defense purposes continues to grow. The material and status interests of each group depend on this. Other mutual assistance pacts characterize areas such as education, health, and highway construction. In his 1973 Presidential Address to the American Economic Association (AEA) (titled *Power and the Useful Economist*), Galbraith commented:

> It requires an organization to deal with an organization, and between public and private bureaucracies—between General Dynamics and the Pentagon, General Motors and the Department of Transport—there is a deeply symbiotic relationship. Each of the organizations can do much for the other.

He goes on to note the entrenched pathways between corporation and government, trodden back and forth by the senior leaders of each; the progress of Robert McNamara from President of Ford Motors to Secretary of Defense was apparent to Galbraith when he also trod the lawns and colonnade of the White House. The power of members of the Technostructure is also manifest in their ability to limit the market pressure to maximize profits. This room for maneuver stems from their power over or relative independence from the shareholders, first stressed by Berle and Means. It enables managers to orient the goals and actions of the corporation to enhance the rewards flowing to themselves, always supposing that they continue to deliver the minimally acceptable returns to the shareholders.

Within that constraint, they are free to pursue their own interests, which Galbraith argues are intimately connected to maximizing the growth of the corporation.

> The stockholders in the large corporation are aroused, if at all, only by inadequate earnings. And profits are important because they bring the supply of capital within the control of the firm. But of greater importance is the more directly political goal of growth.

Growth rewards managers handsomely and by expanding the public scale and scope of their operations enhances their status and capacity to comment on and influence public debate over policy. Control of the growing corporation builds public profile and authority. Galbraith was here responding to the merger and takeover boom during the 1960s that gave rise to the phenomenon of the corporate conglomerate. Growth was sought through broad diversification across industries as well as through vertical and horizontal integration along traditional lines. He was not to know that the next few decades were spent disarticulating the consortia formed as recessionary shocks forced the firms that survived to focus on their core businesses.

Unsurprisingly, he argues that governments came to "bend" fiscal and monetary policy to suit the interests of the Technostructure. The use of monetary policy—impinging least on large corporations able to rely on internal financing—became the preferred tool of macroeconomic policy, ensuring that the costs of slowing an overheated economy would be visited on firms and debtors outside the planning system. Increasingly, the imposition of fiscal cures for the inflationary pressures that characterized the US and other economies in the 1970s called for more and more extreme cuts in government expenditure, cuts that the corporate sector could generally deflect to areas of little significance to itself, while encouraging continuing expenditure in areas like defense, highways, research and development, and communications that did matter to it. Galbraith attacked head on what he called the three legs of the tripod on which orthodox economics stood—consumer sovereignty, profit maximization, and subordination of the firm to the market.

> When the modern corporation acquires power over markets, power in the community, power over the state and power over belief, it is a political instrument, different in form and degree but not in kind to the state itself. To hold otherwise—to deny the political character of the modern corporation—is not merely to avoid the reality. It is to disguise the reality. The victims of that disguise are the students we instruct in error.

Inequalities in wealth and income are reinforced by the operation of the dual economy. Managers and workers in the market system are unable to organize to effectively protect themselves from the naturally unequalizing effects of capitalist development. Small producers cannot easily pass on cost increases;

their workers must accept what their employers can afford to pay under whatever market conditions prevail. Neither can influence government policies on the big issues of taxes and public expenditure. The democratic political system is too blunt an instrument and too compliant with the demands of powerful interests, within and without the corporate sector. The power emanating from the planning system thus undercuts the social settlement on inequality that Galbraith in AS believed had been achieved, just as a proper appreciation of the capacity of the large corporation to absorb wage and other cost rises enables inflation and significant unemployment to coexist.

The development of his ideas on the modern corporation also allowed Galbraith to refine his theory of social balance, bringing out nuances only broadly hinted at in AS. When looked at through the lens of his later work, social imbalance assumes a two-fold character. First, the coexistence of private affluence and public squalor follows from the forces identified in that book. But, second, public provision is itself unbalanced or biased towards those services of most value to large corporations. Chronic under-provision bedevils employers in the market system and poorer communities who suffer the double disadvantage of poor access to private affluence and ready experience of public squalor. Galbraith argues that the growing institutionalized power of the large corporation oriented to growth at all costs necessarily comes into conflict with the general interest of all citizens in maintaining their environmental quality. Where environmental regulations are imposed, their strength can be weakened by corporate lobbying, the regulatory apparatus created to enforce regulations subverted by budget cuts and bureaucratic capture and the more damaging threats to corporate growth and welfare kept off political agendas entirely.*

Having stressed the uneven distribution and application of power in the economy, resulting in the effective subordination of the state to the planning system, Galbraith points to the anomalous situation, that is, all the matters that he wishes to put right—improved social balance, greater economic security, less worrying inflation—are dependent on appropriate state actions. "This is perhaps the greatest question of social policy in our time: is the emancipation of the state from the control of the planning system possible?" Galbraith waxed and waned in answer to this question. In his early days as an active political player—he was, for example, one of the group that started Americans for Democratic Action soon after the Second World War and long hoped to see the Democratic Party move more to the liberal end of

---

* Matthew Crenson's (1972) path-breaking book on "non-decisionmaking," *The Unpolitics of Air Pollution*, was published a few years after *The New Industrial State* and detailed the manner in which the reputed power of US Steel prevented the city government of Gary, Indiana from addressing the problem of polluted air in this steel city.

the political spectrum—he clearly had high hopes for the progressive role of democratic politics.

As he aged and reduced his direct political activities and reflected more on the prospects of liberalism in America, he seemed to become more pessimistic. By the early 1980s he was beginning to answer to being a "socialist." However, he never gave up hope for the creation of a "sensible economics," to use the term suggested by the Cambridge School economist, Geoffrey Harcourt. This commitment was expressed through his ceaseless writings, media stardom, public presentations, and by less visible means, such as his involvement in establishing the *Journal of Post-Keynesian Economics*, the editorial board of which he served as Honorary Chairman from its inception until his death. He also never forgave his orthodox colleagues for pulling the wool over our eyes. The final words of his AEA Presidential Address were unambiguous on the subject. "If the state is the executive committee of the great corporation and the planning system, it is partly because neoclassical economics is its instrument for neutralizing the suspicion that this is so."

III

Galbraith returned to the theme of power in the early 1980s, gathering his earlier thoughts scattered throughout his writings in order to subject the matter to intensive scrutiny. A brief book—*The Anatomy of Power* (1983)—was the result. In it he sought to identify the sources and instruments of power throughout history, a characteristically modest Galbraithian project. "The instruments by which power is exercised and the sources of the right to such exercise are interrelated in complex fashion." His attempt to disentangle the complexities produced "the rule of three"; there are three ways of exercising power and three sources for its exercise. However, there is no simple one-to-one correspondence between instrument and source. In any real world situation power can be expressed through a mix of instruments deriving from a combination of sources.

Taking the instruments first, he distinguished condign, compensatory, and conditioned forms of power. *Condign power* is present when one party causes another to submit to its will by imposing or threatening negative sanctions in the absence of compliance. A powerful actor might impose physical or pecuniary harm on the party whose compliance is required; the mere threat or likelihood of such may be sufficient to be effective. A key condition for the exercise of condign power is that the submissive party would have acted otherwise but for the presence of the coercive force. In that sense, the submissive party's actions—or lack of action if quiescence is required—are "bent" away from their natural destination in ways desired by the powerful. Galbraith gives as a classic example the relation between master and slave.[†] Similarly, one can see this relationship embedded in the social functioning of the medieval guild and the capitalist wage relation. However, as these last examples suggest, other aspects of power are also involved. The wage relation clearly entails the ability of the employer to sack the worker, to impose a negative sanction in the case of non-performance, as judged by the employer; but it also involves a degree of mutual interest in cooperating to produce and sell the product.

The second category is *compensatory power*, being broadly speaking the opposite of condign power. It involves the granting of a positive reward to another in return for that party's submission to the will and interests of the powerful. The reward can be anything valued by the submissive party; in capitalist societies it is most often a pecuniary payment. In both cases submission of one party to another is induced by offering or threatening a reward or punishment, in order to change behavior. The key feature of both instruments is that the party submitting *knows* they are doing so and *why* they are doing so. Power expressed in both its condign and compensatory forms derives its potency from the "objective" manner in which it is expressed. We thus talk about "naked power" when the parties concerned and observers, alike, are under no illusion about what is happening. Such power can also be imposed in more subtle ways, invisible to all but the principal parties. What looks to outside observers as a case of joint agreement and mutual interest may yet, to the actors involved, be clearly recognized as a matter of dominance seeking submission. Indeed, part of the successful imposition of power in these first two forms, resides in the ability of the powerful party to pass off the results of their actions as being in complete harmony with the interests and preferences of the powerless. Only the latter are the wiser!

This leads to the third form of power—*conditioned power*. In contrast to the other ways of imposing one's will, the wielder of conditioned power achieves submission of others by influencing the latter's beliefs, values, or perceptions of what is right, natural, proper, and/or in their interests. There is no awareness that one is or could be acting against one's interest in order to promote the interests of another party. "(t)he submission reflects the preferred course; the fact of submission is not recognized." There is implicit in this form of power the likelihood that if the submissive party *was* aware, then they would act otherwise, and not submit; at least, that would be the preferred path. Of course, even if the scales fell from the eyes, the actions of the submissive may not change, since conditioned power failing, the dominant party may switch to

---

[†] In the air pollution case, the implied threat that US Steel could close or scale down its operations in Gary "encouraged" the city's government to avoid addressing the issue until eventually forced by federal legislation.

other instruments by which to achieve compliance. All parties would then be aware that condign or compensatory mechanisms were in play.

It should be clear that Galbraith proposed his three forms of power as "ideal types" in the sense defined by Max Weber—"pure" concepts that each identified a particular dominant feature of social reality. Indeed, Galbraith explicitly borrows Weber's definition of power as his starting point. The utility of ideal types is that they serve as benchmarks against which to compare the complex social phenomena under investigation. In the real world, social actions and relationships will rarely if ever be explicable in terms of a single ideal type. A full understanding will generally require combining elements of several. Thus, in the case of the capitalist wage relation, one can discern elements of all three forms of power. The worker submits to the will and interests of the employer because: first, not to do so risks the sack; second, doing so attracts a pecuniary reward; and third, a fair day's work is the right thing to do in return for a fair day's pay. The worker is conditioned by historical biography to undertake voluntarily the work duties he is allocated. The society in which he has grown up, the influences of his parents, teachers, sporting heroes, politicians, preachers, and significant events in the wider world, have inculcated a set of values and norms that sanctify the act of labor under the wage relation. To willingly work for a wage is the natural thing to do or aspire to. The potency of conditioned power is, Galbraith proclaims, particularly strong in modern societies, both capitalist and socialist.

Galbraith identifies three *sources* of power. *Personality* compels submission through the force of the individual expressing it. In the political sphere, a dominant leader or Führer galvanizes the masses. Such effects can also be wrought on the smaller scale of school assemblies, rotary club meetings, and sewing circles. Other social groupings, such as the family or local sporting club, can be dominated by the forceful character; in the case of the family the leader may be the mother, the father, or a particularly insistent three-year-old. Galbraith's concept of personality compares fairly closely to Weber's ideal type of *charisma*. Power or authority resides in the claimed and accepted superiority of the exceptional individual. Both argue that this source of power was most important in primitive societies, though also far from absent in the modern world. Weber wrote and died not long before the rise of Hitler and Galbraith worked willingly for Roosevelt.

The second source of power is located in the institution of *property*. Wealth and power go together like a horse and carriage, particularly in capitalist societies. Each feeds off the other. Money and fungible assets form the medium of power. The wealthy are able to use money or its withdrawal to impose their will. Power gained can be used to enhance their wealth. One can peruse history and find few if any cases where wealth and power were not conjoined.

The final source of power is *organization*. "It is taken for granted that when the exercise of power is sought or needed, organization is required."

Individual leadership and accumulated wealth, alone, may not be sufficient to guide developments along preferred pathways, unless they are marshaled strategically and imposed systematically. Organized power occurs at all scales in society, from the family to civil society to the political spheres of government, at the local, regional, national, and supra-national levels. Effective organization is usually necessary to successfully condition large-scale acquiescence in capitalist societies like the US. Clearly, Galbraith's focus on organization stretches back to earlier work, most notably in *The New Industrial State* (1967).

Although it is possible to roughly match a dominant instrument of power to each source—condign power with personality, compensatory power with property, and conditioned power with organization—very little light is cast unless it is recognized that complex societies like the United States must be viewed as the arena for power in all its forms, derived from all its sources.

The will to power emanates from both self-interested and altruistic motivations, or more normally from a combination of both. The powerful wish to impose their priorities to enhance their wealth but often also to further their vision of the way things should be for everyone under their sway. "I rule for their benefit." Politicians, in particular, are masters of (self-)deception, convinced that they are acting "in the general interest." Sometimes they are—or at least, honestly think they are. But, drawing on the work of the French philosopher Bernard de Jouvenel, Galbraith sardonically observes that underlying professions of disinterested public service lays another driver—the intrinsic rewards of power itself. To hold and wield power is a pleasure unto itself. Power underpins feelings of self-importance and self-esteem. It plants a marker in history; by "making a difference," an individual gives some meaning to the fleeting moments of time that he or she troubles the scorer. Before individual morality inevitably brings down the curtain, power casts a spotlight on a bravado performance.

Conditioned power plays such a central role in modern democratic capitalist societies, especially as it reaches the level of affluence that interests Galbraith, because the naked pursuit and use of power runs counter to the dominant ideology of citizen equality before the law and the mutual advantage of market exchange. The twin inheritance of ideas passed down from Adam Smith and the Founding Fathers renders illegitimate the unsubtle forms of power ascendant in earlier societies, particularly those organized along military and theocratic lines. Where once church and military organization ruled, the modern corporation and public bureaucracy now prevail. Consequently, immense resources are now committed to molding beliefs and values to support the routine operation of markets and democratic governance. Galbraith's analysis of how this plays out in the affluent society of corporate capitalism is discussed below.

IV

Organization is the crucial crucible of power in modern America. The other sources of property and personality express their impacts through organized forms of behavior. The main institutional means through which organized power is mobilized and applied are—the political party, government bureau, and large corporation. A range of other organizations jostle for position and influence but the dominant ones are the first three named. Each organization compels a degree of submission internally to a common purpose or purposes but allows for varying degrees of conflict between members over what those purposes are. Thus, a military unit requires strict adherence to orders issued from above, while a political party exacts only loose submission to a continually negotiated set of priorities beyond the foundation platform and origin myths. A trade union leans more toward the military model; "solidarity" is much admired in members. Robust competition for influence over the strategic and tactical actions of an organization, within a formal structure of authority, creates a dynamic environment for the exercise of power, one in which dominant personalities and the liberal application of money can have noticeable effect. In terms of unity of aims and behavioral discipline, the corporation and civilian government agency stand somewhere between the military and the party. The large corporation becomes most powerful when a dynamic CEO directs the considerable assets of the firm to influence the political agenda of government legislators and agencies, in particular with respect to the form, timing, and enforcement of laws and regulations that affect the pecuniary interests of the firm. In such circumstances, organization, personality, and property march in time.

Galbraith saw the apotheosis of power in totalitarian government. Nazism, he remarks, was built on iron discipline of the Nazi party, under its supreme leader, exerting its will outward to (eventually) subjugate or abolish all other organizations—army, security apparatus, business, parliament, trade unions, churches, and other political parties. All the instruments of terror, reward, and propaganda were ruthlessly—though less than fully efficiently—deployed. The jack-boot and the mass rally, the victory parade and the concentration camp came to symbolize the regime until it broke up under the external reality of military defeat and the internal weight of its demands on an increasingly demoralized and cynical citizenry. It was the gradual disillusionment that led to the decline of conditioned power—the fervent belief in the Führer's invincibility—as well as the massed condign power of the allies that contributed to eventual defeat. Hence, we here see the importance, in all organizations, of maintaining member morale.

Organization expresses a form of "symmetry." The extent to which an organization achieves its goals—that is, secures the submission of parties external to itself—depends in part on winning submission within.

...the individual submits to the common purposes of the organization, and from this internal exercise of power comes the ability of the organization to impose its will externally. From the one comes the other. This is the invariable feature of all exercise of organized power.

Thus, the corporation that succeeds in influencing governments to minimize its taxes, dispense subsidies, or relax onerous regulations, will generally enjoy a high degree of internal harmony and commitment to the common cause. Conversely, a leaky ship sinks. Nowhere is this more evident than with respect to the modern political party, where the term "leak" has acquired canonical status and is one of the few activities that demands and receives common assent. Power through organization is therefore most ephemeral and "dynamic" in the political party, where the imperatives of internal discipline run up against the manifold ambitions of its members and supporters. That very fact provides plentiful scope for wealth and personality to thrive. The peculiarly torturous path by which Americans choose their president is the obvious case in point. Aided by another important institution, the media, candidates vie through the expression of character and the depth of their pockets to convince electors that they have the answers. An election is a well-worn occasion for the exercise of compensatory power; buying votes has a long track record. Condign power is applied more subtly, in the suggestion that voting for one's opponent will result in heavy, if vaguely sketched, costs to person and country. Overwhelmingly, however, a presidential campaign is the perfect stage for the arts of persuasion, the currency of conditioned power. Voters are bombarded with slogans and messages designed to convince them, at both conscious and subliminal levels, that their fate and that of the world hangs in the balance and can only be secured by voting the "right" (or left) way.

The corporation, as a container of power, must secure the degree of internal coherence necessary to achieve its defining purposes. That, as just noted, requires the submission of employees at all levels to the legitimate authority of senior management. At lower levels, condign punishment and compensatory reward are generally adequate to secure compliance; but in the higher echelons of management conditioned power rules. Senior managers are under most pressure to "toe the company line." It is unthinkable, asserts Galbraith, for the senior executives of a cigarette company to express any reservations as to the health effects of its products. Repeated public expressions to the contrary reinforce a mindset that represses any such negative thoughts. Internal corporate culture, added to the eye for the main chance (compensatory forces at work), lock the executive into a positive commitment to—if not the health-giving qualities of cigarettes—at least a belief in the absence of harm created by their mass consumption. "High salaries are collected for such submission, but it would be wrong to suggest that these are the decisive factor. Belief in the purposes of the organization—conditioned power—is almost certainly more important."

Since conditioned power in organizations assumes an unconscious dimension, those submitting, being unaware of their submission, avoid the pain of subordination. "There are few people who so willingly and completely submit to the power of the organization with so little consciousness of submission as the modern corporate executive. Not being a conscious act, it is not derogatory or painful." A developed capacity to banish cognitive dissonance by melding personal gain and public benefit is the hallmark of the successful executive and politician. Where conditioned power to internally imposed discipline fails, the organization becomes ineffective. The extreme example of the mass political party has been already noted. Galbraith makes a similar point with respect to the great departments of government; internal divisions of opinion and strategy within the State Department, for example, undermine US foreign policy and spark concerted efforts aimed at their suppression. Symmetry also characterizes the internal and external exercise of power. When the organization seeks to condition customers, voters, or the public at large to particular purposes, then internal members will also need to evince a strong commitment to the same aims.

A true believer makes the most effective propagandist, just as a recent convert makes the best proselytizer, or an enthusiastic consumer the best salesman. Emphasis in many organizations is placed on being "a good team player." This means overtly identifying with the organization's ethos and mission. Dissidents are efficiently identified and neutralized by dismissal, demotion, sidelining, or, simply, neglect. It can be noted in passing that the visible existence of a few sidelined mavericks helps to shore up the commitment of the majority, both because of the exemplary example displayed (toe the line or you too will join them) and the cover provided (see how inclusive and open we are, we even allow dissent).

Military organizations, like corporations, make much use of all the instruments of power and exhibit a pronounced symmetry of form. Condign power—in the extreme, rape, pillage, and mayhem—is deployed externally to subdue and defeat the enemy. Serving officers and lower ranks are aware that failure to do their duty, in accordance with orders down the line, will result in similar unpleasant personal consequences, though not always as severe; this is only part of the picture. Although mercenary armed forces operate primarily under the sway of compensatory power, regular military forces necessarily are conditioned to act, in part, from deeply ingrained motives of patriotism. These motives are developed through the primary socializing experiences of individuals growing up in a particular culture and from deliberate processes of indoctrination practiced within the military milieu.

A third general factor characterizes the effective use of power—to add to the impact of linking the three instruments and the force of symmetry in their application. Organizations are powerful to the extent that they pursue a limited number of aims. For the corporation, this means maximizing profit or growth of the enterprise; for the party, winning elections and distributing the spoils of office; for the army, winning wars and increases in the military budget; for the trade union, achieving improved conditions for members and growth in membership. Galbraith increasingly came to see the common interests of the Technostructure as the guiding purpose of the corporation. The rewards, pecuniary and status-related, of the executives who rule the large firm depend on being able to limit uncertain future eventualities in the market and public policy environment by careful planning. This requires systematically bringing the instruments of power to bear on customers, employees, suppliers, elected representatives, and government agencies in order to achieve predictably acceptable financial results and growth.

Following this line of argument, the most effective organizations within government are likely to be those with the clearest and most focused public function, whether this relates to provision of services or regulation of the actions of others. Perhaps the whole apparatus of the law and judiciary best demonstrates the functional success—in liberal democratic jurisdictions—of government's role, albeit that this sector is highly complex and internally differentiated. At a more modest level, the sale and policing of fishing licenses is generally well handled. At the other extreme, the convoluted and disjointed operations of the State Department—Galbraith seemed to reserve special contempt for this agency—almost guaranteed regular failure. Much the same could be said for the "war on drugs." Single-issue interest groups often have considerable political success. Galbraith instances groups like the National Rifle Association and pro-life organizations. In such cases—"(i)nternal submission is strongly in the service of external power." However, single-issue politics is often small scale, leaving little impact on the wider policy world. It is also prone to trigger opposition groups to enter the lists, an example of the tendency to countervailing power Galbraith identified decades before. The example of the political battles fought over abortion demonstrates both the focused ferocity of the conflict and its marginality beyond the immediate constituencies mobilized, though, of course, the consequences for the lives of many women are immense.

The final distinction Galbraith draws concerns the difference between real and illusory conditioned power. Because this form of power is subjective and obscured from the submissive party, it is not always possible to be sure that submission is not the preferred path that would have been taken. Nor is it always possible to sheet home the locus of domination. Some organizational leaders may *believe* that their actions have conditioned submission, whereas other forces unknown to either themselves or their targets are decisive in this regard. Galbraith held that politicians, journalists, and public prophets are especially prone to confuse the reality and illusion of power.

Galbraith's focus on the increasing importance of organization has recently been endorsed by Hacker and Pierson (2010: 113):

In our fragmented political system, victories without enduring organization are almost always fleeting. To influence the exercise of government authority in a modern democracy generally requires a range of formidable capabilities: the capacity to mobilize resources, coordinate actions with others, develop extensive expertise, focus sustained attention, and operate flexibly across multiple domains of activity. These are the attributes of organizations, not discrete, atomized voters.

V

In a chapter titled, "The Dialectic of Power", Galbraith returns to and underlines his earlier theory of countervailing power. This tendency he generalizes to all spheres in which power is exercised. "The usual and most effective response to the unwelcome exercise of power is to build a countering position of power." Wherever and whenever the instruments of power are mobilized and deployed, forces are set in motion to oppose or ameliorate their effect. For every power there is an opposite though not necessarily equal push back. Power contains within its very nature seeds of its negation. This essentially ontological position resonates a kind of watered down version of Newton's third law, as well as a more than passing resemblance to Friedrich Engels's *Dialectics of Nature*. Perhaps a better metaphor from physics would be the notion of political resistance or friction. The way in which this deep tendency to conflict plays out is open-ended in the sense that the outcome will depend on the relative strengths of the power wielded on each side. Whoever most effectively mobilizes and uses the instruments of condign, compensatory, and conditioned power wins. Each case must be carefully analyzed in order to determine the sources drawn upon, the instruments deployed, and the outcomes observed.

Galbraith applies this framework to examples drawn from economics, history, and politics, including many cases treated in earlier books. For example, the analysis can be used to elucidate and better understand the forces resulting in the extremes of social imbalance highlighted in *AS*. Automobile manufacturers were successful in establishing a growing mass market for their product, from the initial decision of Henry Ford to pay his workers high wages to facilitate their purchases of the Model-T (compensatory power), to the immense amounts of money spent on design features and advertising the Model-T's successors (conditioned power). Automobile makers also organized and spent money to acquire and close down public transit alternatives, and to join the defense sector in lobbying for major highway development.

These and countless other cases demonstrate, claims Galbraith, another general tendency. "A very large part of all modern political activity consists in efforts to capture the state in support of, or resistance to, some exercise of power." The modern state as the major and most complex organizational structure claims the legitimate monopoly of violence and through the legal and regulatory apparatus is foremost in the exercise of condign power in general. Government taxation and spending policies, the target of continuous pressure by private organizations, generate crosscutting currents of compensatory power. Through the actions of government agencies involved in education, public debate and information, and propaganda activities, conditioned power is both expressed and molded in private spheres. In many battles to impose one's will and bend others to one's purpose, capture of the state—or at least, its neutralization—is the main prize.

A further constant can be discerned. The dialectic expresses another aspect of symmetry. The instruments and sources used in the initiating exercise of power tend to be played back by resisting parties, like opposing like. Thus, in the early days of struggles between employers and unions, violence was a common form of condign power on both sides of the barricades. Nowadays, however, the battle is more likely to be fought around the table in long-winded negotiating sessions, with actual (as opposed to threatened) strikes and lock-outs measures of last resort. Organization also effectively overtook personality as a dominant source of power in industrial relations in the twentieth century. In the major political parties, competition for office is dependent on the relative abilities of candidates to raise large amounts of money to support campaigning for the hearts and minds of voters.

Similar resort to conditioned power is apparent in the efforts of interest groups opposing the advertising campaigns of large companies in the cigarette, energy, and agricultural chemical industries. Groups in favor of "truth in advertising" struggle in support of general consumer rights. The most dramatic example of symmetry Galbraith provides is in the sphere of international relations, where both sides in the Cold War accumulated vast stocks of nuclear weapons capable of annihilating life on the planet many times over—creating a tense situation captured in the apt acronym, MAD (mutually assured destruction).

On this point Galbraith was—blessedly—more prescient than the inventor of game theory, polymath John von Neumann. The latter, in keeping with the logic of "the Prisoner's Dilemma," urged the US to a nuclear "first strike" on the Soviet Union before it got in first. In the final chapter of *AS*, Galbraith urged governments to forgo the terminal use of condign power in favor of more sustainable measures. "If the possibility exists, the risks of negotiation and settlement, however great these may be, would still seem to provide a better prospect for survival than reliance on weapons which we can only hope are too terrible to use." Like all Washington habitués of his generation, Galbraith was much affected by the Cuban missile crisis and Kennedy's actions in dealing with it.

The tendency towards symmetry in the dialectical clash of powers is strong but not universal. Galbraith notes the success of deliberately asymmetrical responses, especially in situations where the opposing forces are badly mismatched in relative access to political resources. Gandhi's use of passive resistance to the might of British imperialism avoided pitting nationalists against imperial overlords in a conflict that the former was bound to lose. Similar tactics were used extensively in the US civil rights movement of the 1960s, drawing (then and since) on the personality of Martin Luther King. The refusal of guerilla forces to fight pitched battles is a similar case, one that should resonate with Americans in light of their experiences in both the American Revolution and more recently, on the other side of the coin, in Vietnam, Iraq, and Afghanistan. "Nevertheless, symmetry in both the sources of power and the instruments of enforcement remains the rule."

VI

Galbraith's forensic reflection on the nature of power culminates in his analysis of its exercise in the modern world of "high capitalism", earlier termed "the affluent society" and "new industrial state." The key elements of this view have been slipped into earlier commentary in this chapter. They include the following points. First, capitalist societies have moved, historically, from a situation in which the application of condign power—punishment—meted out by dominant personalities of property, including kings and others claiming the legitimate use of violence, to one in which impersonal markets and a complexly organized state (democratic or authoritarian) condition citizens from all social classes. Second, in this latter world, the large corporation plays a central role. The force of dominant personalities engaged in the corporate, civic, and government spheres still matters, though much less than in the past—their role largely usurped by committees of technical experts and processes of negotiation. Third, wealth and property are still crucial to success but increasingly only when mobilized and strategically applied through effective organizations. The capitalist state mediates competing claims on the material and symbolic (status) rewards of economic activity, while influencing many aspects of life associated with morality and belief. Fourth, symmetrical arrangements characterize the sources and instruments of power; in high capitalism, the ubiquity of organization ensures the triumph of conditioned power. In order to convince government and citizen to act in ways beneficial to the corporation and its managerial elite, the latter must demonstrate a high degree of conditioned commitment to the benign mission of the organization as realizing the true interests of all. In consequence, corporations have centralized a growing control over the levers of compensatory and conditioned power. Finally, as always, concentration in one direction creates resistance and mobilization in opposition. Countervailing forces of varying strengths are at work.

It should be clear from earlier chapters that Galbraith's extended treatment of power in society draws on and codifies ideas informing his preceding work, including the main themes of *AS*. I have already mentioned the light it casts on the theory of social balance. The importance of recognizing the grip of conditioned power helps to explain the ubiquity of advertising and government lobbying. It also renders comprehensible the widespread acceptance of extreme inequality. Uneven shares are seen to reflect relative economic contribution to total production, the maximization of which is essential to continuing economic security. The naturalization of market-determined incomes and the associated accumulation of wealth is thoughtfully assisted by the economics profession—by the economic ideas enshrined in the central tradition. Conditioned power in high capitalism is instantiated through the conventional wisdom.

VII

Although Galbraith's analysis of power is consistent with his earlier work and allows a fuller appreciation of his critique of orthodox economics, it is neither fully original nor altogether satisfactory. On the first point, he acknowledges his debt to Jouvenel (1993) and Weber (1948). However, his typology is also similar to that offered a decade before by the British political sociologist Steven Lukes, particularly with respect to the concept of conditioned power. In his book *Power: A Radical View*, Lukes (1973) distinguished between three dimensions of power. The first two dimensions related, like condign and compensatory power, to the "visible" (though not necessarily overt) influence over the actions of subordinate actors. The third dimension, like conditioned power, stressed the capacity to influence others without their full consciousness that this is happening. Lukes also noted that some parties benefit without the need to overtly act in their own interests by virtue of "the logic of the situation," that is, by the existing institutional structure of social and economic arrangements.

The notion that class structure conditions outcomes was, of course, dominant in the works of Marx and Weber, and thus in the founding and development of sociology as a discipline. This raises an irresolvable tension in Galbraith's treatment of power. On the one hand, he wishes to elucidate the manner in which power matters in capitalist societies, creating and reinforcing the dominant role of the modern corporation; on the other hand, in keeping with his liberal faith in the project of civilizing capitalism, he is desperate to find the footholds of resistance and reform. He looks to the theory of countervailing power, introduced in his first important book, to partly carry the weight of this ambition. But he can't have it both ways. In spite of occasional demur, Galbraith's choice of the term "countervailing" implies the existence of a roughly equal balance of power, when the overwhelming direction of his argument in his key works points to the greater and growing power of the corporation over government, consumer, and citizen. If it was not so, then the problem of the primacy of production, the scourge of inflation and coexistence of private affluence and public squalor, papered over by the comforting truths of the conventional wisdom, would not exist.

The final attempt to resolve this political impasse was to draw on the idea of a new class of technical and professional workers, increasingly independent of the old power of capital, working primarily for the intrinsic personal satisfaction of the job and the supplementary benefits of achieving worthwhile social outcomes. This idea reprised Veblen's opposition of "the instinct of workmanship" to the pecuniary goals of business. The spread of education and the desire to find interesting and fulfilling work would swell the ranks of the new class, building a political constituency increasingly sympathetic to reforming the economy and government. This class, rather than Marx's proletariat, would be the harbingers of a better society in which the fruits of increasing affluence would be more fairly shared and the imbalances more effectively righted. Galbraith also draws on Keynes's speculations, as noted earlier, that work in general would recede as the all-consuming focus of human activity, partly replaced by various leisure and spiritual pursuits. This hope, as also noted in preceding chapters, has been dashed over the past few decades. More and more people in the developed economies have been locked into conventional work practices, and time-urgency has created new forms of scarcity. The decay of social capital, as people strive to meet the rising costs of living and debt repayment, has eaten away at the capacity of people to diversify their lives and undercut their capacity to participate in political reform of the type Galbraith favored.

> The 1980s "yuppies" and their 1990s successors—the SUV-driving, McMansion-dwelling suburbanites and habitants of chicly restored urban lofts, whose chief passions are for expensive restaurants, exotic vacations, and investment in the latest technological trend, and whose politics exhibit a quasi-libertarian contempt for government—show how wrong he may have been. (Parker, 2005: 292)

At the macro-level in the United States, power, in step with income and wealth, has become progressively more unequal during the neoliberal era. *Asymmetric power relations* mark modern American capitalism. This is the basic message of analysts like Hacker and Pierson (2010) in *Winner-Take-All Politics* and Robert Reich (2008) in *Supercapitalism*. Both authors, as noted earlier, tie asymmetric developments in the American political economy to the outbreak and severity of the global economic crisis, as does James Galbraith (2008: xii).

The latter—in this book, *The Predator State*—more specifically charges the state with abandoning its post: "(m)arching under the banner of free markets, the state turned the regulatory function over to agents of a predatory class.... It is the nature of predators, when unchecked, to run wild." The particular constitution of the US political system has facilitated this outcome. Thus, E.J. Dionne, Jr (2012) describes the historical context in which the recent and continuing lurch to the right by both major political parties—the internal polarization within the Republican Party between traditional conservatives and tea party partisans; and the weak-kneed response by traditional liberals—has fractured what he calls "the long consensus," causing gridlock in important fields of public policy. This is not the result of the much-lauded "checks and balances" of America's political system, still less a case of countervailing power at work, but the unintended and unwanted consequence of an economy and society in crisis.

Much attention has focused since the GFC on the one percent, the super-rich targets of the Occupy movement. But asymmetric power is also exerted at levels lower down the income ladder. This is the message of Martin Gilens's (2012) detailed empirical study in his aptly titled book, *Affluence and Influence: Economic Inequality and Political Power in America*. He does this by comparing the impact on policies of citizens at the ninetieth income percentile with that of lower- and middle-income groups. His conclusion is telling:

> What I find is hard to reconcile with the notion of political equality is Dahl's formulation of democracy. The American government does respond to the public's preferences, but that responsiveness is strongly tilted towards the most affluent citizens. Indeed, under most circumstances, the preferences of the vast majority of Americans appear to have virtually no impact on which policies the government does or does not adopt. (Gilens, 2012: 1)

Although Galbraith's particular analysis of power in the affluent society may have distinct weaknesses, especially from the standpoint of today, nevertheless he must be credited with a lifelong commitment to opposing its exclusion from the purview of economists. It was not he who was responsible for "instructing the students in error." Another lasting lesson resides in Galbraith's insistence that the large corporation is the key arena of power in modern capitalism and that senior executives wield excessive power over the broad political economy. It is true that his notion of an independent Technostructure able to routinely exert decisive influence over events has proved to be a considerable overstatement. The powerful corporate core is much smaller, typically, than Galbraith suggested. Moreover, the chaotic economic environment is much more uncertain and less tractable than he envisaged. But the ability of corporate leaders to treat the corporation as a vehicle for extracting maximum personal gain and for influencing public policy is, if anything, even more marked than he would have allowed, since many of the countervailing forces he looked to have withered away.

*   *   *

Power is a theme running throughout *AS*, as it did throughout its author's political and intellectual life. The decision by generations of economists to strictly segregate the analysis of the economic from other spheres of social life—what Duncan Foley (2006) called *Adam's [Smith] Fallacy* in his book of the same name—was precisely what separated Galbraith from his colleagues. This lacuna in the central tradition provides part of the explanation for Galbraith's vehement dismissal of orthodox economics as a useful tool in understanding the world as it is and how it might be; symmetrically, it also accounts for the reverse—Galbraith's dismissal by the economics profession. At base, Galbraith's appreciation of the impacts of power provided a spur to pursue what the world should be, to reflect on the moral order of a just society.

13

The Moral Order

If put in sufficiently general terms, the essence of the good society can be easily stated. It is that every member, regardless of gender, race or ethnic origin, should have access to a rewarding life.

(J.K. Galbraith)

The economist, like everyone else, must concern himself with the ultimate aims of mankind.

(Alfred Marshall)

* * *

John Kenneth Galbraith was America's public intellectual number one. Over a period spanning seven decades he bombarded his fellow countrymen and women with a steady stream of commentary on their fears, hopes, and foibles. Along with the seemingly cool disinterested analysis, laced with ironic, sometimes cynical, reflections, came a consistent flow of advice on how to live better and more fulfilling lives. His last substantive book, published not long before his death, was titled *The Good Society: The Humane Agenda* (1996). The aloof persona of a Harvard academic and member of the East Coast intelligentsia was cover for a man who burned with a sense of injustice on behalf of the less fortunate of his fellow citizens and who also harbored a cynical disregard, bordering on contempt, for the pretensions of the rich and contented elites who controlled the heights of the economy, polity, and dominant culture. His self-constructed position as an amused bystander also belied the strenuous efforts he made throughout his life to influence what governments did and did not do. He was a committed social reformer, not merely a social prophet content to criticize from the sidelines. In this penultimate chapter I attempt to stand back from the text of *AS* in order to reflect on this aspect of this remarkable man and how his concerns still resonate in a world perhaps entering the dark side of the affluent society.

I have earlier argued that Galbraith's approach to economics and public policy stems from his early upbringing and education in a small, remote

Canadian farming district. As a relative latecomer to the hustle of urban life, this meant that he arrived with a well-formed world view and moral compass. Perhaps his suspicion of big-city wheelers and dealers, both business and political, was fed by the small farmer's experience of market rigging and other forms of chicanery practiced by untrustworthy buyers, brokers, and bankers. This wariness seems to have spilled over into a general suspicion, if not active dislike, of those in authority in other spheres, including his chosen discipline of economics. He was, as we have seen, a relentless critic of the orthodox economics that evolved after the Second World War, tracing its tottering foundations back to Adam Smith. It is, I think, for these reasons that Galbraith is often bracketed with that other iconoclast in the discipline, Thorstein Veblen. This is only a partly accurate depiction, mostly with respect to the negatively critical dimension to their work. Although there are superficial similarities in their positive analyses of capitalism—as in their focus on consumption and the leisure class—Galbraith's dissection of modern capitalism is far more developed and relevant to today's world. This is not a criticism of Veblen; it's just that Galbraith had the good fortune to live a long life through a century in which much happened.

Galbraith was a committed liberal (or social) democrat. In the "Afterword" to the 1998 edition of *AS*, he identified "the two major effects of affluence that I would now wish to especially emphasize." The first related to the need to oppose the tendency to ignore the plight of the disadvantaged; the second to the need to defend the freedoms hard won from "those who, in the name of defending it, would leave the planet only with its ashes." His first imperative has been given urgency by the developments in the world economy since his death, the second by the global growth of terrorism and the responses unleashed. As he himself would undoubtedly have agreed, the two developments are not unrelated. Globalization is creating an increasingly polarized world of haves and have-nots. Many of the have-nots live in societies riven and driven by a religious ideology affronted by the liberal democratic societies whose haves control the main levers of global power.

In *The Good Society* Galbraith set out to provide a guide to how we should today live our lives in order to meet the two imperatives just noted. More specifically—

> How can economic policy contribute to this end? What of the public services of the state; how can they be made more equitably and efficiently available? How can the environment, present and future, be protected? What of immigration, migration and migrants? What of the military power? What is the responsibility and course of action of the good society as regards its trading partners and neighbors in an increasingly internationalized world and as regards the poor of the planet?

To argue for the good society it is necessary to refrain from speculative flight to some envisioned utopia. Certain realities of human nature and the world as it is must be respected. But, argues Galbraith, some basic elements can't be denied. These include personal liberty in the western sense, racial and ethnic equality, opportunities widely available to all citizens for a "rewarding life", and a reasonable and secure basic income. "Nothing, it must be recognized, so comprehensively denies the liberties of the individual as the total absence of money. Or so impairs it as too little."

Galbraith is aware of the hold that the motive of self-interest exerts in society and the models of economists. He notes the tendency of those who would defend the status quo and their own self-interests by finding ways of hitching those interests to some conception of the common good. However, he does not allow this constraint posed by human nature to prevent deploying arguments designed to demolish its manifestations in policy debates and development. A morally reconstructed society enjoying increasing affluence requires a concerted attack on the bastions of privilege and power in order to defeat the forces of social exclusion, environmental devastation, and the illiberal threats to personal freedom. The political and intellectual project must be focused on overcoming what Galbraith called in an earlier book "the culture of contentment." Increasing affluence in the United States has led to a class of wealthy and "wanna-be wealthy" content with their lot, oblivious to the growing numbers of poor and excluded people who barely exist in "a democracy of the fortunate." The politics of contentment has resulted in a sharp swing to the right in American politics. The attack on the state, entailing concerted attempts to shrink government, has, as noted in earlier chapters, become the hallmark of the rise of neoliberalism, the ruling ideology of high capitalism.

Consequently, progress toward the good society requires a reversal of the trends evident since the 1970s. The social foundation of the good society entails the following factors—many of which reprise arguments put forward in *AS*. First and foremost, the economy must deliver modest and stable growth supporting relatively high levels of employment. Second, the inevitable trend towards income and wealth inequalities must be recognized and limited through appropriate state intervention, both financial and regulatory. Those people unable to work for an income that would support a reasonable standard of living are to be helped do so by supplementary government assistance. This diverse group includes the elderly, the young, the frail, the disabled, and those who care for some or all of the preceding. Third, universal medical insurance is vital to make real the opportunities for gainful employment and a rewarding existence over the life course. Fourth, education, basic and advanced, is equally important, both to fit the individual for intrinsically satisfying work and to boost productivity and sustainable growth in the economy. Fifth, illegitimate means of getting ahead must be curtailed; not all aspirations to succeed in the affluent society are allowable. Galbraith here had firmly in mind the excesses of the savings and loans scandal, the dot.com boom, insider trading, and like financial pathologies infesting recent US history. Had he lived a couple of years longer, his list of pathologies would have multiplied. Sixth, governments have particular responsibilities in the field of environmental protection. Seventh, the internationalization of capitalism, resulting in increasing capital mobility and global migration, forced and voluntary, requires much greater international cooperation between national governments. The established supra-national institutions—World Bank, IMF, World Trade Organization, and the various arms of the United Nations—have become less able to ensure reasonable stability and harmony. New architectures of collaboration will be necessary to supplement existing institutions, a development apparent in the relatively recent appearance of the new forums such as the G-20, European Union and Asia-Pacific Economic Community (APEC). Eighth, the imbalance between public and private provision must be redressed in favor of the former, while also limiting the grasp of the military on public resources. Requirements seven and eight are closely interrelated. Reduced military expenditure at the national level depends on improved peaceful collaboration internationally. Likewise, improving relations between nations requires verifiable reductions in the military threat each poses to the others.

II

None of the above will be novel to readers of Galbraith's earlier books, especially *AS*. He was faithful in his views, values, and analysis over a long period. The philosophical underpinning to his vision of the good society is based in the modern liberal tradition running from John Stuart Mill to the later (post-Hayekian) works of the British political philosopher John Gray. The latter's book, *Two Faces of Liberalism* (2000), stresses the two key traditions in liberalism—the priority of personal freedom and the virtue of toleration. Gray argues that in the modern world with its diverse cultures, ways must be found to entrench a robust *modus vivendi*, a situation of benign coexistence of cultural traditions and conceptions of the good life. Mutual respect, or at least prudent acceptance, for the other's way of life is, in this view, a basic requirement for global harmony; this, of course, includes religious toleration.

The requirements of toleration may rub up against the freedom of individuals to dissent from the dominant moral and religious precepts in a particular society. Some cultures are more comfortable with moral and political dissent than others. Liberal democratic societies echoing the Enlightenment credo of a Voltaire or the mid-Victorian precepts of J.S. Mill defend—in theory at least—the right to oppose the majority view on matters of personal belief and morality. In other societies and times, dissent brings punishment of varying severity. Gray seems to go further than this and argue against the traditional lexical order of freedom and toleration, in fact to reverse the order of priorities.

Tolerating the morally reprehensible beliefs and practices in other countries may be necessary to ensure stability and harmony in a complex world. One then has to speak not of *the* good society but of many good societies that are incommensurate one with another. In this way it may be possible for peace, however uneasy, to persist between liberal democracies, theocracies, military dictatorships, and hereditary ruling monarchies—between the United States, Iran, and Saudi Arabia. Galbraith is not, therefore, an unalloyed proponent of human rights, and in particular of the special role of the United States in bringing democracy to the world. (He might even have subscribed to the sentiments of the Leonard Cohen song—"Democracy is Coming to the USA"—based on the heretical notion that America, after all, is not great, not the very model of a major modern democracy, but an imperfectly and partly developed work in progress.)

It is not clear that Galbraith's good society and the moral order that he would like to see entrenched pay much attention to the virtues of toleration, especially when they impinge negatively on individual freedom. Nevertheless, throughout his career he was strongly opposed to the military adventurism of half-a-dozen presidents. He had witnessed the long history of successive US governments using military means to further national interests under the cover of freedom and democracy—most notably in South and Central America and South-East Asia. His ire was democratically spread across the two political parties; Johnson, as much as Bush major and minor, felt the sting of his withering criticism. The military establishment was a favorite target—and he rarely missed his mark. This was a talent that he developed early, a taste first acquired when serving on the commission reviewing the (in)effectiveness of aerial bombing over Nazi Germany. His son James Galbraith recently found evidence that just prior to his assassination President Kennedy was about to act on Galbraith's written advice to withdraw American troops from Vietnam. It is clear that Galbraith did not subscribe to the neoconservative commitment to imposing democracy and the American way of life on other countries and culture; he was not a fan of "shock and awe" in international relations.

Neither is it possible to see Galbraith implicitly committed to the morally based social order proposed by his Harvard contemporary based in the Philosophy Department—namely John Rawls. It is true that there are some superficial similarities—both thought that an absence of money (primary goods) was a basic impediment to the individual's opportunity to live a rewarding life; and both looked to political institutions to counter the inherent capacity of capitalist societies to generate self-reinforcing economic inequalities, with a resulting loss of self-esteem for the least favored. However, Galbraith's essentially pragmatic stance, seeking practical ways of improving outcomes in a world riven by conflicting interests, inconsistencies, and contradictions, would not sit well with Rawls's transcendental social contract approach. Although Galbraith would have endorsed many of the policy outcomes flowing from an application of Rawls's (1971) two principles of justice—especially those that equalized opportunities and boosted the life chances of the most disadvantaged (Rawls's second principle)—he would not have based his acceptance on the abstract thought experiment from which they derived.

Galbraith was a reformer very much anchored in the real world, dealing with the politically possible (if difficult) task of challenging and changing minds. In this context, his implicit view of justice more closely approached that proposed by another Harvard philosopher and economist, Amartya Sen. In *The Idea of Justice* (2009), Sen proposes a conception of justice designed to confront the barriers to leading a rewarding life that stem from the uneven capacities individuals inherited, socially and biologically, in real existing societies. Sen's emphasis is on reducing actually existing injustices, rather than constitutionally wiring up a perfectly structured mechanism and allowing it to work without further engineering.

Whereas Rawls was content to prioritize the right over the good—to set up the institutional rules that would garner universal consent by rationally self-interested individuals—Sen and Galbraith preferred attacking injustices head on in the hope of reducing their malign impacts. The latter were proposing strong conceptions of the good, and weaker or supporting conceptions of the right. By adopting a broadly pragmatic stance on social ethics Galbraith can also be seen to stand in the American philosophic tradition stretching from Thomas Dewey to Richard Rorty. It may even, at a further stretch, be possible to trace his conception of social justice back to the Scottish Enlightenment and the "moral sentiments" of Adam Smith. Galbraith may not have been the latter's ideal of "the impartial spectator" but there is a persistent strand of dogged if rueful detachment in his social analysis.

The theory of justice or public morality implicit in Galbraith's work can be seen in the way he consistently endorsed policies that would improve the access of the working majority and the marginalized poor to key public services that would open up opportunities—develop capacities—to directly improve their lives while boosting long-term productivity in the economy. He believed that affluence was too important to leave it to the rich. The coming of affluence provided the material possibility of creating a fairer and more just society. Existing taxation regimes were dysfunctional and unfairly skewed because they allowed the rich to keep far more of the fruits of collective production than they either needed or deserved—and in doing so stunted the opportunities for a rewarding life of the non-rich.

Although this familiar outcome is explicable in terms of the calculus of power, noted in Chapter 12, it cannot be acceptable in Galbraith's *Good Society*. At a more subtle level, Galbraith's analysis of the Dependence Effect carries moral overtones. Intelligent and compassionate citizens are being conditioned into becoming consuming automatons, captive of several of the seven deadly sins—to wit, greed, envy, gluttony, and pride. Retail therapy is worse than the disease. An over-emphasis on the consumption of goods to satisfy manufactured wants demeans the person, undermining the moral authenticity and autonomy of human existence. Like Keynes and Mill before him, Galbraith saw in the stunted lives of the disadvantaged and forgotten, unrecognized potential for a flowering of human capacities and personal liberation. The life of a squirrel is not to be envied—or aspired to.

It was, ultimately, the underlying moral or value foundation to Galbraith's economics that allowed economic orthodoxy to attack and discount his professional work and question his credentials as an economist. Postwar economists bought into the pernicious "scientistic" position that economics was (and should be, note the irony) a "value-free" discipline—a rigorous body of work committed to establishing what is, not what should be. Galbraith's willingness to explicitly deny this neat division of the positive and normative dimensions of the discipline incurred the fury of those who wished to establish the discipline of economics on the same epistemological and political basis as the natural sciences—to promote economics as "social physics." In this way, economists could hope to be influential politically and well rewarded materially for their enhanced relevance.

Other economists had dismissed the value freedom argument, notably the Swede, Gunnar Myrdal (1953), who spoke of "the beam in our eyes" to capture the manner in which established economic theory was blind to matters beyond its ken. Galbraith's analysis of the implicit political support that a value-free economics—based on the naïve view that governments would always act without fear or favor to ensure economically efficient outcomes— would provide to powerful conservative interests, was also a source of displeasure and unease to his colleagues. The ambition of economists of a liberal bent to operate with "hard heads and soft hearts" was a worthy but difficult act to pull off. Nevertheless, Galbraith himself never gave up trying to do so.

III

However progressive Galbraith was in his thinking, however liberal his moral scruples and political leanings, he was too much of a pragmatist to rely over much on the tendencies of real existing capitalist societies like his own to realize the good society. "Because in the modern polity there are two groups that are unequal in power and influence, democracy has become an imperfect thing." The power of the rich and those commanding the heights of the corporate sector and public bureaucracies overwhelm the interests of the deprived and their supporters. "It can be, and most clearly is, an unequal contest."

For Galbraith, then, the most important task is to make democracy a more inclusive system, one that mobilizes and engages those whose interests have been ignored or heavily discounted. The greatest barrier to this occurring is the perennially low turn-out at elections by poorer voters. Consequently, the money and influence exerted in favor of the wealthy is perpetually reaffirmed by the outcome of elections in which many do not participate. The need to court the favor of those who do vote and who listen to the pro-affluent voices of the popular media requires both major parties to lean to the right and implement policies favoring (or steer away from policies harming) the already blessed. The clear way forward, he suggests, is for the excluded and disadvantaged to form coalitions to exert organized pressure through the Democratic Party to shift the political agenda leftwards. In effect, this strategy called for a new future modeled on the past. He saw the Democratic Party of the New Deal and, perhaps, the New Frontier, as the organizational goal to pursue. The Democrats have, in the past, stood up for the interests of the disadvantaged and resisted the attack on the legitimate role of the state in economic and social affairs.

The Good Society ends at this point. Galbraith, no more than anyone else, has no simple strategy for bringing about the state of greater popular engagement and voter-driven reform he proclaims. He admits that critics of his position will claim that the affluent and their supporters are firmly in power, that opposition is fruitless and bound to fail. But he disagrees that this always need be the case. His early commitment to the concept of countervailing power never fully fades, even after a lifetime in which the uneven expression of power has consistently biased outcomes in favor of the rich and powerful. He characteristically concludes on a hopeful note.

> Let there be a coalition of the concerned and the compassionate and those now outside the political system, and for the good society there would be a bright and wholly practical prospect. The affluent would still be affluent, the comfortable still comfortable, but the poor would be part of the political system. Their needs would be heard, as would the other goals of the good society. Aspirants for public office would listen. The votes would be there and would be pursued.... With true democracy, the good society would succeed, would even have an aspect of inevitability.

IV

Looking back at the last few decades, especially since the beginning of the new century, it is difficult to share Galbraith's confidence in the victory of a new progressive politics—a new New Deal—in the US or elsewhere. The charge sheet of economic, social, and environmental misdemeanors is lengthening, as discussed at various points earlier in this book. Perhaps, had he lived to see the GFC and its aftermath, Galbraith himself would have been surprised at how quickly the very people and institutions responsible for the crisis—and the ruling ideas that legitimized their power—were back in charge. But, then, maybe he wouldn't.

The attack on the state has not subsided, in spite of the fact that global depression and chaos was only avoided (and that, barely) by large-scale government intervention. The power of the wealthy (and those who would ape them) to manipulate existing political institutions and reinforce values and beliefs in the broad public congenial to their positions and interests has ensured that the strongly conservative policies of governments have prevailed. In the United States, Democratic administrations at the federal and state levels have moved further to the right of the political spectrum. This is particularly evident in the case of the drive to lower taxes. Federally, the most dramatic manifestation of this is the rise of the Tea Party and its partial capture of the Republican Party.

As I write, a re-elected president is facing down a stubborn Republican rearguard action to resist tax rises on the rich, part of the administration's strategy to reduce the federal budget deficit without penalizing middle-income households. Even if Obama wins and the economy avoids toppling over "the fiscal cliff," further battles loom over pushing out the public debt limit. At lower levels of state and county, initiatives like "the taxation bill of rights" that result in popular endorsement of caps on any rise in taxes without explicit majority citizen agreement are forcing governments to cut back on public services, even essential ones like police, fire brigades, and street lighting. In the town of Colorado Springs, the city privatized maintenance of parks and gardens with a noticeable decline in the reach and quality of access; one is reminded of the travelers in the mauve and cerise automobile falling asleep in a public park injurious to their health and morals—is this, indeed the American genius?

There is some evidence in support of Galbraith's claim that high voter turnouts result in policies more inclusive of the interests of disadvantaged groups. Australia, for example, has compulsory voting at federal, state, and local levels. It has a strong Labor Party with a social democratic history and a record of introducing most of the progressive legislation around social security, mass education, and, above all, health. A federal Labor government introduced a universal health insurance scheme—Medibank (later relabeled Medicare)—in the 1970s, funded by a surcharge on the income tax. The current government (and federal opposition) is committed to introducing a similar scheme that would cover all people with disabilities, however acquired.

On the other hand, successive Australian governments of all political colors have enthusiastically embraced the domestic policies of neoliberalism and the foreign policies of the United States. Compulsory voting has indeed made a difference, but hardly overturned the grip of the privileged on the levers of power—especially the power to condition the beliefs, fears, and aspirations of the majority. Elements of Galbraith's good society peep through in countries like Australia that evolved a functioning welfare state prior to the rise of neo-liberalism. It is not clear that these progressive elements, and the values from which they emerged, will survive.

*   *   *

AS was Galbraith's first major success in engaging a wide readership beyond the discipline of economics. His earlier forays into journalism had fitted him with the tools and appetite to reach the thoughtful general reader. His intention was not merely to inform and entertain—though these outcomes were certainly achieved, as the long weeks of the book on the best-seller list attests—but to persuade people of the need to aspire to a better world that increasing affluence made possible. An affluent world *should* be a good society—there were no excuses for *not* making it so. The time-honored claims of economists that scarcity prevented such advance, inculcated through the many currents of the dominant conventional wisdom, no longer held. This barrier to the *Good Society*, at least, could be consigned to the dustbin of history.

14

Concluding Thoughts

This, as only death can, exonerates him.

(J.K. Galbraith, in reference to President Warren Harding)

* * *

John Kenneth Galbraith died on 29 April 2006. A few years earlier another Harvard luminary departed this planet. Steven Jay Gould was, in some ways, Galbraith's equivalent in the life and earth sciences. He was a prolific writer of popular essays on the nature and history of science, as well as an important technical contributor to the disciplines of evolutionary biology and paleontology. In the first role he produced a staggering 300 essays for publication in the magazine *Natural History*. These brilliant essays were produced at the regular rate of one a month for thirty years. This amazing feat of intellectual endurance was accomplished despite the fact that he battled a deadly disease diagnosed in his late thirties, to which he eventually succumbed in his early sixties. Like Galbraith, Gould was a passionate champion for the progressive uses of science and a stern critic of those conservative forces that would bend scientific arguments in favor of narrow political agendas. He frequently appeared in public and before the Congress to oppose the misuse of science by creationists attacking evolution and the teaching of biology in schools. He also argued in public on the dangers to universal survival posed by nuclear proliferation in light of the debates over the prospects for a "nuclear winter."

Both also shared a particular misfortune—they died a little too early. Gould was a life-long Red Sox baseball fan, a member of a large club of frustrated supporters. The Boston Red Sox had not won the World Series since the First World War—not since the club had traded Babe Ruth to arch enemies, the New York Yankees. The "Curse of the Bambino" was finally broken in 2004, two years after Gould's demise on 20 May 2002. Boston again won the World Series in 2007.

Galbraith's misfortune was to miss the demise of Lehman Brothers on 15 September 2008, two years after his death. The dreadful scale and suddenness of the events that followed—the flurry on Wall Street and in Washington DC;

the confusion, missteps, and reversals; the confident public pronouncements that all was under control (eerily reminiscent of Herbert Hoover's claim that "recovery was just around the corner"); and above all, the exhortations not to panic while panic ensued behind mahogany closed doors—all this would have come as no surprise to Galbraith. He would have understood immediately that this was a case of history repeating itself, as both tragedy and farce. He would have extracted some grim enjoyment from the shocked and bewildered faces of his economist colleagues and would not have been human had he not derived some satisfaction from the public discomfort of political and financial leaders. Nor would he have been surprised at the clear demonstration of the inadequacy of the theories and models of orthodox economics; after all, hadn't he been saying so for sixty years?

What would have saddened him was the degree of harm inflicted on ordinary people throughout the world, the lives blighted by people who had trusted the villains responsible. Complacent politicians and contented elites had much to answer for but appear to be escaping the wrath of the masses; this would have angered but not surprised him. He never underestimated the power of outdated ideas in the service of powerfully organized interests to impose their will and bend that of the rest to their continuing advantage. In November 2008 the Queen of England opened a new building at the London School of Economics (LSE). Referring to the global financial crisis or credit crunch she commented—"it's awful. Why did no one see it coming?" The answer offered by two LSE professors was that it was all due to "a failure in the collective imagination of many bright people" [i.e. orthodox economists]. Galbraith would have concurred, and added that the power of entrenched interests might also have had something to do with what befell all of us.

II

For much of this book I have discussed the many contributions of Galbraith under the shadow cast by John Maynard Keynes. As a young economist, keen to establish his reputation for relevance and originality, Galbraith adopted a respectful but critical attitude to the master from the "other Cambridge." He refused to be carried away by the revolution sweeping through economics immediately after the war, admittedly having earlier been hit by the tidal wave (his words) unleashed by Keynes's *The General Theory* (1973/1936) in the 1930s. In *American Capitalism* (1952) and *AS* he laid down the basis of his concerns with a macroeconomics, divorced from its microeconomic foundations, that was soon to be rendered harmless to the central tradition and later to be defenestrated. Eventually, in the later years of his career, Galbraith acknowledged his indebtedness to the master and proclaimed a close affinity with the group of American and English economists attempting to build on the foundations of *The General Theory*. Fifty years after the original publication of *AS* and two years after his death, a special issue of the *Review of Political Economy*, edited by the prominent American post-Keynesian Steven Pressman in 2008, reviewed some of Galbraith's key contributions to economic theory and policy, as well as celebrating his life and achievements on the centenary of his birth.

Pressman's introductory paper identified three aspects of his contribution to establishing a sounder micro-foundation to Keynes's macroeconomics. The first was to insist on the importance of understanding how individuals, firms, and governments acted to reproduce the institutional structure of the economy and to make strenuous efforts to do so. To properly capture the complexities of modern economies the economist had to go beyond the comfortable confines of models based on "rational individualism;" to encompass social and political forces influencing behavior on the ground. The second contribution was to stress the ineluctable presence of uncertainty in economic life and the efforts, rational and otherwise, of economic actors to deal with the consequences. This position requires the economist to take history seriously, to see real people making decisions in historical time using the information, habits, and rules of thumb available at the time; the need to so do was eventually conceded by the prominent British economist John Hicks (inventor of the IS-LM model), the person partly responsible for turning the "Keynesian revolution" towards its eventual dead end. The final contribution noted was Galbraith's insistence on the relevance of "income effects on consumption, rather than orthodox economics'" concern with substitution effects. The latter mattered less and less in a world where scarcity was being overtaken by affluence as the focus for (morally) sound economic policy. Galbraith saw this earlier and more clearly than anyone. This paper and its accompanying ones offer thought-provoking reading for the interested reader.

Galbraith, as noted in Chapter 13, believed to the end that real human beings were able to rise above mere self-interest to behave in ways that improved the lives of all citizens in democratic societies. In this, he followed the lead of seventeenth-century thinkers such as Immanuel Kant, Adam Smith, and Jacques Rousseau, who held dualistic conceptions of human nature—the motive of self-preservation and a capacity for sympathy and compassion toward others, culminating in the ability, even imperative, to develop rationally a moral conception of the good. The political scientist Paul Clements, in his recently published book, *Rawlsian Policial Analysis* (2012), has formalized this approach, arguing that an adequate understanding of how real human behavior emerges and political systems work requires an equal focus on the causal force of both "the good" (interests) and "the right" (principles), rather than a sole focus on the former. (Tellingly, the sub-title to Clements book is: *Rethinking the Microfoundations of Social Science.*) Dionne too, in *Our*

Divided Political Heart (2012), points to the endemic struggle in America, on both sides of politics, to reconcile the nation's twin commitment to individualism and republican "virtue." Communitarian sentiments battle naked individualism in a never-ending dance to the music of time.

John Kenneth Galbraith had the optimistic outlook of an abiding liberal. He believed that democratic societies harbored within multiple centers of countervailing power that would offset or at least constrain the overwhelming force of those occupying the commanding heights. His vision of America was, in many ways, the negative image of Herbert Marcuse's one-dimensional society. Like Keynes and other liberals he underestimated the reality of social class inequalities and overestimated the goodwill of honest, disinterested citizens. Galbraith's politics is similarly incomplete. His contribution was primarily analytical; he was able, through books like *AS*, to diagnose the disease but not cure it.

AS is a justly famous book. Its main ideas and suggestions for reform echo down to the present day. Many of the problems of affluence Galbraith pinpointed still require solution but a number of new and more complicated ones have emerged. The endless pursuit of economic growth based on rising productivity is intensifying the inequalities within and between nations, hardening class divisions and the lines of political conflict. Globalization in the era of modern finance is intensifying global insecurity, economically and politically. In a world of nuclear proliferation and terrorism, state and non-state, people still face the threat of annihilation, once thought to have disappeared with the end of the Cold War. Macro-environmental problems of climate change and resource depletion complement national and localized issues of pollution, desertification, and blight. Historically unprecedented movements of people driven by wars, environmental change, famine, religious persecution, and the hope of a better life are creating social tensions and new scarcities. Uncontrolled immigration to western countries is also creating a defensive, sometimes rabid, right-wing political response in inappropriately named "host" countries, where the modern equivalent of concentration camps are springing up, many operated by private multinational corporations.

New patterns of inequality are overlaying and reinforcing long-established ones. Inequality of opportunities and power between men and women continue to mark life in the early decades of the twenty-first century. As older doors are opened to women in countries like America—for example, access to paid employment—other doors are kept firmly closed. Hence, although female workforce participation has increased substantially since the Second World War, the proportion of women occupying the top executive positions in industry, government, and major institutions, such as churches, the professions, and the armed forces, remains low and unmoving. Women who do achieve powerful positions are still overwhelmingly caught in a culturally imposed dilemma—avoid having children or try to "have it all." Daughters, of course, are implicitly assumed to take on the responsibilities of caring for ageing and infirm parents. The thought that men might actually share the joys and challenges of juggling both domestic and paid labor escapes most (men). Although women are increasingly becoming the majority on university campuses, their representation at senior faculty level lags, and not just in the "hard" sciences; economics as a discipline remains a boys' club, as Deirdre McCloskey (1997) has forcefully reminded us. Until the relatively recent emergence of feminist economics, Galbraith was one of the few in his profession to notice this persisting and massive source of injustice in the affluent societies of our time.

What is not new is the irrelevance of much of the old economics that Galbraith attacked with such verve and modest effect. Fortunately, the various strands of heterodox economics that have prospered since *AS* was published are continuing his attempt to both understand and change our world for the better. And that, after all, is what matters.

III

Finally, we can summarize why reading *AS* and reflecting on its messages, overt and implicit, still reward today's reader. Why, in short, write a book about a long ago published tome, albeit an elegantly crafted and famous one? The first answer is, like a number of other "classics," time does not weary it; Galbraith, half a century ago, was onto something. Orthodox economics then as now simply did not adequately explain the human condition, even in its narrowly confined gaze. We now have some idea as to why. The social and economic future is radically unpredictable. Orthodox economics, then and now, struggles under the twin burden of a commitment to the ergodic fallacy that knowledge of the future can be gleaned from knowledge of regularities in the past *and* to a model of the discipline as a branch of classical physics. For this reason economists and the hapless policy makers they advise are forever being surprised when their confident forecasts fall to dust—"all that is solid melts into air." The bewilderment accompanying the global financial crisis, like the many unexpected crises before—"why did no one see it coming"—offered a rare and temporary moment of self-awareness in a discipline in which the majority of practitioners resolutely avoids facing reality.

Galbraith's determination to analyze modern economies in terms of how people actually interact allowed him to escape some of the pitfalls of his orthodox colleagues. In doing this he raised important features emerging from the most advanced economies of the postwar period, even where he overstated or misstated their significance. But this did not mean that he was able to accurately foresee the future—our fifty-year past—with a high degree of success.

That leads to a second valuable payoff. Reflecting on where he was right and where wrong gives us some purchase on the underlying social, economic, and political events that made up our experience of the recent past, understandings that eluded economists of a more orthodox persuasion. As a corollary, recognition that hubris doesn't pay, that economic policy comes with no guarantee, can sensitize citizen and decision maker to a more cautious and watchful approach to life in an uncertain global environment. The economy is not a machine but a complex system embedded in social layers of complexity. By all means let us gather and interrogate data, make forecasts, and act on them. But let us all be under no illusion that the analysis generated, the advice offered, and the policies enacted stem from an unassailable font of technical wisdom, denuded of sectional interests, heuristic bias and political influence. It is possible that the more we know about how economies function, the more likely we and our governments can exert some degree of control over our collective futures. However, it is also likely that, with the best tools, models, and data, we will still miss critical conditions and drivers that will result in surprising and unwelcome outcomes. If the recent past has taught us anything it is that individual rationality can lead to collective or systemic irrationality, that is, to unexpected and undesired outcomes. Unfortunately, we only get to see this in hindsight.

At a deeper level, *The Affluent Society* is indeed "one of those books" that asks us to confront basic questions and dilemmas. To what extent is the untrammeled pursuit of material well-being the ultimate aim of human kind? Can the material welfare of seven billion people on the planet be assured in a world of limited resources and bio-physical environmental changes? Is it too late? Are their alternative paths to the future not predicated on "the paramount position of production?" Is the word "Affluent" in the title an ironic comment on its negation? If *The Affluent Society* is lodged in a time capsule to be retrieved two or three hundred years hence, what will the readers of the future make of it? Will they exist? When H.G. Wells's hero returned from the future to the turn of the twentieth century, he chose a book from his library before jumping into his time machine to head back to save the future. If you or I were he, would we choose *The Affluent Society*? Probably not. But if there was were room in the boot for a few more volumes—perhaps.

A Reader's Guide

The following guide points the interested reader towards references relevant to the discussion informing this book. They are offered, of course, in addition to Galbraith's prolific output. A full list of references mentioned or quoted in the text follows.

*   *   *

The first port of call must be the superb biography by Richard Parker, *John Kenneth Galbraith: His Life, His Politics, His Economics* (2005). See also the special issue of the journal, *Review of Political Economy* (20(4), 2008) published to celebrate the centenary of Galbraith's birth and edited by Steven Pressman.

For well-balanced and informative accounts of developments in postwar economics see Roger Backhouse, *The Puzzle of Modern Economics: Science or Ideology* (2010) and Diane Coyle, *The Soulful Science* (2007). Backhouse's *The Penguin History of Economics* (2002) is a useful contextual reference.

John Quiggin, *Zombie Economics: How Dead Ideas Still Walk Amongst Us* (2010), provides a devastating critique of mainstream economics from a broadly post-Keynesian perspective. So too does Steve Keen, *Debunking Economics: The Naked Emperor Dethroned* (2011).

Michel Beaud and Gilles Dostaler, *Economic Thought Since Keynes: A History and Dictionary of Major Economists* (1995) is an excellent compendium of major developments in the discipline, coupled with biographical sketches of the main cast of characters.

Keynes's essay on "Economic possibilities," together with a number of contemporary commentaries on it, is published in Pecchi and Piga (eds), *Revisiting Keynes: Economic Possibilities for our Grandchildren* (2010).

The global financial crisis and its aftermath have created a veritable publishing industry. From the many excellent books on offer, try Paul Krugman, *The Return of Depression Economics and the Crisis of 2008* (2008) and *End This Depression Now* (2012); Joseph Stiglitz, *Freefall: America, Free Markets and the Shrinking of the World Economy* (2010); C. Reinhart and K. Rogoff, *This Time Is Different: Eight Centuries of Financial Folly* (2009); R. Posner, *A Failure of Capitalism: The Crisis of '08 and the Descent into Depression* (2009); R. Rajan, *Fault Lines: How Hidden Fractures Still Threaten the World Economy* (2009); G. Tett, *Fool's Gold: How Unconstrained Greed Corrupted a Dream, Shattered Global Markets and Unleashed a Catastrophe* (2009); J. Lanchester, *Whoops! Why Everyone Owes Everyone and No One Can Pay* (2010).

For an entertaining but technically sophisticated critique, see S. Das, *Extreme Money: Masters of the Universe and the Cult of Risk* (2011). The analysis by Posner is particularly striking, coming from one of the intellectual leaders of the "Chicago School" of free market economics. Tett is a financial journalist with a PhD in anthropology, suggesting the value of a critical eye outside the economics discipline.

Behavioural economists have not been slow to comment: see R. Shiller, *The Subprime Solution: How Today's Global Financial Crisis Happened and What To Do About It* (2008); Akerlof and Shiller, *Animal Spirits: How Human Psychology Drives the Economy and Why It Matters For Global Capitalism* (2009). A number of classic papers, including those by Kahneman and Tversky, appear in Cammerer, Lowenstein and Rabin (eds), *Advances in Behavioural Economics* (2003). A useful compendium of the many ways people attempt to value things in real-world markets is provided by Poundstone, *Priceless: The Myth of Fair Value (and How to Take Advantage of It)* (2010). The more adventurous may care to consult Glimcher et al., *Neuroeconomics: Decision Making and the Brain* (2009).

Paul Omerod in his (2012) book *Positive Linking: How Networks Can Revolutionise the World* questions the very foundations of economics as a discipline tied to methodological individualism. His approach is drawn from a developing body of theory termed "social physics," concerned with how systems as a whole function.

In the shadow of the GFC, critiques of economics from a post-Keynesian perspective are offered by Keynes's biographer Robert Skidelsky, *Keynes: The Return of the Master* (2009), and Paul Davison, *The Keynes Solution: The Path to Economic Prosperity* (2009), Keynes's foremost US champion. For a less committed, more nuanced view, see Backhouse and Bateman, *Capitalist Revolutionary: John Maynard Keynes* (2011).

Explicitly Marxist critiques are presented by David Harvey, *The Enigma of Capital and the Crises of Capitalism* (2010), and Chris Harman, *Zombie Capitalism: Global Crisis and the Relevance of Marx* (2010).

Useful discussions of the sub-discipline of evolutionary economics are presented by Beinhocker, *The Origin of Wealth: Evolution, Complexity and the Radical Remaking of Economics* (2006); and Hodgson and Knudsen, *Darwin's Conjecture: The Search for Principles of Social and Economic Evolution* (2010).

There is a renewed and much overdue interest in understanding the scale, scope, and impacts of growing economic inequalities in capitalist societies. See Barry, *Why Social Justice Matters* (2005); Wilkinson and Pickett, *The Spirit Level: Why Equality is Better for Everyone* (2010); Organization for Economic Cooperation and Development (OECD), *Growing Unequal: Income Distribution and Poverty in OECD Countries* (2008). Reich, *Aftershock: The Next Economy and America's Future* (2010) explicitly charges the increasing scale of economic inequality since 1980 with the primary blame for America's collapse into the GFC. Hacker and Pierson in *Winner-Take-All Politics: How Washington Made the Rich Richer and Turned its Back on the Middle Classes* (2010) trace the political dynamic reinforcing the inequalities generated under neoliberalism. On the link between equality and fairness, see W. Hutton, *Them and Us: Changing Britain—Why we Need a Fair Society* (2010). Recent books that focus on the importance of growing inequality in the current context of globalization are: Joseph Stiglitz, *The Price of Inequality* (2012); James Galbraith, *Inequality and Instability* (2012); and Bowles, *The New Economics of Inequality and Redistribution* (2012).

On economic insecurity, see Hacker, *The Great Risk Shift* (2008); and Standing, *The Precariat: The New Dangerous Class* (2011).

There is a huge and growing literature on the economics and psychology of happiness. See Coyle, *The Economics of Enough* (2011); Kay, *Obliquity* (2010); and Layard, *Happiness: Lessons from a New Science* (2005).

References

Akerlof, G and Shiller, R 2009 *Animal Spirits: How Human Psychology Drives the Economy and Why It Matters For Global Capitalism*, Princeton University Press, Princeton, NJ.

American Society of Civil Engineers 2009 *Report Card for America's Infrastructure*. Available from: <https://apps.asce.org/reportcard/2009/grades.cfm> [7 August 2011].

Arrow, K and Debreu, G 1954 "Existence of an equilibrium for a competitive equilibrium," *Econometrica* 22: 265–290.

Backhouse, R 2002 *The Penguin History of Economics*, Penguin, London.

Backhouse, R 2010 *The Puzzle of Modern Economics: Science or Ideology*, Cambridge University Press, Cambridge.

Backhouse, R and Bateman, B (2011) *Capitalist Revolutionary: John Maynard Keynes*, Harvard University Press, Cambridge, MA.

Barry, B 2005 *Why Social Justice Matters*, Polity Press, Cambridge.

Beaud, M and Dostaler, G 1995 *Economic Thought Since Keynes: A History and Dictionary of Major Economists*, Routledge, London.

Beinhocker, E 2006 *The Origin of Wealth: Evolution, Complexity and the Radical Remaking of Economics*, Random House, New York.

Berle, A and Means, G 1932 *The Modern Corporation and Private Property*, Transaction Publishers, New York.

Boettke, P and Leeson, P 2007 "The Austrian School of Economics, 1950–2000," in W Samuels, J Biddle and J Davis (eds) *A Companion to The History of Economic Thought*, pp. 445–453, Blackwell, Oxford.

Bowles, S 2012 *The New Economics of Inequality and Redistribution*, Cambridge University Press, Cambridge.

Cammerer, C, Lowenstein, G and Rabin, M (eds) 2003 *Advances in Behavioural Economics*, Princeton University Press, Princeton, NJ.

Clements, P 2012 *Rawlsian Political Analysis: Rethinking the Microfoundations of Social Science*, Notre Dame University Press, Notre Dame, IN.

Coyle, D 2007 *The Soulful Science: What Economists Really Do and Why it Matters*, Princeton University Press, Princeton, NJ.

Coyle, D 2011 *The Economics of Enough: How to Run the Economy as if the Future Matters*, Princeton University Press, Princeton, NJ and Oxford.

Crenson, M 1972 *The Unpolitics of Air Pollution: A Study of Non-Decisionmaking in the Cities*, Johns Hopkins University Press, Baltimore, MD.

Das, S 2011 *Extreme Money: Masters of the Universe and the Cult of Risk*, Penguin, Melbourne, VIC.

Davison, P 2009 *The Keynes Solution: The Path to Economic Prosperity*, Palgrave Macmillan, New York.

Dionne, E J, Jr 2012 *Our Divided Political Heart: The Battle for the American Idea in an Age of Discontent*, New York, Bloomsbury.

Fisher, I 1933 "The debt-deflation theory of Great Depressions," *Econometrica* 1: 337–357.

Foley, D (2006) *Adam's Fallacy: A Guide to Economic Theology*, Harvard University Press, Cambridge, MA.

Friedman, M 1971 *A Theoretical Framework for Monetary Analysis*, National Bureau of Economic Research, New York.

Friedman, M and Schwartz, A 1963 *A Monetary History of the United States, 1867–1960*, Princeton University Press, Princeton, NJ, for the National Bureau of Economic Research.

Galbraith, J K 1952 *American Capitalism: The Concept of Countervailing Power*, Houghton Mifflin, Boston, MA.

Galbraith, J K 1955 *The Great Crash, 1929*, Houghton Mifflin, Boston, MA.

Galbraith, J K 1960 *The Liberal Hour*, Houghton Mifflin, Boston, MA.

Galbraith, J K 1967 *The New Industrial State*, Houghton Mifflin, Boston, MA.

Galbraith, J K 1979 *Annals of an Abiding Liberal*, Houghton Mifflin, Boston, MA.

Galbraith, J K 1981 *A Life in Our Times: A Memoir*, Houghton Mifflin, Boston, MA.

Galbraith, J K 1983 *The Anatomy of Power*, Houghton Mifflin, Boston, MA.

Galbraith, J K 1996 *The Good Society: The Humane Agenda*, Houghton Mifflin, Boston, MA.

Galbraith, J K 1998 *The Affluent Society*, Houghton Mifflin, Boston, MA.

Galbraith, J K and Dennison, H S 1934 *Modern Competition and Business Policy*, Oxford University Press, New York.

Galbraith, James 2008 *The Predator State: How Conservatives Abandoned the Free Market and Why Liberals Should Too*, Free Press, New York.

Galbraith, James 2012 *Inequality and Instability: A Study of the World Economy Just Before the Great Crisis*, Oxford University Press, New York.

Gilens, M 2012 *Affluence and Influence: Economic Inequality and Political Power in America*, Princeton University Press, Princeton, NJ.

Glimcher P, Fehr, E, Cammerer, C and Poldrack, R A 2009 *Neuroeconomics: Decision Making and the Brain*, Academic Press, London.

Goodwin, R 1967 "A growth cycle," in C Feinstein (ed.) *Capitalism and Economic Growth*, pp. 54–58, Cambridge University Press, Cambridge.

Gray, J 2000 *Two Faces of Liberalism*, Polity Press, London.

Hacker, J 2008 *The Great Risk Shift*, Oxford University Press, New York.

Hacker, J and Pierson, P 2010 *Winner-Take-All Politics: How Washington Made the Rich Richer and Turned its Back on the Middle Class*, Simon & Schuster, New York.

Harman, C 2010 *Zombie Capitalism: Global Crisis and the Relevance of Marx*, Haymarket Books, Chicago, IL.

Harvey, D 2010 *The Enigma of Capital and the Crises of Capitalism*, Oxford University Press, Oxford.

Haskins, R and Sawhill, I 2009 *Creating an Opportunity Society*, Brookings Institution, Washington DC.

Hirsch, F 1976 *Social Limits to Growth*, Harvard University Press, Cambridge, MA.

Hodgson, G and Knudsen, T 2010 *Darwin's Conjecture: The Search for Principles of Social and Economic Evolution*, University of Chicago Press, Chicago, IL.

Horwitz, S 2007 "The Austrian Marginalists: Menger, Bohm-Bawerk and Wieser," in W Samuels, J Biddle and J Davis (eds) *A Companion to the History of Economic Thought*, pp. 272–277, Blackwell, Oxford.

Hutton, W 2010 *Them and Us: Changing Britain—Why We Need a Fair Society*, Little, Brown, London.

Jouvenel, B de 1993 *On Power: Its Nature and the History of its Growth*, Beacon Press, New York.

Kalecki, M 1939 *Essays in the Theory of Economic Fluctuations*, George Allen and Unwin, London.

Kay, J 2010 *Obliquity*, Profile, London.

Keen, S 2011 *Debunking Economics: The Naked Emperor Dethroned*, Zed Books, London.

Keynes, J M 1973/1923 *A Tract on Monetary Reform*, Collected Writings vol. IV, Macmillan, London.

Keynes, J M 1973/1930 "Economic possibilities for our grandchildren," in *Essays in Persuasion,* Collected Writings vol. IX, pp. 321–334, Macmillan, London.

Keynes, J M 1973/1936 *The General Theory of Employment, Interest and Money*, Collected Writings vols VII, XIII, Macmillan, London.

Krugman, P 2008 *The Return of Depression Economics and the Crisis of 2008*, Penguin, London.

Krugman, P 2012 *End This Depression Now*, WW Norton, New York.

Kuhn, T 1962 *The Structure of Scientific Revolutions*, University of Chicago Press, Chicago, IL.

Lanchester, J 2010 *Whoops! Why Everyone Owes Everyone and No One Can Pay*, Allen Lane, London.

Layard, R 2005 *Happiness: Lessons from a New Science*, Penguin, London.

Lowenstein, R 2008 "Triple-A failure," *New York Times,* 27 April.

Lukes, S 1973 *Power: A Radical View*, Macmillan, London.

McCloskey, D 1997 *The Vices of Economists, the Virtues of the Bourgeoisie*, University of Amsterdam Press, Amsterdam.

Marcuse, H 1964 *One Dimensional Man*, Routledge & Kegan Paul, London.

Marx, K 1976/1867 *Capital: A Critique of Political Economy*, vol. 1, Penguin, Harmondsworth.

Megalogenis, G 2012 *The Australian Moment: How We Were Made for These Times,* Hamish Hamilton, Camberwell, VIC.

Minsky, H 1975 *John Maynard Keynes*, Macmillan, London.

Moss, R 2002 *When All Else Fails: Government as the Ultimate Risk Manager*, Harvard University Press, Cambridge, MA.

Myrdal, G 1953 *The Political Element in the Development of Economic Theory*, Routledge & Kegan Paul, London.

Myrdal, G 1957 *Economic Theory and Under-developed Regions*, Gerald Duckworth, London.

Omerod, P 1994 *The Death of Economics*, Faber and Faber, London.

Omerod, P 2005 *Why Most Things Fail: Evolution, Extinction and Economics*, Pantheon, New York.

Omerod, P 2012 *Positive Linking: How Networks can Revolutionise the World*, Kindle edn, Faber and Faber, London.

Organisation for Economic Cooperation and Development (OECD) 2008 *Growing Unequal: Income Distribution and Poverty in OECD Countries*, OECD, Paris.

Organisation for Economic Cooperation and Development (OECD) 2011 *Divided We Stand: Why Inequality Keeps Rising*, OECD, Paris.

Packard, V 1957 *The Hidden Persuaders,* David McKay, New York.

Packard, V 1959 *The Status Seekers,* David McKay, New York.

Parker, R 2005 *John Kenneth Galbraith: His Life, His Politics, His Economics,* Farrar, Straus and Giroux, New York.

Pecchi, L and Piga, G (eds) 2010 *Revisiting Keynes: Economic Possibilities for Our Grandchildren,* MIT Press, Cambridge, MA.

Pigou, A C 1927 *Industrial Fluctuations,* Macmillan, London.

Pigou, A C 1932/1920 *The Economics of Welfare,* 4th ed., Macmillan, London.

Posner, R 2009 *A Failure of Capitalism: The Crisis of '08 and the Descent into Depression,* Harvard University Press, Cambridge, MA.

Poundstone, W 2010 *Priceless: The Myth of Fair Value (and How to Take Advantage of It),* Scribe Publications, Melbourne, VIC.

Pressman, S 2008 "John Kenneth Galbraith and the post Keynesian tradition in economics," *Review of Political Economy* 20(4): 475–490.

Quiggin, J 2010 *Zombie Economics: How Dead Ideas Still Walk Amongst Us,* Princeton University Press, Princeton, NJ.

Rajan, R 2009 *Fault Lines: How Hidden Fractures Still Threaten the World Economy,* Princeton University Press, Princeton, NJ.

Rawls, J 1971 *A Theory of Justice,* Harvard University Press, Cambridge, MA.

Reich, R 2008 *Supercapitalism: The Transformation of Business, Democracy and Everyday Life,* Alfred A Knopf, New York.

Reich, R 2010 *Aftershock: The Next Economy and America's Future,* Alfred A Knopf, New York.

Reinhart, C and Rogoff, K 2009 *This Time Is Different: Eight Centuries of Financial Folly,* Princeton University Press, Princeton, NJ.

Robbins, L 1932 *An Essay on the Nature and Significance of Economic Science,* Macmillan, London.

Robertson, D H 1926 *Banking Policy and the Price Level,* King, London.

Rodgers, D 2011 *The Age of Fracture,* Harvard University Press, Cambridge, MA.

Romer, P 1986 "Increasing returns and long run growth," *Journal of Political Economy* 94(5): 1002–1037.

Rutherford, M 2007 "American institutional economics in the interwar period," in W Samuels, J Biddle and J Davis (eds) *A Companion to the History of Economic Thought,* Blackwell, Oxford.

Samuels, W, Biddle, J and Davis J (eds) 2007 *A Companion to the History of Economic Thought,* Blackwell, Oxford.

Schumpeter, J 1934/1912 *Theory of Economic Development,* Harvard University Press, Cambridge, MA.

Schumpeter, J A 1954 *History of Economic Analysis,* Oxford University Press, New York.

Schumpeter, J 1962/1942 *Capitalism, Socialism and Democracy,* 3rd ed., Harper Perennial, London.

Sen, A 2009 *The Idea of Justice,* Harvard University Press, Cambridge, MA.

Shiller, R 2008 *The Subprime Solution: How Today's Global Financial Crisis Happened and What To Do About It,* Princeton University Press, Princeton, NJ.

Skidelsky, R 2009 *Keynes: The Return of the Master,* Allen Lane, London.

Smith, A 1961/1776 *An Inquiry into The Nature and Causes of the Wealth of Nations*, ed. E. Cannan, two vols, Methuen, London.

Smith, A 2009/1759 *The Theory of Moral Sentiments*, Penguin, New York.

Solow, R 1956 "A contribution to the theory of economic growth," *Quarterly Journal of Economics* 70: 65–94.

Sraffa, P 1960 *Production of Commodities by Means of Commodities: Prelude to a Critique of Economic Theory*, Cambridge University Press, Cambridge.

Standing, G 2011 *The Precariat: The New Dangerous Class*, Bloomsbury Academic, London and New York.

Stiglitz, J 2000 "The contributions of the economics of information to 20th century economics," *Quarterly Journal of Economics* 115(4): 1441–1478.

Stiglitz, J 2010 *Freefall: America, Free Markets and the Shrinking of the World Economy*, WW Norton, New York.

Stiglitz, J 2012 *The Price of Inequality: How Today's Divided Society Endangers Our Future*, WW Norton, New York.

Tett, G 2009 *Fool's Gold: How Unconstrained Greed Corrupted a Dream, Shattered Global Markets and Unleashed a Catastrophe*, Little, Brown, London.

Wapshott, N 2011 *Keynes Hayek: The Clash that Defined Modern Economics*, Scribe, Melbourne, VIC.

Weber, M 1948 *From Max Weber: Essays in Sociology*, ed. H H Gerth and C Wright Mills, Routledge & Kegan Paul, London.

Wilkinson, R and Pickett, K 2010 *The Spirit Level: Why Equality is Better for Everyone*, Penguin, London.

Index